*"We have one wish in our hearts,
one wish in our souls—
to bring peace to our people."*

So said Prime Minister Menachem Begin in his address before the Israeli Parliament on the historic occasion of Egyptian President Sadat's visit to Israel in November 1977.

The man chosen to lead his country to peace after so many years of hostility came to power only six months earlier to the surprise and shock of most of the world. But for Begin it marked the culmination of a twenty-nine-year quest. . . .

Now at last we have the full and amazing story of the dynamic man who embarked on that dramatic path to greatness.

MENACHEM BEGIN
The Legend and the Man

MENACHEM
BEGIN
The Legend and the Man

BY EITAN HABER

A DELL BOOK

Published by
DELL PUBLISHING CO., INC.
1 Dag Hammarskjold Plaza
New York, New York 10017

For information contact:
Delacorte Press
1 Dag Hammarskjold Plaza
New York, New York 10017

Dell ® TM 681510, Dell Publishing Co., Inc.

ISBN: 0-440-16107-X

Reprinted by arrangement with
Delacorte Press

Printed in the United States of America

First Dell Printing—April 1979

Acknowledgments

In writing this book I sought assistance from a number of different sources, including books, newspapers, archives, and written testimonies. I would like to pay special tribute to those who were particularly helpful to me in obtaining a full and proper description and understanding of the hero of my work, Menachem Begin, prime minister of Israel.

My heartfelt thanks are due to Mrs. Rachel Halperin, the premier's sister; Mrs. Hasia Milo, the premier's daughter; Yehiel Kadishai, head of the Prime Minister's Bureau; Dr. Eliahu Ben-Elissar, Director-General of the Prime Minister's Office; Haim Landau, cabinet minister and former Knesset member, and former head of the IZL headquarters; the late Amihai Paglin, former chief operations officer of the IZL and advisor to the prime minister on counter-terrorism; the late Aharon Propes, former leader of the Polish *Betar;* Natan Yallin-Mor, former member of the Polish *Betar* leadership, and former commander of *Lehi;* Dr. Meir (Marek) Kahnan, a former member of the IZL command; David Yutan, a former member of the Polish *Betar* leadership; and to many others —comrades of the prime minister from his youth, former members of *Betar* and the IZL, past and present MKs and cabinet ministers, whose contributions to this book have been of the utmost importance.

Many thanks to my colleague Shlomo Nakdimon for his good advice, and to my colleague Aviezer Golan, whose comments on the manuscript were of the greatest help. I want to pay tribute also to my co-workers Yitzhak Schweitzer, Sima Ella, Tali Shalev, and Yoram Tal. A final tribute remains. My thanks to my dear wife Gilla and our children, Michal and Ilan, for tolerating my moods and for silently enduring my labors.

Contents

MENACHEM BEGIN
The Legend and the Man

Prologue

At 7:58 P.M. on November 19, 1977, the wheels of the presidential aircraft "Egypt 01" touched down at Ben-Gurion International Airport, near Tel Aviv. By 8:00 P.M., the pilot had switched off the engines of the red and white Boeing 707 bearing the Egyptian standard on its tail; two maintenance men pushed the steps toward the plane. "Operation Gateway," as Israeli officials called it, was under way and a new era in Middle Eastern history about to begin.

The eyes of hundreds of millions of people throughout the world were focused on the ensuing spectacle brought to them by courtesy of the communications satellite hovering over the Israeli airport. Out of the plane emerged Anwar el-Sadat, president of the Arab Republic of Egypt. As he stood at the top of the steps taking in the historic scene he had brought into being, he wore a serious, almost closed expression reflecting his inner tension. Facing him across the terminal building was a huge banner proclaiming "Welcome

President Sadat" in Hebrew, Arabic, and English. The entire tarmac leading to the terminal was a sea of faces and flags illuminated by brilliant lights. Over 2,000 newsmen from all parts of the world waited in serried ranks for the biggest story of the year; one of them felt that this was the second most important moment in the history of our generation, the other being man's first landing on the moon.

Everyone applauded as the president of Israel, Professor Ephraim Katzir, and the prime minister, Menachem Begin, walked along the red VIP carpet to welcome the leader of the country with which they had fought for thirty years and which was still their enemy.

The Israeli leaders shook hands with their guest, enveloped by security men and photographers. "I am waiting for you, Mr. President," Begin said with a warm smile, "and all the ministers are waiting for you . . ." They looked at each other as the cameras whirled, and no one could tell what passed through their minds at that very first moment of their meeting.

The Egyptian president, faultlessly dressed, presented an elegant picture as he surveyed the honor guard of detachments from the Israel Defense Forces, men he had fought against over the past three decades. In his ears still echoed the sound of the welcoming trumpets and the thunder of twenty-one salvos of cannon. He was facing, for the first time, those people whom he had opposed most of his life: Begin and Golda Meir, Moshe Dayan, Yigael Yadin, Shimon Peres, Yitzhak Rabin, Yigal Allon, Ariel Sharon, and Mordechai Gur.

Thirty years of wars, 80,000 Egyptian and 14,000 Israeli dead, and ruined economies in both countries were all part of the heavy price that had been paid to reach this emotional moment at Ben-Gurion International Airport. As the world watched, Sadat and Begin were asking not to be forced to pay any more blood money of that kind ever again.

The two men who shook hands on that warm November night are two outstanding and tough leaders who resemble one another to a remarkable extent. Begin is a man of principles, not easily budged. His election to the premiership of Israel was only possible because during thirty long years he refused to sacrifice any of his principles. Sadat, too, is a man of principles. Until now his years in power have shown that he stood by each of them, fulfilling all of his promises to the letter. Begin lived beneath the shadow of a great Israeli statesman, David Ben-Gurion. Sadat also lived in the shade cast by the great Egyptian leader Gamal Abdul Nasser. Both these earlier leaders were obliged to concentrate on making war, and almost all their years in office were enveloped in the smoke of battle. Begin and Sadat want to enter the history books along a route that has been blocked until now—the path of peace. Both are charismatic leaders, and both enjoy tremendous popularity among their peoples.

Commentators claim that only leaders as strong as these two could demand of their peoples the heavy price they will have to pay for peace. The fate of the Middle East has never hung so dramatically in balance as it does now in the hands of these two men alone.

Sadat, in his outstanding speech to the Israeli Knesset, stressed that "The first duty is to exhaust all means possible in order to remove from my Egyptian people and from the Arab nation all the likely catastrophes

13

ensuing from dreadful and destructive wars." And Begin is well aware of this: "We have one wish in our heart, one wish in our souls—to bring peace to our people," he said in the address that followed Sadat's.

During a visit to Israel that lasted only forty-four hours, Sadat managed to break down towering walls of enmity and distrust, to smash myths, and to eliminate many psychological obstacles. The enthusiastic welcome he received from the Israeli people demonstrated more than anything else how much they yearn for the day referred to by King Hassan of Morocco, when "The Jewish genius and the Arab genius can turn the area into a veritable paradise."

The man who intends to lead Israel to peace was elected prime minister, to the surprise of most of the world, just six months before, almost to the day.

At eleven in the evening of Tuesday, May 17, the streets of Israel suddenly emptied. The polling stations were closing their doors, and the election for the ninth Knesset was at an end. All that remained was to count the votes.

The election campaign had been short and very intensive. It was provoked by the sudden resignation of Prime Minister Yitzhak Rabin at a moment when the battle for public opinion was at a peak, and was colored by his stepping down from the candidacy for premiership—in the middle of the campaign—as a result of accusations that he was hiding a bank account abroad in contravention of Israel's strict foreign currency regulations. This was only the last in a chain of revelations of corruption in high places. On the international scene, the relationships between Israel and the United States were nearing the breaking point.

Minutes before entering the polling booth there were still many thousands of Israelis who had not yet made up their minds. Now they were settling down in front of their TV sets to watch Israel Television indulge in some forecasts on a wider scale than ever attempted before in Israel. At selected polling stations throughout the country thousands of citizens had been asked to place a repeat of their vote, in sealed envelopes, in dummy ballot boxes belonging to the broadcasting authority. A team of statisticians intended to predict the final results almost immediately.

Promptly at eleven o'clock Haim Yavin, Israel's most popular newscaster, appeared on the screens in thousands of homes. But the famous smile was conspicuously absent—and he wore an expression as if he himself could not quite believe what he was about to report.

"Based on the television sampling, there is an indication of a decisive victory for the *Likud* Party in the elections just over—and a crushing defeat for the ruling party. I repeat that this is a sampling by television, not based on official results. According to this sample, Menachem Begin will be at the head of the next government."

There were three instantaneous reactions. One camp cheered, another remained in oppressive silence, and the third—far the biggest, composed of members of both right and left—simply dismissed the forecast as too speculative to credible. Now there was nothing for it but to wait for the trickle of official results.

Far from the crowd milling around in *Likud* election headquarters—a crowd that included almost all the

15

leaders of his party—the man for whom the prediction spelled victory sat in front of his TV in a small apartment in Tel Aviv. Three weeks earlier he had suffered a severe heart attack. Nevertheless he had spent Election Day touring the suburbs of Tel Aviv and Jerusalem, shaking hands, patting shoulders, trying to appear optimistic. For him, this ninth attempt could only be the last. It was now or never.

His sole reaction to Yavin's startling prediction was a whispered "Hush" to his wife and daughters. He stirred the ever-present cup of tea without taking his eyes from the screen. That tea had become his trademark, even though a mild diabetes had forced him to give up the habit of sipping it through a lump of sugar.

Begin had returned exhausted from his tour. Changing into pajamas he lay down to rest in the room that served as living room, bedroom, and study, while his family sat in the tiny kitchen to avoid disturbing him. His daughter Hasia was more on edge than her mother and sister; she was scared of yet another failure for her father. Aliza Begin, Menachem's wife, was optimistic. She remembered the impression he brought home from the last-minute tour: "I have never had a reception like the one I got today. I think there is a change among the electorate."

There was no real tension in the house. Towards evening Begin had asked for something to eat, and Aliza served his usual bread and white cheese with a cup of tea. Two old friends, Yehudit and Max Ferber, arrived, and joined the Begin women in the kitchen. Nobody wanted to disturb Menachem. Most of the phone calls were intercepted by Hasia. Benjamin, the eldest of the Begin children, was thousands of miles

16

away in Denver, Colorado, working on a doctoral thesis in geology.

The call at 10:45 was intended for Menachem Begin personally. Eliezer Zhurabin, the public relations man who headed the *Likud*'s propaganda campaign, told his boss: "Mr. Begin, you can prepare your victory speech . . ." He had received advance information from the news department of Israel Television.

"Slow down, Eliezer," Begin responded calmly. "Don't take it so seriously."

At eleven Begin moved into the old yellow armchair that had graced their living room for many years. As Yavin began his announcement, Hasia exploded: "I don't believe it. They're lying!"

"And I do believe it," Aliza said. "I told you I was optimistic."

Yehudit Ferber bolted back into the kitchen and burst into tears.

"We're still waiting," Begin declared, as if the man on the screen meant nothing to him.

Next Yehiel Kadishai, Begin's secretary of many years' standing, phoned to say that the party was waiting for him at headquarters.

"Yehiel, it's too early. We have time. This is only a guess by the boys at television."

The calls were more frequent now, and voices filled the tiny apartment on the corner of Rosenbaum and Yosef Eliahu streets where Begin had lived since his days in the underground and which he had promised himself he would leave only for the prime minister's residence in Jerusalem. Apart from a convertible couch crammed up against his desk, the room contained a bookcase and photos of Zeev Jabotinsky, Garibaldi, old-time underground friend Yisrael Epstein, Menachem's grandchildren, and finally one of Begin himself in disguise as a religious Jew.

Hasia answered the doorbell to find Arye Giladi, Begin's chauffeur for the past two months and the son of Yoske Giladi, his closest associate for over thirty years. Yoske Giladi had driven, protected, and been a friend to the family until his death from cancer three months before the election. The son took over a month later. Both Hasia and Arye were in tears. She took his hands in hers and said: "It's a pity your father isn't here to see this."

"Hasia, do you know that there are already policemen outside the house?"

That was an early confirmation of Begin's changed status. Meanwhile the street was full of people and television crews were arriving. Two more old friends, David Grosbard and Moska Stein, made their way through to the door. Stein announced that they had not come to disturb Menachem, but only to pronounce the age-old Jewish prayer: "Thank the Lord that we lived and survived to see this moment." Tears were in his eyes also.

By midnight the actual results were confirming the forecast with a precision that amazed even the statisticians. Television cameras focused on the face of Shimon Peres, the Labor Party's favorite in the race, and his expression told the whole story—the same disappointment that had been there months earlier when Peres lost, by a handful of votes, in his ambitious attempt to replace Rabin as leader of the party. He was now saying that he would accept the electorate's decision with a good grace. Then the camera panned down the corridors of 110 Hayarkon Street, the Labor Party headquarters. The building,

18

which had been at the center of power for three decades, was deserted and lifeless.

The contrast between the rejoicing at *Likud* headquarters in Tel Aviv and the stunned amazement, even despair, in the Labor camp made striking viewing. Some commentators noted that Yitzhak Rabin was absent. To him had fallen the unlikely task of handing over the reins of power to his party's traditional adversary. Rabin was sitting at home, chain-smoking.

Hasia worried lest the excitement should affect her father so soon after his heart attack. She considered calling in the family doctor—but Menachem seemed relaxed. He was now explaining to the friends packed into the room how his party had been constantly gaining from election to election while Labor dropped. He did not seem at all surprised.

Kadishai called again, and again Begin insisted that he was not going to party headquarters until there was some official confirmation of the news.

At the *Likud* headquarters on King George Street there could be no doubt that this night belonged to Begin's men. They had waited twenty-nine years— maybe longer. Until tonight all their hopes had foundered on the rocks of an unshakable political reality: Israel belonged to the parties of the left. But the *Likud* leaders in their campaign had asked to be given a chance, and now at last they appeared to have it.

Begin still would not join the celebration. Not that he was not sure of the victory. In fact as he paced the floor, his hands crossed behind his back, his family knew from long experience that he was preparing the speech he would make sometime during the night. At times like this it was as if a wall shut him off from

the rest of the world. Suddenly he turned to the book
case and pulled out a volume to look for a quotation
from Abraham Lincoln.

In the high-rise building on King George Street
his supporters were waiting. They formed a circle
of dancers, pulling in Major General (Res.) Ezer
Weizman, ex-head of Israel's air force and chairman of
the *Likud* Election Committee. Weizman restrained
his colleagues, who wanted to break open the cham
pagne. "We must wait for Begin." He asked his assis
tant, Mordechai Zipori, to quieten the place down a
bit.

"I suggest a little order," Zipori's parade-ground
voice boomed out. "We're on live television. The
whole country is watching us."

But no one was listening. The only person they
would listen to now was Menachem Begin. Finally
at close to one o'clock in the morning, he decided
the time had come. He came out of his house into a
street floodlit with television lamps, and climbed into
the white Peugeot driven by Arye Giladi. Five min
utes later, at the *Likud* headquarters, he was greeted
by an overwhelming crowd; they pushed in close to
touch him, shake his hand, share in his great moment.
A police officer held Begin's arm and tried to force
a way through, but the *Likud* leader turned to him.

"Sir, let them be. Let them be."

At the doorway to the building he passed down a
long line of beaming men, hugging each other—the
veterans of his underground army days and childhood
friends from Poland. While his wife looked on, his
daughter Leah was having trouble of her own.

"Lady, no one can shove in here," said the door-
man, who did not know Leah Begin.

"But that's my father. I'm Begin's daughter," she protested.

"We've heard that one before," he said with an air of finality. It was Yitzhak Shamir, chairman of the *Herut* faction in the *Likud* Party, who heard the argument and came to Leah's rescue.

In the upstairs hall Menachem Begin looked around at the mass of political colleagues, brothers in arms, old friends, all those who had remained faithful during the long years of political wilderness and opposition—those he affectionately called "the fighting family."

A television commentator thrust a microphone at him, but he brushed it aside politely.

"I will not say a word until I have spoken to my colleagues."

"It's the biggest moment of your life, isn't it?" the commentator persisted.

"Oh, no! There were bigger in the underground, in the war for Israel's independence."

After making the rounds of his close associates, Menachem Begin was ready to speak to the television audience:

"Today is a historic turning point in the annals of the Jewish people and of the Zionist movement—one such as we have not seen in the forty-six years since the Seventeenth Zionist Congress, in 1931, when Zeev Jabotinsky suggested that the objective of Zionism should be the establishment of a Jewish State in our time. Zeev Jabotinsky devoted his whole life to that aim. He did not live to see the establishment of the State, or the turning point that has taken place today. His students, who in the name of his doctrine and for its realization fought for the liberation of the nation, and continued patiently and with absolute faith in democracy to aspire to change the shape of things in our country by means of the ballot slip—and the ballot slip alone—have arrived thus far."

Begin surveyed his road in opposition, mentioning his partners from the various factions that made up the *Likud* Party and then, as a man to whom the trappings of respect were part of life, made some warm remarks about his wife. His voice trembled as he said:

"My first thanks are to my wife, to whom more than any other person on earth apply the eternal words: 'I remember thee, the kindness of thy youth, the love of thine espousals, when thou wenteth after me in the wilderness,' to which I add, 'sown with mines.' "

He paused to plant a kiss on Aliza's hand, then thanked his son and two daughters, his sister Rachel Halperin, and their children.

"And now I want to thank my friends and comrades of the underground, of the *Irgun Zvai Leumi* and of the Fighters for the Freedom of Israel, the vaunted heroes. We have come a long way and they never ceased to believe that a day like this would come, that a night like this would come . . ."

The Labor Party headquarters, across Tel Aviv, was as silent as a battle headquarters after a resounding defeat. The few people who sat there watching their old adversary make his victory speech did so without any comment.

A new spring day was in the air as Begin went home. This time he was accompanied by two secret service bodyguards. The street, which had been relatively empty when he left, was now packed with people.

"Begin! Begin!"

As the prime minister designate waved to the crowd, not even the fatigue of a long day was able to prevent the smile on his face.

With the dawn, Israel Television ended its long marathon. The last word went to Haim Yavin, who appeared every bit as exhausted as Menachem Begin.

"From now on we will all have to get used to a new style."

CHAPTER 1

Bloody Pogrom

Before World War I few people in the West had ever heard of Brest Litovsk, and even fewer knew how to find it on the map. Brisk, as the Poles and Germans called it, was during the first decade of the century the provincial capital of Polesia. Its population was mixed and its history a long succession of border disputes. Then, almost overnight, about a year before the official ending of World War I, the town entered world history when the representatives of Germany and of the new Bolshevik régime in Russia met to sign the Brest Litovsk Treaty that formally brought to a close war in the East.

It was altogether fitting that the treaty signed in this town was linked with the name of a Jew—Commissar of Foreign Affairs Leon Lev Trotsky—for the historic site already occupied an important place in contemporary Jewish affairs. Jews formed half the population, and were at times even in the majority. The greatest pride of the Jews of Brest Litovsk was their network of educational institutions. Of the four secondary schools in the town, two were Jewish—and the language of instruction was Hebrew. Alongside these two—the "Tarbut" and "Tachkemoni" gymnasiums—there were primary schools, hospitals, a large library on biblical subjects, welfare institutions, and mutual aid funds.

After World War I Brisk was restored to Polish jurisdiction. There was a short period of postwar depression, then life returned to normal. In the marketplaces and streets of the town the Polish farmers and merchants were so accustomed to the ring of Hebrew that some of them could even use a few words in their daily commerce.

Dov Zeev Begin, the father of Menachem, was a leader of the town's Jewish community, widely known and liked. The eldest of nine children of a timber merchant, he was a typical product of the local Jewish culture. Until the age of seventeen he studied the Bible in one of Poland's best known *yeshivas*, from which came among others Rabbi Dov Soloveichik of Boston—whom his son Menachem would consult before his first meeting as prime minister with President Jimmy Carter. Persuaded by a German auditor who worked for his father, Dov Begin at seventeen tried to run away to the university in Berlin. His father caught the boy at the railway depot; he needed help at work, so Dov's studies were completed by "teach yourself" techniques. Dov traveled a lot for his father's timber interests, frequently visiting Warsaw, Danzig, and Berlin; this broadened his mind far beyond the confines of a provincial Jewish environment. Traveling also brought him into contact with,

26

and under the influence of, most of the active leaders of Zionism.

The traditional Judaism of Brest Litovsk was still remote from the new Jewish ideology. The deeply religious Jews were not ready to believe in nationalist solutions to their problems. Their ancient daily prayers were influenced by the reference to Divine Providence that governed Jews everywhere and accorded them the role from time immemorial as bearers of the godly message. The same prayers made mention of nations that had risen to destroy the Jews yet had vanished from the stage of history, while their intended victims survived. One of the most important motifs of their life was the "Chosen People" concept, which was entirely free of any nationalistic undertones. For the Jew, being "chosen" is not a privilege but a burden that must be borne. Under its precepts a good Jew is the one who obeys the commandments, observes the Sabbath, eats only kosher food, maintains the purity of the family, and preserves all the other ordinances that regulate daily life.

Zionism was attempting to define Jewish existence and to confront its problems through the use of a modern yet classic nationalism. Thus it was no wonder that the Zionists' first conflict was with their immediate environment, which viewed their conception as a dangerous heresy that sought to place Jewish survival on a foundation contrary to tradition. Indeed the extreme orthodox circles in modern Jewry still view Zionism as a heretical movement, and still wage their own brand of warfare on it both from within Israel and from outside—even to the extent of cooperating with the Palestine Liberation Organization, solely because it is committed to the eradication of

Zionism. The new Jewish nationalist ideal needed time to absorb the mainstream elements of orthodox Judaism—a process that was begun by the father of modern Zionism, Theodor Herzl.

On the day that Herzl died, July 3, 1904, the rabbi of Brest Litovsk Great Synagogue, a member of the Soloveichik family, took the keys of the synagogue home with him to prevent any attempt at a memorial service within its walls.

Dov Zeev Begin came to the synagogue armed with an ax. He broke the lock and opened the doors wide. With a friend named Sheinerman, he held a somewhat sparsely attended service dedicated to the memory of the newly departed Zionist patriarch. Sheinerman was the grandfather of the Israeli general, Ariel Sharon, who would achieve military glory as the leader of Israel's commandos and who would serve Begin's son as his Minister of Agriculture.

In 1906 a young, quiet girl with dreamy blue eyes named Hasia Kosovsky arrived in Brest Litovsk. She came of a family of rabbis well known in Wolin. Her father, also a timber merchant, had died when she was very young, so she was brought up by her grandfather in strict orthodox Jewish fashion. One Friday night she was the Begins' guest at dinner. Her meeting with Dov Zeev proved to be love at first sight.

As was the custom of the time, Dov Zeev had been unwillingly married at a very young age to a local girl. The arrangement made by the parents of the couple did not last long. Like all acquaintanceships made under the wedding canopy, compatibility was a matter of luck. But Hasia was different.

"If a woman has beautiful eyes, then it's a sign that she's beautiful," ruled the rabbi as he gave his blessing to the couple. They were married at Wolin railway station a few weeks later. Then the young Begin, complete with top hat and white gloves, brought his new bride home to his father's house in Brisk. Dov Zeev found work as a departmental manager in a bank. He intensified his activity in *Hovevei Zion,* an offshoot of the Zionist movement, and threw himself wholeheartedly into the passion of his life: playing chess. He spent hours bent over a chessboard at the local club. Another board enjoyed pride of place at the center of his desk at home. Indeed he was more attached to the massive pine desk on brass wheels than to any other piece of furniture in the house. Apart from the privilege of polishing its brass wheels, the children were never allowed near it.

The Begins' first child, Rachel, was born a year and a half after the wedding. Soon after her birth the couple moved into their own home, a spacious four-room apartment in a wooden house on Gobol Street. Like the other homes of Brest Litovsk, there was no running water. A neighbor made his living by carting water from the town's central faucet, while the burghers of Brest Litovsk took their baths at the local bathhouse. There was no electricity in town.

The birth of their second child put an end to a family argument. Dov Zeev had wanted his firstborn to be a son, and had planned to name him after the late lamented Zionist leader. As luck would have it, their first child was a girl. He proposed to call her "Herzlia," but his wife wouldn't hear of it. So "Rachel" it was—in memory of Hasia's grandmother. But the new child was a boy, and Dov Zeev was free to name him Herzl.

The name of their second son, who was born on

Friday, August 16, 1913, was a foregone conclusion. August 16 happened to be the 13th of *Av* on the Jewish lunar calendar. *Av* is by tradition a sad month; the Temple in Jerusalem was twice destroyed on the 9th of *Av*—once by the armies of Babylon, and the second time by the legions of Titus. Over the generations the dual significance had become symbolic of the pogroms suffered by Jews in their dispersion. On the 9th of *Av*, wherever they may be, orthodox Jews spend their day in fasting and in reading from the Book of Lamentations. The first Sabbath following the sad day is known to Jews as "the Sabbath of Consolation" from the prayers said during the daily service, and from the implication that—having wept for the destruction of the Temple—the time has now come to herald the resurrection. The theme has run through Jewish life for 2,000 years, and still prevails in the connection between the Holocaust and the resurrection of the State of Israel in 1948.

So the Begins called their third child "Menachem" which, in Hebrew, means "consoler." Eight days later, according to Jewish tradition, Menachem Begin was introduced into the covenant of Abraham. At a ceremony in which his godfather was the Chief Rabbi of Brisk, the Zionist leadership presented a gigantic cake in the shape of a bouquet of flowers. The Chief Rabbi and the cake together indicated that the hosts of the celebration were to be classified somewhere between orthodox Judaism and the nascent nationalism. And these were to be the formative influences in Menachem Begin's life that still remain to this day.

Mere months later the world was at war. The Begins, like the other Jews of Brest Litovsk, did not particularly feel it, even though the town was surrounded by Russian army camps. The exception was perhaps Menachem's nurse Natasha, herself a Russian, who flirted happily with almost every soldier who crossed her path. By early 1915, however, the war was becoming an oppressive presence in Brisk. The Begins' neighbor on the floor above was a Russian officer, and the children were home on the day that strange soldiers brought back his kit, saying he had been killed. In a slow but steady trickle Galician refugees—most of them Jews—began to arrive. Dov Zeev used to go out and mingle with the refugees and invite some of the less fortunate ones into the house. Eventually he developed the habit of serving a meal for them twice a week. Although he had no love for Russia or the Russians, he did not hesitate to share his bread with the occasional soldier who struggled past exhibiting all the marks of war. Yet his sympathies were with the Germans, and he often said: "The day will come when the Germans will arrive, and then you'll see the difference!"

Menachem's father was suspected by the authorities of Brest Litovsk of cooperating with the German enemy. Many of the townspeople had heard him speak in praise of all things German, and he did not hide his expectation of a German victory. His words sometimes fell on the wrong ears. Eventually the Russians expelled him from Brisk. His fellow leaders in the town chess club tried to intercede, but to no avail. The response was that Dov Zeev Begin should be thankful he wasn't being hung in the marketplace as a spy. Forced to depart, he went first to Moscow, then on to St. Petersburg, leaving Hasia behind in Brisk with the three children.

On one occasion at the height of the war, somebody

told the family that Dov Zeev would be passing through town on a train. They went to the station hoping to see him wave from a window, but it hurtled through at too high a speed and they saw nothing.

The next day Rachel wrote a letter to the local governor: "Please return Father to us." She received no reply. A few days later Hasia packed her belongings and moved with the children into her in-laws' home—a spacious house set in a vineyard on the banks of the local river. But her stay was destined to be a short one. A relative arrived one morning, excited and out of breath: "They've plastered an announcement on every wall in town that all the citizens of Brisk must leave within three days!"

Again it seemed like an illustration of the Jewish fate, yet one tinged with irony. The head of the family had been forced to abandon his family because he expected the Germans, and now his family was being compelled to leave for fear of the Germans who might arrive at any moment. Once more Hasia packed her belongings and loaded her children on a horse-drawn wagon; she and her mother-in-law set off for the home of a cousin in Drohiczyn. It was a long and tiring journey, but the children quite enjoyed it. Menachem reveled in the sights on this, the first trip of his life, and his first encounter with the Jews' nomadic destiny. Two days later Brest Litovsk went up in flames, and nothing was left of the Begin home except charred embers. The front line of a war that had seemed remote was drawing steadily nearer. The Begins' refuge at Drohiczyn became very cramped as more and more refugees flocked in.

Meanwhile Menachem's grandfather also left the rubble of Brest Litovsk in the small boat that, before the war, had hauled his timber and other wares down the River Bug. Loading it up with the family furniture, including Hasia's, he sailed downstream as far as Kobrin. In the thick forests on the banks of the river the two armies were drawn up facing each other. The old man hoisted a white flag from his boat and hoped for the best. His first contact was with the Germans, whom he regaled with tea and jam. In return they showed him a small house alongside a nearby dam. Before the war it had belonged to the damkeeper, but he had fled as the armies approached. The elder Begin moved in.

Elsewhere the Germans reached Warsaw, where Dov Zeev Begin now was. Once the way was clear he decided to try to make contact with his cousin in Drohiczyn. The rumor from Brisk was that the Russians had slaughtered the entire population, so, with no hope of finding his own family, he set out to walk from Warsaw to Drohiczyn.

One morning Rachel, accompanied by a friend, went to the local dairyman to fetch milk for the young Menachem. As she stood waiting her turn, pitcher in hand, she heard a familiar voice.

"Perhaps someone can tell me where the Begin family lives?"

"That's my father," Rachel shouted, throwing herself into his arms.

The Begins' Drohiczyn sanctuary did not last long. Despite the historians' propensity for presenting World War I as a static conflict, when it moved, it moved fast; the battlefront was approaching.

One morning, a column of weary peasants, carrying their worldly goods, trooped past the house. The Begins' cousin walked out to meet them.

"What happened? Where are you going?"

"The Cossacks are rampaging back there. They're driving everyone away and setting fire to the fields."

The following morning a Cossack cavalryman approached the house.

"Who lives here? Jews or Russians?"

A moment's silence, permeated by the sense of impending tragedy.

"Russians," answered the cousin in a passable imitation of the local farmers' dialect, then added, "and the Governor lives in the house across the way."

The Cossack departed and the Jews of Drohiczyn set to work digging shelters.

In the late afternoon of the following day the Cossacks arrived in force. They drove the occupants out into their fields and set fire to the homes. It was cold and rainy. Rachel slept under a wagon while young Menachem found shelter in a stack of straw. Hasia stayed awake all night. In the morning the Germans came and distributed sugar-coated cookies to the children.

Dov Zeev Begin took his family and various relatives and friends to the house that his father had found by the dam on the Bug. They walked all the way. A German soldier, from the detachment that was to guard the dam, held the hand of the young child who was to be the prime minister of Israel. Menachem did not cry or complain. In fact he was delighted with his new friend and enjoyed every minute of their trek.

Their new haven contained only two rooms, but there was food and the children had plenty of things with which to amuse themselves. They picked mushrooms in the nearby forest, and adopted a lonely raven whom they called "Hans."

34

The Begins spent a year here. Then they moved into a one-room apartment in the nearby town of Kobrin. Rachel started school, and Herzl was sent to *heder*—the traditional institution of East European Jewish children, where they learned to read and write Hebrew and memorized the Holy Books. Dov Zeev returned to his Zionist activities.

After four years in Kobrin Dov Zeev went back to Brest Litovsk, armed with a permit to restore the ruins of the town synagogue, which he stretched to include the building of a hospital. Each week on the Sabbath he returned to his family in Kobrin. A year later he moved Hasia and the children back to Brisk, into an apartment in a non-Jewish district of the town. As the Jews of Brisk began to return to the town, Dov Zeev devoted himself to reconstructing the community's homes. It was the classic Jewish situation of destruction followed by redemption. The community prospered, and Dov Zeev Begin became one of its leaders.

But the happiness of returning home proved short-lived. Brisk changed hands with each new treaty that carved up Europe at the end of the war. The Germans were followed by the Poles; then, in 1920, the Bolsheviks arrived. They did not stay long, but they left a strong impression in the mind of young Menachem, an impression he would repeat whenever anyone asked about his childhood. Two images remained particularly clear: that of a Russian soldier knocking on their door to ask for a crust of bread; and that of a Jewess who was the commissar of a unit billeted in their house. Menachem felt pity for the soldier, with his rumpled uniform and sad face. And even though he was only seven, he could discern the high motivation of this scruffy army. In the evenings he heard them singing the songs of their revolution, and listened to their voices gaining power after a few drinks.

The commissar was something else again. She awakened revulsion both by her stern expression and by the fact that she behaved like a man among men. He was particularly repelled by her stories of the Bolshevik Revolution, and her open hints that she could shoot human beings without batting an eyelid.

Maybe it was that casual conversation, at which Menachem Begin sat in as a passive and perhaps unnoticed listener, that formed his deep detestation of communism. Many years later, when he was a member of the Knesset, he treated even the bitterest of his political opponents with courtesy. Begin's speeches could be scathing, yet he always addressed his adversaries with utmost politeness. The Communists were the exception to his rule. Throughout his years in the Knesset Begin for the most part ignored their remarks. But when he did take note of their presence, he shed all vestige of politeness, mocked them cruelly, calling them "traitors" while lashing out, though with a deal more parliamentary courtesy, at the Soviet Union as the prime example of a totalitarian state.

In 1923, when he was ten, Menachem won his first notice as an orator. It was at a *Lag B'Omer* festival organized by his father. He stood on a table and, in a mixture of Hebrew and Yiddish, spoke of the festival's significance. *Lag B'Omer* is a popular festival, traditionally associated with the heroism of the last Jewish revolt against Rome, in A.D. 70. In normal times the children were taken out into the fields and forests and taught to use bows and arrows. The evening was spent around a bonfire, singing the songs that went with this particular festival. Over generations it had lost much of its meaning, and few people remembered its origins. However Dov Zeev Begin, the ardent Zionist, was well aware of its ancient significance, and so was his son. The adult listeners were open-mouthed. They had never expected such oratorical talent in a child so young. And it is perhaps significant that Menachem's first speech was made at a Jewish festival of both religious and nationalistic importance, for it was this mixture that would bring him to the peak of power fifty-four years later. Furthermore *Lag B'Omer* with its traditional parade was perhaps instrumental in fashioning Menachem Begin's love of the ceremonial. He thrilled to the sight of the marching men and the flames of the festive bonfire. He listened eagerly to the men telling tales of bravery and heroism. And he was already learning that words put together into sentences, delivered with a particular intonation, possess an almost magical power of their own.

Menachem completed his primary education in Tachkemoni School, which was sponsored by the Mizrahi religious Zionist movement. The atmosphere at home complemented his traditional education. On Friday nights he accompanied his father to synagogue and was intensely influenced by the environment there. These influences shaped the viewpoint of a man who is today deeply pious, who observes all the commandments, will not travel on the Sabbath, and intersperses his speeches with references to his adherence to traditional ways. His remarks often conclude with the phrase "if God wills it."

Even at that age, the young Menachem displayed a particular love for the Jewish festivals. For him then, these were moments of spiritual uplift—moments when one could look back and remember a world that was no more but could perhaps come again, the great period of Jewish history. For the adult Begin there would be moments of looking back on a world that was indeed no more—that of his parents' home, of the landscapes of his childhood, of an entire Jewish world wiped out by World War II. Perhaps the most vivid memory of all was of Passover in his father's home. The first evening of the festival is an occasion when all Jewish families, without exception, sit down together to read and sing the story of the Exodus, the breaking of the chains of bondage, and of God's promise to his Chosen People.

In the Passover service were words that particularly aroused the emotions of the young boy in Brest Litovsk, verses that collectively form a psalm of praise to the Almighty who, throughout the ages, has rescued his nation from persecution: "Not one alone, but in every generation, those who rise against us to destroy us, and the Holy One—Blessed be He—rescues us from their hands." As the years passed Menachem came to believe fervently in this eternal truth, and it is this as much as any other credo that can be called his political motto. In his refusal to talk to the Palestine Liberation Organization, or to contemplate Israeli withdrawal from the West Bank, Golan Heights, and parts of Sinai—territories conquered in the 1967 war—Menachem Begin as a politician has been guided by that same premonition of a world rising up to destroy Israel. In every generation there is someone—and in this generation it is the Arab world—who seeks the destruction of all things Jewish. This is the kernel of Begin's belief.

At fourteen he transferred to a Polish governmental

school, and it was perhaps here more than anywhere else that he acquired the patina of Polish aristocratic behavior, learning to refer to and address his fellow men with respect. To a certain degree it was here, also, that his national consciousness was forged—an awareness permeated by the East and Central European tradition, with its aura of mysticism and medieval chivalry, coupled with the love of symbols and pageantry.

Although there were only three Jews in the school, Menachem made no attempt whatsoever to subdue or hide his Jewish background. Indeed it was the cause of a failing mark in Latin, a subject at which he excelled. The Latin exam was set for a Saturday. He politely informed his teacher that he could not desecrate the Sabbath by writing on that day. His classmates laughed.

"I might have given in and written the exam," Begin later remarked; "but they laughed, and I wasn't going to let them think that I surrendered because of their laughter."

The Begins brought up their children to respect tradition and God, but they did more than that. On the Sabbath eve, upon their return from synagogue, the children heard their father tell of that distant land on the eastern Mediterranean coast, the source of the historical memories recorded in the holy writings and the inspiration of Jewish prayers. Still a place somehow distant and abstract, it had occupied the dreams of multitudes of Jews throughout the ages, yet none dared to believe that they would live the dream and tread the soil of the Holy Land. The Jewish belief in the "other Jerusalem"—the city of the spirit suspended somewhere beyond this world—could perhaps console the dreamers, and unite the aspirations of Jews scattered throughout the world. Others found solace in calling the places where they lived by the beloved name. Vilna, for example, was referred to in Jewish literature as "the Jerusalem of Lithuania."

Political Zionism, conceived by its leaders as a nationalist revival, sought to release the scattered communities of Jews from the captivity of their dreams. It posed them the challenge of return to the land of their forefathers as something both tangible and possible.

But there were many who refused to believe, and others who were frightened by it. Jewish history was full of such trauma-inducing attempts. One of them had ended, in the Middle Ages, in an economic holocaust. An eccentric rabbi of Izmir in Turkey by the name of Shabetai Zvi had disseminated through the Jewish communities of Europe and North Africa the revelation that he was destined to lead the Chosen People back to their Promised Land. Jews, seeing in him the Messiah, flocked to his banner. They sold their homes and property, and waited for his signal to start their voyage. Then he was exposed as a crazed charlatan. Shabetai Zvi converted to Islam and was buried in a Moslem grave. He left behind him split communities and masses of Jews who were now homeless, their only possession an unfulfilled dream. No one intended to take them to Palestine—and certainly nobody would let them settle there. So great was the trauma that the rabbis declared a boycott on anyone rash enough to weave the fabric of dreams.

In the early twentieth century the antagonists of early Zionism tried to attach to Theodor Herzl and his colleagues the label of false messiah. Those entrenched within traditional Judaism argued that the return to the biblical "Land of Israel" was in the hands of heaven, and that until the coming of the true Messiah, born of King David's line, no mere mortal had the right to preempt salvation. Others grasped with both hands the solution offered by Bolshevism— the rejection of nationalism and a new division of mankind by classes.

Menachem Begin was still a child when he heard his father speak of the "Land of Israel" in terms of tangible reality. He could not understand the implications, yet the idea took its place in his awareness, together with things heard in *heder* and at Tachkemoni School. The holy writings provided confirmation for his father's words. Begin still uses those writings today to justify Jewish ownership of the entire Land of Israel, including those areas occupied in June 1967. It is written, and it bears the seal of a commandment from God. Begin believes that with all his heart. He can display humanitarian feelings for the Arabs of the West Bank—perhaps far more so than his predecessors of the labor movement—and can sincerely work toward granting that population its maximal rights under military government. With the same sincerity he believes in its right to reside in the country. But the historic right is the sole preserve of the Jews.

The Polish educational system was always the cradle of nationalist spirit. Polish teachers—with their intimate knowledge of the frequent partitioning of their homeland, of the strips torn off to satisfy ravenous neighbors, of the invasions by hostile armies—preached love of homeland, loyalty, the pride of belonging, and the eternal message that Poland had always survived and would continue to do so. Begin, armed with his father's message, was quick to find Jewish implications —particularly in the history lessons.

"The day will come when we will all be in the Land of Israel," his father declared. Menachem, at fourteen, listened with sparkling eyes. He had a vision of himself setting foot on that distant soil, and he believed that the day was not so far off.

One way or another the intellectual seeds were already there in the growing youth. While his classmates were roaming around outside, Menachem preferred to sit at the chessboard with his father, a game he had played well since the age of seven.

There are those who say that Menachem Begin's talents at chess stand him in good stead today in politics. He is not only a statesman with a vision, who loves to speak in the name of higher principles and lard his pronouncements with historic and legal references, but also a skilled politician, who pulls strings deftly and prepares traps for his adversaries with the utmost elegance.

The boy destined to lead an armed underground in defiance of the might of the British army never excelled at sports. Books were more important to him than games. So deep an impression did the written word make that decades later he was capable of reciting from the podium of the Knesset verses by Adam Mitzkevitz, Poland's national poet—verses learned back in school that had captured his imagination for their nationalistic sentiment.

Menachem's relationship with his mother was founded on honor and esteem. Having heard his father address her with the greatest respect that a man could offer his wife, mingled with deep affection, Menachem himself learned to treat her and all women with the same courtesy and tolerance. Like all Jewish mothers Hasia was the overseer of her children's education. Hers was the familial duty of supervising their development into educated, enlightened, and cultured human beings.

His image of his father was of a man of courage, unmarked by sin. Menachem was very small when Dov Zeev was forced to leave Brisk. As time passed he attributed this to an act of personal courage and boldness in siding with the Germans when it involved considerable danger.

In the early 1920s the young Begin witnessed another example of his father's courage. Polish soldiers roaming around Brisk were in the habit of assaulting Jews, beating them, and cutting off their beards. One day Dov Zeev was walking with a bearded rabbi when a Polish sergeant accosted them. Pulling out a knife, the man threatened to shave the rabbi's beard. Dov Zeev raised his walking stick and hit the sergeant—an act unheard of in those days. It was to cost Dov Zeev and the rabbi dearly. Both were arrested and taken to a military fort across the river, where they were cruelly beaten.

To his son's eyes Dov Zeev appeared as a gentleman, respected by his fellow men and always able, in turn, to treat others with equal respect. This reinforced what Dov Zeev told him. Perhaps it also taught him to pay attention to appearance. Throughout all his wanderings and distress Dov Zeev was always dressed with immaculate care.

Menachem's first steps in politics now seem strange, even ironical and a little amusing. At twelve he joined the local branch of *Hashomer Hatzair*. The few Israelis who know this detail of the prime minister's life derive considerable humor from it, for *Hashomer Hatzair* youth movement is an offshoot of Zionism's extremist left-wing Mapam Party, and possesses a decidedly Marxist orientation. Today it would be difficult to find two more confirmed adversaries than Menachem Begin and *Hashomer Hatzair*. But in 1925 the movement was in its infancy and Menachem and Rachel both joined, with their father's blessing. For him *Hashomer Hatzair* represented an opportunity for his children to complete their Zionist education; the movement's secular trend was not yet evident.

Menachem and Rachel fitted in well with the group's activities. She took part in the drama circle, and both were active in the literary trials staged in the clubhouses, where they made their first social contacts. Among the teachings of the movement were aspects well designed to attract Menachem. The instructors taught their charges to be respectful of others, to tell the truth, and to maintain honest relations with those around them. Basically the movement taught good citizenship, much like that inculcated by all scout movements. Its uniqueness lay in its indoctrination of the youngsters to Zionism.

But at the end of 1926 *Hashomer Hatzair* took a turn that repelled the young Menachem. The first sign was a brochure written by Mordechai Orenstein, which said that the road for the Zionist youth movement was that of communism. Many years later this same Orenstein would be sent on a mission from Israel to Prague, where the Czechoslovak authorities arrested him for anti-Communist activities. He was tortured into a false confession, sentenced to a long term of imprisonment, then finally released after being cleared of all guilt. Ironically it was this man's communism that drove Begin away. He agreed with his father when he argued with members of *Hashomer Hatzair*, "First fight for your own freedom, then worry about the freedom of other nations."

Though he left the movement, Menachem did not lose interest in the Jewish affairs of his town. The Begin home was a center for the local leaders. He heard his father discussing public matters, debating with friends the items that were on the agenda of the Zionist movement, and occasionally he watched him at the community club listening intently to the speakers on culture.

Menachem would later say that up to this point his childhood memories were all colored green—the green of thick forests and fields stretching as far as the eye could see. And with the green were memories of the houses where the family lived and of a few faces that made some deep impressions. But the real turning point of his youth came with his departure from *Hashomer*. Had he not left that movement, Menachem might well have been influenced by Marxist idealogy; he might even have turned his back on politics.

Almost immediately he joined another youth movement, *Betar,* founded by Zeev Jabotinsky in 1923. This was a movement dedicated to the memory of, and named for, Yosef Trumpeldor (the name is formed from the initials of Brit Yosef Trumpeldor), a Russian Jew and officer in the czarist army who distinguished himself in the Russo-Japanese War. Organizing some of his comrades, Trumpeldor went to Palestine with the intention of driving out the Turks and establishing a Jewish State. But he found that the dream was too grandiose for immediate fulfillment, so he settled with a pioneer group at a place called Tel Hai. It was here that he died, fighting off armed Arab gangs.

Trumpeldor's death shook the Jewish world. The heroism displayed in the defense of Tel Hai became a part of the legends of the new Israel—synonymous with the concept that Jews could fight back. And it was this heritage that *Betar* wanted to pass on to its young members.

When Menachem joined, there was no way his new instructors could have known how big a change it would make in the life of the bespectacled and retiring youth. Nor could they know that his joining would be a major milestone for the movement itself.

This was Menachem Begin's first step along the road that would lead him, half a century later, to the prime ministership of Israel.

CHAPTER 2

The Slanting Curl

Menachem Begin's first act on assuming the premiership of Israel was to hang a large portrait on his
office wall. The face staring out is stern, the expression penetrating, with eyes prominent behind round-
framed glasses, pinched lips, and curl slanting across
the forehead.

The man in the portrait is the Zionist leader Vladimir Zeev Jabotinsky, one of the most controversial
figures in the military and political struggle that was
to culminate in the establishment of the State of Israel. So controversial was he that even today, thirty-
five years after his death, his image can still arouse
old hatreds between his supporters and his opponents.
David Ben-Gurion, the first prime minister of Israel,
carried this hatred over into his feelings about Begin
with an intensity far beyond that customary even between political enemies. In his wildest nightmares
Ben-Gurion could not have conceived that, four years
after his death, Menachem Begin would be occupying

his old shoes as prime minister, and that Jabotinsky's portrait would adorn the walls of the office from which he ran the affairs of Israel.

Begin's admiration for Jabotinsky exceeds even Ben-Gurion's hatred. Jabotinsky was the first name mentioned by Begin in the very first sentence of his victory speech after the 1977 election. In Jabotinsky Begin sees far more than leader, politician, poet, and thinker. He sees something akin to a modern oracle. For the present prime minister of Israel the writings that Jabotinsky left behind him rank with the volumes that describe Moses leading the Children of Israel to the Promised Land. Like all oracles, his writings and personality are not entirely free of contradictions; but they merge into one entity that inspired a political camp created in the 1920s in East Europe, and continue to inspire those who now hold the helm of state in Israel.

Without appreciating his attitude to Zeev Jabotinsky Menachem Begin cannot be understood. He himself has explained the relationship often enough, but one speech expresses it better than all the others—a speech made at an airport near Tel Aviv, over a coffin draped with the Israeli flag. The coffin contained the remains of Zeev Jabotinsky, flown back from New York for retirement in 1964, twenty-four years after his death:

> I hereby proclaim to the Jewish nation—to its cities and villages on the mountains and in the valleys, in their places of dispersion East and West—and to the fighters for freedom among the nations of the world both near and far, that forty-six years after fighting with a battalion of Hebrew

soldiers founded in the Hills of Ephraim and on the fords of the Jordan in order to return the Land of Israel to its eternal owner—the People of Israel; thirty-five years after being sentenced by the foreign ruler to exile because of his war for a Jewish State in our time, and to save millions of Jews from extermination; twenty-four years after his demise in the Holocaust of which he had warned; sixteen years after the driving out of the foreign régime from our land and the resurrection of Israel—Zeev Jabotinsky has returned to the homeland.

Honored head of *Betar*, our father, teacher, and rabbi—you have returned to the land of your fathers and your sons. You delayed. We have waited for you ever since that day when the flag of Israel was hung among the flags of the liberated countries by the hands of its fighting sons. Many of the members of the nation you so loved, and of the students you reared—too many of them to count —did not live to see this great and sacred day for all Israel. They are no more, for they were exterminated by alien and enemy, they fell in battles for the sake of the nation and its redemption, for the country and its liberation, went to the gallows to sanctify its freedom, and lost their lives. The spirit of all of them is with us.

Begin saw Jabotinsky for the first time in Brest Litovsk. He was only a boy of sixteen then, but the man with the slanting curl took his heart by storm. There was something hypnotic in his sweeping rhetoric, something that touched a hidden nerve in the youngster brought up in traditional Judaism at home and

49

romantic nationalism in the Polish gymnasium—the nationalism that swept East and Central Europe between the world wars.

Menachem had already read a book that had given new hope to millions of Jews worldwide. Theodor Herzl was no longer alive, but his book *Altneuland* (*Old-New Land,* written between the years 1899 and 1902) had become a banner. Even those who had not read it knew its contents. Like Thomas More's *Utopia,* Herzl's Jewish State seemed a distant and perhaps utopian dream. But Begin was impressed by the detailed description of that dream.

If he discerned any difference between himself and his classmates—and he did indeed—then it lay mainly in the fact that they identified with the national poetic epics, the heroes of Polish history, the heritage of their country, and even with its anti-Semitic tradition.

Menachem as a Jew was not only a stranger to all that, but his upbringing actually fostered and encouraged its rejection. Teenagers growing up in an environment that nourishes nationalistic emotions usually tend to identify with their national heroes. Who then were Menachem Begin's heroes? He could choose from among biblical figures, but they were far off in terms of time. He heard talk at home, and particularly at festivals, of Jewish heroes throughout the ages in one place or another, but mostly in the land of his dreams. Herzl's book held out the hope that there was a tract of land where young Jews like himself could renew the web of a national life, returning to where it began sometime at the dawn of human history. Often enough he had heard his father say that the ancient hope of returning to the Holy Land had never died away. But this book described it all as something possible, something that could be done.

Menachem's departure from *Hashomer* was not only a result of an instinctive dislike for Marxist ideologies. He disliked any idea that denied nationalism, and was looking for another way to classify human beings. Now it seemed that Zeev Jabotinsky's *Betar* could offer him what he was seeking, so he joined its ranks. The Jewish nationalist education offered by the movement changed Begin's image of himself. The delicate and fragile boy suddenly straightened his back and stood up to his classmates, giving as good as he got—whether in words or blows. He acquired a national pride of his own that gave him new strength.

"From time to time they descended on me at school," he has said, "but I learned to defend myself. I never bowed my head. If someone raised his hand to me, I paid him in the same coin. There were times when I came home bruised and bloodied—but with the feeling that my honor was intact. As time went by I learned that the ones who hit me treated me with respect when I hit back. They learned their lesson."

A famous Jewish poet of the romantic period, Saul Tchernikowsky, wrote that man as an adult becomes an exact reflection of his childhood. The Israeli-born youth who still learn Tchernikowsky's poetry in school can bear witness to that truth from their own experience. In Israel more than in any other immigrant country, the gap between parents and their children is immense, and it must be measured not only in time but also in space. The parents brought to Israel their childhood memories, which for the most part were of persecution and alienation, of anti-Semitism, pogroms, and harsh decrees. Many young Israelis believe that their parents suffer from a collective paranoia, and that they interpret any military or diplomatic threat as a plot to destroy them. To a certain extent Begin's viewpoint and his political platform are an exact reflection of his own childhood memories of the Polish gymnasium.

In speaking of the PLO as a neo-Nazi organization, and in ascribing to the Arab rulers intentions no less evil than those of Hitler, Begin is seeing in his mind's eye the Polish classmates who called him "Zhid" and tried to thrash him. He fights for his political views with those same methods that he adopted in school: an eye for an eye, and defend one's honor no matter what the price. To Western eyes such a struggle must seem anachronistic, particularly in the light of a total disillusionment with nationalism. To an American, living in a multiethnic environment, the concept must appear strange and obsolete. But for Menachem Begin there is nothing more tangible than this approach. His speeches, both as leader of the opposition and as prime minister, have contained sermons on the need for a national "upright stance," for the defense of national honor, for a show of muscle in the face of muscle. He truly believes that Israel's enemies will respect her only if they respect and recognize her power—exactly as his classmates came to respect him after they felt his fists.

When, in 1923, Jabotinsky founded the *Betar* youth movement, he was already a well-known and controversial Zionist leader. His political horizons encompassed all Europe. Moreover he was one of the very few Jewish leaders who could claim first-hand experience of life in Palestine. For him, the Promised Land was no abstract dream; he was even familiar with the country's prisons. Consequently the youth movement that he created was in some ways a precise mirror of his own accumulated experience.

Jabotinsky was born in October 1880 in Odessa. His father, a prosperous grain merchant, gave him a liberal Russian education, which was not exceptional among the Jews of Odessa, who had broken through the walls of conservatism. Indeed the orthodox rabbis who bitterly criticized the permissiveness of the community were frequently heard to say that the fires of Hell were burning a mere 2 or 3 kilometers from the outskirts of Odessa.

When already a leading light in the Zionist movement Jabotinsky loved to talk about his first steps toward what became the turning point in his life, and particularly about a conversation with his mother that took place when he was only seven:

"Tell me, Mother, will we Jews also have a kingdom sometime?"

"Of course, stupid."

He did not repeat his stupid questions, preferring to grow up as a Russian. His knowledge of Russian literature, coupled with his natural intelligence, made him an outstanding pupil at school, and ensured his popularity among his classmates. At seventeen he was acquiring publicity and fame through a series of articles printed in the local press. His command of language was phenomenal and a place of honor among contemporary Russian journalists was assured; but the anti-Semitism of East Europe, which gnawed away like a cancer, accorded him a different role. Perhaps history owes a debt to one of Jabotinsky's teachers in the local gymnasium—a man of decided anti-Semitic opinion. A particularly virulent remark of his caused the proud youngster to give a sharp response, and Jabotinsky left school rather than apologize.

Thus at seventeen—the outstanding student of his class—Jabotinsky went to Italy to complete his studies, though he continued to send his articles to the Odessa newspapers. His stay in Italy, a country almost devoid of Jews, was paradoxically the experience that complemented his Zionist awareness. Like Menachem Begin and other Jewish youths who were destined for the first ranks of the Zionist movement, Jabotinsky's nationalist convictions were formed from a study of his non-Jewish environment.

In Italy he was enchanted by the fierce romanticism of the Italian revivalist movement, and particularly by the towering figure of Garibaldi. Mastering the Italian language at an amazing pace, he adopted the theatrical manners of the Garibaldians which reached somewhere deep inside him to the nerves of the Judaism.

When he returned to Odessa in 1903, Jabotinsky was an established figure in Russian journalism. His articles sent from Italy, signed with the pen name *Altalena*, had been widely read. And for the Jews of Russia he was a man of promise. He had returned far more imbued with national spirit than he ever could have been had he continued a liberal Russian education. That same year he joined other young Jews in setting up a self-defense organization to combat the pogroms that were sweeping Odessa and its surroundings. He also became very active in the local Zionist organization, and was elected as its delegate to the Sixth Zionist Congress at Basel, Switzerland, in 1903 where, for the first time, he saw Theodor Herzl.

The Sixth Congress was an important milestone in the struggle to revive the Jewish nation, and it took place under the shadow of a threat of a split. Herzl as the father of modern Zionism, backed by a slight majority of the delegates, favored acceptance of an offer made by the British to set up a Jewish State in Africa, in what was then called Uganda but is today a part of Kenya. Their argument was that in the prevailing political conditions it would be most difficult to bring to fruition the Zionist vision of Jewish national revival in the historic homeland. They wanted to postpone the idea for a more propitious time, but demand an immediate sanctuary until that time came. Herzl brought his full moral and personal prestige to bear on the Congress, but the East European and Russian delegates were violently opposed. Their argument was that the African solution was likely to destroy any chance of ever returning to the land of Israel, that there was no point in replacing a European diaspora by an African version. The Zionist movement was about to break into two. That it did not was the result of an impassioned plea by Herzl in which he declared his loyalty to the "Zionism of Zion." Nevertheless the search for alternative solutions would go on in some Jewish circles for the best part of a decade after the formal abandonment of the Uganda idea at the Seventh Zionist Congress.

Jabotinsky was deeply impressed by the stormy debate in the Congress and in the corridors outside the main hall—a debate that was casting the Jewish world into a whirlpool of dispute and hate. Personally he was opposed to Herzl's Uganda plan, but he was still a young and insufficiently known delegate. Greater and better known leaders were ascending the platform to pour forth flame and brimstone on Herzl and his supporters.

Three years later, at the 1906 Russian Zionist Conference in Helsinki, Jabotinsky was among the main speakers—and his proposal was to act immediately to establish a Jewish State in the Land of Israel. His audience concluded that this was a young man with a powerful command of persuasive rhetoric.

By 1909 he was already a member of the Zionist Executive, entrusted with the Portfolio of Information and Propaganda. He was sent to Constantinople to set up four Jewish newspapers. Jabotinsky got to know the local Jewish community, whipped up sympathy for the Zionist cause, and made a study of the prevailing moods in the administration of the Ottoman Empire, which still included the territory of Palestine. He returned to Russia a year later firmly convinced that the Jews could rebuild the Land of Israel only if that empire fell and lost its Palestinian domains. Meanwhile, since he could hardly influence that process, he set about propagating Hebrew as the language of Jewish youth. Given his own skill in languages—by then he was fluent in ten—this was a task tailored to his talents. He wrote a Hebrew textbook and translated the best of European literature; he also set up a publishing house.

In World War I Zeev Jabotinsky became military correspondent for a big Russian paper. His beat was the Western Front, and eventually he accompanied the British Expeditionary Force to Egypt—an event that proved to be another milestone in his life. It was here that Jabotinsky met the one-armed ex-czarist officer named Yosef Trumpeldor who was soon to enlist in the British army to fight the Turks. Trumpeldor had visions of a Jewish military force that would share in the conquest of Palestine, and Jabotinsky was enthusiastic about the idea. He brought it to the attention of the British High Command in Egypt, but was told that the British as yet had no interest in opening a new front in Palestine. Their headquarters was overflowing with experts on Arab affairs who believed that British Intelligence could incite the countries of the Arabian Peninsula to revolt against the Turks. These men, or at least the majority of them, were against any cooperation with Zionists. But the High Command did have an alternative to offer: If the Jews really wanted to fight, why shouldn't they put together a battalion for the Gallipoli front? Trumpeldor agreed. He was willing to fight Turks anywhere. Jabotinsky declined politely. He was not seeking some anonymous battalion but a Hebrew force dedicated to one defined objective: the conquest of Palestine.

"Indirectly, we can serve that purpose," Trumpeldor observed at their last meeting before each went his separate way.

"Perhaps you are right, sir," replied Jabotinsky, "but I am not joining such a battalion."

In fact history proved both of them right. The battalion fought in Gallipoli, was eventually disbanded, and did not reach Palestine. But its outstanding performance in battle convinced the British that Jews could take their place on the battlefield, and was instrumental in their decision to establish the Jewish Legion.

While Trumpeldor served in Gallipoli, Jabotinsky was in London trying to convince the Jewish leadership to press the British government for a Jewish army to conquer Palestine. This activity did not sit well with the leaders of the Zionist movement, who were trying to preserve a cautious neutrality. After all, a considerable proportion of the Jewish nation was living under the control of Germans, Austrians, and Turks, and deviation from a neutral position could endanger them. Jabotinsky decided to make his appeal directly to the Jewish people. The step marked the beginning of a rift between him and the Zionist establishment—a rift that would widen into bitter competition tinged by hatred.

The Jews to whom Jabotinsky turned in London were mostly refugees from czarist Russia who had come to England to find sanctuary from persecutions and pogroms. The only privilege they enjoyed, as foreign aliens, was exemption from military service. They mocked this short, bespectacled man who wanted to turn them into soldiers; they broke up his meetings and pelted him with rotten tomatoes.

In 1916 there were no more than 200 volunteers willing to serve in a Jewish battalion within the British army if and when it was created. But one year later, after a concerted campaign by Jabotinsky, the Zionist group—which was now leaning toward the Allies—agreed to try the idea; and eventually the British government gave formal approval to the establishment of the all-Jewish 38th Battalion of the Royal Fusiliers. The refugees from Russia were given the option of joining the 38th Royal Fusiliers or of returning to their own countries.

On September 21, 1918, Jabotinsky, who had enlisted and was later promoted to lieutenant, was with the 38th Battalion when they seized the Jordan fords 3 miles north of Jericho. For him it was a highly significant action. The Promised Land lay before his eyes—he was even sharing in its conquest, together with his comrades from England and the United

States, and those Palestinian Jews who had enlisted in Egypt and in southern Palestine, already in British hands.

But his hopes that the Jewish Legion would be garrisoned in Palestine, and would thereby be able to dictate somewhat what would happen politically, were doomed to failure. Most of the men of the 38th wanted to be demobilized, and return home. In fact the British had never entertained the idea of keeping the force in Palestine. Released from the army, Jabotinsky settled in Jerusalem.

The city gave Jabotinsky a vantage point from which to study a problem of which most contemporary Zionist leaders were unaware—or had deliberately ignored: the relationship between the Jews who wanted to return to the land of their forefathers, and the Arabs who had arrived by slow migration over centuries. Of course the problem is still at the core of the Arab-Israeli dispute, but Jabotinsky was there when it first began to take shape.

The Jewish and Arab national movements were growing simultaneously at a time when the Arab world, while recovering from the war, was turning its back on nationalism simply as an ideal, and seeking a far more comprehensive objective. A collision in Palestine was unavoidable; Jabotinsky grasped that fact from the moment he set foot in Jerusalem. Lord Balfour, the British Foreign Minister, had promised a Jewish National Home in Palestine. Although the promise was still far from realization, it had aroused the Arabs of the country, who were obviously opposed. Jabotinsky could see that, sooner or later, this opposition would lead to violence. As a way of preparing for this violence, he proposed something which in principle was similar to the solution that Menachem Begin would later offer, as prime minister of Israel, as a means of solving the Arab-Israeli conflict. Jabotinsky presented his proposal for a Jewish defense force to Justice Louis Brandeis, a leader of U.S. Jewry, who was then visiting Palestine.

"Anyone who envisages a pogrom in Palestine is dreaming wildly," Brandeis answered.

"Your honor may indeed be an excellent judge, but you cannot see what is going on under your own nose—a sign that you lack even minimal political sense," Jabotinsky told Brandeis tersely.

Jabotinsky then went ahead on his own. He bought weapons, hid them in his own apartment, and began to train his men in secret. In April 1920 a nucleus of *Haganah* ("Defense") existed in Jerusalem and Tel Aviv. By the summer of that year Jabotinsky's nightmare had come true. A Moslem procession on its way to the Mosque of Omar in the Old City attacked Jewish bystanders and tried to loot Jewish homes. The Arabs launched a pogrom with the cry "The Government is with us," knowing they enjoyed British support. Riots continued the next day. There were 180 Jewish casualties, but *Haganah* defenders kept the Arabs out of Jewish neighborhoods. On the third day the British army intervened, imposed a curfew, and began a search for weapons primarily in the Jewish areas of the city. There, in a small attic, they found 3 rifles, 2 pistols, and 300 rounds of ammunition. Nineteen people were arrested but they refused to reveal the identity of their leader. However Jabotinsky, learning of the arrests, turned himself in. He was arraigned for trial before a military court, charged with illegal possession of firearms.

Jabotinsky's trial began on the day that the Jews of Palestine were to go to the polls to elect a representative assembly. As an act of identification the left-wing party (from which the Israel Labor Party would later evolve) placed Jabotinsky at the top of their list of candidates. But his election did not prevent his being sentenced to nineteen years in the fortress of Acre. Jabotinsky spent his time in prison teaching English to his fellow prisoners and translating Dante's *Inferno* into Hebrew.

Three months after Jabotinsky went to prison, the first High Commissioner for Palestine, Sir Herbert Samuel, arrived to take up his post. He granted pardons to Jabotinsky and his comrades, though Jabotinsky was deported and declared *persona non grata* for life.

Jabotinsky had gone to prison as a very popular figure in the small Jewish community of Palestine. But when he came out he became involved in a major controversy with the Zionist leadership, directed by Dr. Haim Weizmann, because of his opposition to the concept of selective Jewish migration to Palestine. The leaders of the Jewish community were deeply influenced by the social and political model of the Bolshevik Revolution in Russia. Some of them had witnessed the abortive revolution of 1905, and now wanted to apply its main lesson in Palestine: that a select, small, and united élite could, by force of its unity and determination, accomplish things beyond the reach of an entire nation. It was such a Zionist avant garde that they wanted in Palestine. Most of these men had fled from the Jewish reality of East Europe and Russia, which had forced their fathers to become small merchants, shoemakers, and tailors. The answer for Palestine was a new Jew, returning to the soil, using the sweat of his brow to conquer the wastelands and swamps of a country that had been virtually deserted for 2,000 years. And for that they needed to attract Jewish youngsters imbued with the same vision and ideals. The last thing they wanted was an influx of shopkeepers. The time for them would come when the infrastructure was already there.

Jabotinsky argued that the shopkeepers and tradesmen were no less entitled than the pioneers who were draining swamps and building the first *kibbutzim*— communes—on the banks of the Sea of Galilee and in the Vale of Esdraelon. His conflict with the community leaders began to acquire social overtones. He was condemned as a reactionary, and the rift deepened and broadened to the point where it embittered the entire Zionist movement for decades.

In January 1923, Jabotinsky resigned his membership in the elected assembly of Palestinian Jewry; and in 1923 he founded a new youth movement— *Betar*. The founding congress of *Betar* took place in Riga, and its ideas spread from there across East Europe. Two years later Jabotinsky set up an independent Revisionist Party within the Zionist Organization, whose purpose was to demand a revision of the definitions of Zionist aims.

Menachem Begin was sixteen when the new party caused a crisis in the Zionist movement and the entire Jewish world. Although the roots of the crisis lay in the differences of opinion between Jabotinsky and his adversaries, the immediate cause was a statement made to a British journalist by Dr. Haim Weizmann, to the effect that Zionism did not aspire to a Jewish majority in Palestine. Jabotinsky demanded of the Zionist Congress a vote of no confidence in Weizmann—who was its leader. When the conference rejected Jabotinsky's motion by a vast majority, he asked to speak and, in front of everyone, tore his delegate's card into pieces, then led his colleagues out of the hall.

He swiftly set up an opposing organization called the New Zionist Organization. The establishment labeled them "dissidents," and the name stuck for a good many years. (Menachem Begin inherited it, and his opponents still resort to its use to this day.)

When Jabotinsky came to Brest Litovsk he found plenty of supporters, among them Dov Zeev Begin. For years in the Begin household there was a blue box of the sort used for contributions to the Jewish National Fund. This one was for the Zionist Organization to purchase lands in Palestine. At the end of each week Dov Zeev would drop in a few coins, and he would collect, as well, from his friends and neighbors. But the box vanished after Jabotinsky's visit, to be replaced by another bearing the legend: "Tel Hai Fund"—the financial arm of the New Zionist Organization.

In 1931, at the age of eighteen, Menachem Begin went to Warsaw to attend law school at Warsaw University, but he continued to be active in *Betar*. He was offered a paying job in the movement's central office, and quickly revealed his talents as an organizer. He also established a reputation as an impersonator who could imitate anyone's voice and mannerisms. He was particularly good at imitating Zeev Jabotinsky, though it would be many years before people realized that Begin was really trying to copy his mentor's voice and style in his own speeches. One thing was clear from the very beginning, however. For Begin, Jabotinsky's words were not to be disputed, and this devotion helped to strengthen his position among the local heads of *Betar*.

CHAPTER 3

Blood Libel

In the early 1930s, while Menachem Begin as a young law student was being watched and considered a promising youth in Jabotinsky's movement, Jabotinsky's own conflict with the Zionist Organization was taking on even sharper dimensions of overt hostility. The result was a painful shadow hanging over world Jewry. The arguments were at once ideological and political, and personal and emotional—and they persist into the party politics of present-day Israel. Issues such as the future of the territories taken by Israel in 1967, the structure of society, and the place of labor unions in economic disputes all somehow revert back to the old antagonisms.

Since the demise of the "Uganda solution," and despite the fact that splinter factions continued to seek other territorial answers, the consensus among Zionists was that the way lay in a national home in the biblical "Land of Israel." And this was their common platform in the continuing war against anti-

Zionist elements such as the Jewish "Bund" and pro-Communist organizations who argued for the total integration of Jews into their non-Jewish environment. But the Zionists could not agree as to what methods to use to achieve their aim. The Zionist center, led by Dr. Weizmann, pinned its hopes on Great Britain, in the belief that the British would not go back on their promise of a Jewish National Home when the time was right. Both the British Zionist Federation and the Jewish Agency for Palestine had strong lobbies in London.

The left-wing faction, from which the Israel Labor Party would evolve, put its faith in practical Zionism—having no illusions about the power of diplomacy. Its leaders tried to attract to Palestine the young Jewish intelligentsia and to convert them into a pioneer force to reclaim the deserts in the name of those who would follow. In what had been swampland they sought to create a new generation of Jews, who could both farm and defend themselves. As far as possible, the labor faction avoided annoying the British and ducked conflict with the Arabs. Much of what they did was achieved under the nose of the British.

The Revisionists favored a radically different approach. They sought an immediate solution through the conquest of Palestine. "We must turn illegal immigration into our national sport," preached Jabotinsky, and he gave *Betar* a paramilitary appearance, saying: "Our movement is a blend of school and army camp." The members of *Betar*, like other nationalist youth movements in East Europe, wore uniforms and held summer camps under army-like discipline. The structure of the movement was along classic military lines, and members were required to obey orders and address their superiors in correct military fashion.

The social ideology of *Betar* took shape, to a certain degree, in response to the left-wing faction in Zionism. It favored an extreme monism—a total denial of class differences and a merging of all social resources in one national stream. This view is evident today in the social and economic program of Menachem Begin's government. The prime minister is often moved to tears when he stands, straight-backed, at the conferences of his party to sing Jabotinsky's poem, which has become the *Betar* anthem. The second verse speaks for itself:

> Hadar—
> Even in poverty a Jew is a prince;
> Whether slave or tramp
> You have been created a prince
> Crowned with the diadem of David
> In light or in darkness
> Remember the crown—
> The crown of pride and tagar

The two decades that separated the global wars were marked by a continual ideological conflict between the extremist elements of the Zionist right and left, each of which challenged the social order, and each of which swore to destroy the existing order and build a new society on its ruins. The Zionist movement did not take sides in the ideological struggle that cast its shadow over Europe and paved the way to World War II. But Jews as individuals were unable to stand aside. The leftist faction of Zionism detested communism, but its social position was clearcut; many of its leaders were the products of European social democratic traditions, and they sought to integrate the national redemption of their nation with a social redemption—to put an end to Jewish self-imagery as petty traders and moneylenders. For them, Jabotinsky was a reactionary. The military behavior of his movement led them to suspect him of leaning toward the European ultra-nationalists, at a time when Munich beer cellars were echoing with the words of an ex-corporal in the kaiser's army. Jabotinsky's movement was also notable for its military ceremonial, its preaching against class differences, and its emphasis on national uniqueness. His opponents were not above labeling him "Vladimir Hitler," while some of them made less than flattering comparisons with Benito Mussolini.

But the words of Jabotinsky's song caught the imagination of Polish Jews, many of whom—like Menachem Begin—were seeking a proud identity for themselves amid the stormy nationalist sea:

> Tagar—
> To all obstacles and hindrances,
> Whether you go up or down
> In the flame of revolt—
> Carry the flame to kindle: "Nevermind,"
> For silence is mud;
> Give up blood and soul
> For the sake of the hidden glory.

In the 1930s the Polish Jewish community was the largest and most important of the Jewish factions—a center of creativity and culture. Its relative influence, always considerable, had increased after Russian

Jewry virtually vanished behind the Soviet curtain of silence. None of the Zionist parties could allow themselves the luxury of ignoring Polish Jewry, or of leaving the field open to adversaries.

In Palestine the handful of men who joined Jabotinsky's movement, together with the occasional reinforcements of new immigrants of the same mind, remained isolated and outnumbered. The labor unions, established as an arm of the Zionist left wing, denied the Revisionists the shelter of professional protection. Labor exchanges, operated by the same unions, were closed to Jabotinsky's supporters. Men were careful not to be seen in their company. At the same time the parties of the left used their influence overseas to have the same kind of pressures applied. As a result Jabotinsky's movement began to become militant as its members accused their opponents of clouding the Zionist objective, of betraying the educational and political heritage of Herzl, and of denying the needs of the Diaspora.

On the eve of the 1933 elections for the Zionist Congress, Labor leader David Ben-Gurion was sent from Palestine to campaign throughout Poland. In those towns where Jabotinsky's supporters were powerful, he was greeted with tomatoes and insults. Ben-Gurion retaliated, using every insult in the book to describe Jabotinsky and comparing him with the worst of the political monsters who stood ready to seize power in Europe. While Jabotinsky cried out in his speeches and articles that the ground was burning beneath the very feet of Poland's Jewish community and that the only alternative to massacre was emigration to Palestine, Ben-Gurion accused him of fostering vain illusions and holding out messianic hopes that led nowhere.

The battle for Jewish public opinion in Poland, and elsewhere in the world, was finally resolved on the beach at Tel Aviv. There, on June 16, 1933, a pistol shot changed the course of history. Even today the mere mention of the victim's name is enough to arouse cries of mutual accusation.

The man who fell on the hot sand was Dr. Haim Arlosorov, chairman of the Jewish Agency Political Department and a key figure in the Zionist left-wing movement. Two days earlier he had returned from a mission to Nazi Germany, where he tried to convince the Jewish community to emigrate before it was too late. He came back to Tel Aviv in a depressed frame of mind, anxious about the developments in Germany and the implications for her Jews. On the evening he was murdered, he had dined with his wife Sima at the Kaete Dan Hotel on the waterfront, and afterwards they had strolled along the beach. When they were a few paces from a Moslem cemetery, someone came out of the dark, shone a flashlight, and shot Arlosorov in the stomach. Some time elapsed before passers-by could get him to the hospital. As his condition was critical, he was questioned by the police about what had happened and who had shot him before undergoing emergency surgery. But he could tell them nothing and he died on the operating table.

Four decades later the question of "Who killed Arlosorov?" can still stir up bitter recriminations in Israel. What happened in those few minutes from the time Arlosorov and his wife stepped out of the hotel to the moment when he lay dying on the sand is still shrouded in mystery.

Sima Arlosorov identified—though not with absolute certainty—two young Revisionists, Avraham Stavsky and Zvi Rozenblat. They were arrested and tried, together with Dr. Abba Ahimeir, a Revisionist leader. All three were acquitted after a long trial, and the relationship between the opposing camps reached new heights of antagonism and overt hostility.

The workers' movement in Palestine, the bastion of the Zionist left, was convinced that Revisionists were responsible. Youths who dared to appear in the streets in *Betar* uniforms were beaten up. Across the Jewish world left-wing propagandists, including Ben-Gurion, used the murder to shame and rout their opponents. Now they could indeed accuse Jabotinsky and his movement of Fascist tendencies. At times Jabotinsky himself faced physical threats. His opponents broke up his meetings, pelted him with rotten eggs, and heckled him with vile abuse. The Revisionist Party found itself on the defensive.

The impression left on Revisionist minds was a bitter one, and for Menachem Begin, it was traumatic. He recalled years later standing alongside Jabotinsky at a meeting in Brest Litovsk, with a living wall of *Betar* members around them: "An inflamed crowd tried to stone him, and we surrounded him, created a human wall to absorb the stones instead of him."

Begin accompanied Jabotinsky on his campaign across Poland. In Pinsk, the hometown of Avraham Stavsky, Begin, by his own admission, listened open-mouthed, his flesh covered with goose pimples, as Jabotinsky said: "The inciters tell you that I educated young Jews to murder one of their own people, while I have devoted my whole life to saving Jews from murder, to defending them from pogrom and assault."

Begin sat behind him, ready at any moment to leap in front if anyone in the crowd threw a stone. He looked across at his friend Shimshon Yunichman, sitting beside him. Shimshon's shoulders were shaking and the tears poured through the fingers he held to his eyes.

In Revisionist historiography the witch-hunt was given what is for Jews the most poignant of names—"the blood libel." The associations of those words were obvious to all East European Jews, exactly as they are today to all Israelis. Anti-Semites, hiding behind Christian theology, fabricated the theory that Jews baked their Passover matzah with the blood of Christian children, and this according to a commandment in the Bible. Though the argument was transparently foolish, it served the purpose of inciting the rabble whenever their leaders felt like provoking a pogrom. Their timing was in itself a masterful stroke of cruelty: the *Seder* night, when Jewish families everywhere gather round a festive table to commemorate the Exodus of the Children of Israel from Egyptian bondage. This so-called blood libel had sent shivers down the spines of countless generations of Jews.

So at the accusation of fascism the response was a resort to the traditional terminology of pogrom. Nonetheless, with the spectacular rise of fascism in Central and Eastern Europe, the leftist propaganda was certain to fall on attentive ears, and one immediate result was a dramatic decline in the popularity of the Revisionist Party. Jews who had been entranced by the masterly rhetoric of Zeev Jabotinsky now turned their backs—and the left wing made the most of the suitation. Even when the evidence linking the three men in the Tel Aviv courtroom to the assassination was shown to be weak and inconclusive, the left would not let up. The opportunity was too good to miss. The records of internal debates among the Labor leadership in Palestine accurately record the degree to which they tried to ride on the back of the anti-Revisionist wave that swept world Jewry. And whenever it seemed about to die away, they did all in their power to add new impetus.

The hatred between the camps would remain with Begin almost to the moment that he entered the prime minister's office in Jerusalem. In all his years as leader of the opposition, the Arlosorov murder hung over his relationship with the Israeli establishment, and in particular, in his frequent and sharp clashes with David Ben-Gurion.

Back in the 1930s Menachem Begin was in the vanguard of those who rejected any compromise. Even the radical Revisionist Abba Ahimeir called for a truce within the Zionist movement from his detention cell, terrified that the confrontation heralded tragedy for the entire Jewish community.

"With all due respect for a brave fighter like Ahimeir," Begin observed to a friend, "we cannot accept his view. It is a serious breach of movement discipline."

The militant stance of Begin and others could not save the Revisionist Party from crushing defeat in the July 1934 elections of delegates to the Zionist Congress. Well before the votes were counted, Ben-Gurion planned the next move that would finally crush the extreme right-wing camp.

"After the elections," he wrote to a friend, "we must

see whether there is a firm anti-Revisionist majority, and that majority must convene to decide our future course. There will be no concessions to those outside that majority. If they want to leave the Zionist Congress—let them leave!"

The results gave the workers' movement 44 percent of the total delegates, while Jabotinsky's party only received 11 percent. There could no longer be any doubt. Menachem Begin was ascending to the leadership of a small, defeated, and hated party. But it was also a united and determined group, certain of the justice of its cause.

CHAPTER 4

The Storm Approaches

In the early years of Menachem Begin's association with *Betar*, his close friends could already attest to his affinity with the spirit of Jabotinsky's movement. It was as if the movement was tailored to fit him personally.

Begin was so delicate in his teens that people seeing him for the first time assumed he was tubercular. Yet his unimpressive exterior hid an inner flame. He was never a brilliant conversationalist, but his speeches flashed with rhetoric magnetism—and that was a most precious commodity in *Betar*. So effective was his delivery that his listeners went away convinced the boy knew what he was talking about. His style was polished, literate, and lucid. He loved to display his command of Jewish history and international politics. Every speech gave fresh evidence of the meshing of his traditional Jewish and general Polish education.

But most of all Menachem Begin stood out for his devotion to Jabotinsky's movement and ideas. His appearances in the *Betar* club in Brest Litovsk, dressed in the movement's brown uniform, were never for social reasons merely to pass the time or engage in some recreational activity. The club was his mission, and he was utterly dedicated to it. To the same degree his personal mannerisms, even the courteous behavior, were appropriate to those of the movement.

In a paramilitary organization like *Betar,* qualities such as these could not remain a secret long. The national leadership of the movement were quick to notice this promising youngster, as Jabotinsky already had done during his Brest Litovsk election campaign appearance. The second time that Jabotinsky had visited the town, Begin was already the local leader of *Betar,* and all roads led to his active participation in the movement center at Warsaw. He began to devote every spare moment there while he studied law.

Warsaw University was housed in a number of ancient buildings in the Cracow Quarter of the city, not far from the Vistula River. Begin on occasion allowed himself the luxury of skipping lectures and learning the material out of books. His grasp was quick, and his motivation anything but laziness. He simply had other things to do—and most of them were at 9 Granitza Street, the headquarters of *Betar,* where he served as head of the Administration Department.

The movement was suffering from a chronic deficit, as was evident from the dreariness of its offices. The courtesy with which the members behaved to each other was in complete contrast to the dinginess of their surroundings. Even the small rent for these quarters was so hard to come by that the staff made do with a salary below the average wage in Poland, often paid days late. Begin earned 100 zlotys a month, well below the average, but he wasted no time in thinking about that. He was far too busy. His work was anything but exciting—and Menachem Begin has never been an outstanding administrator; details and routine cause his concentration to flag. Unable to type, he wrote all his correspondence laboriously by hand, in a handwriting that still remains almost illegible. (In the years before his rise to power Begin wrote a weekly column for an Israeli paper, but it was as a matter of course dictated to his male secretary because the typesetters complained that they could not decipher his hieroglyphics.)

However boring his mornings, the evenings, when he spoke to groups and at meetings in and around Warsaw, brought full recompense. His speeches were electrifying. He was learning to use the spoken word as a sharp and effective political weapon—one on which he would rely heavily in years to come. But this in no way detracted from the devotion with which he carried out the mundane administrative work. He arrived each morning armed with slices of thick buttered bread and a hard-boiled egg. Only rarely did he take the time to go out with his comrades to a nearby restaurant that extended them credit.

He was becoming a well-known figure even beyond the Jewish student circles in Warsaw. The only person who tried to cut him down to size occasionally was his elder brother Herzl, who was studying mathematics in the same university. After a particularly forceful speech, he would tell Menachem: "You talked so much, but what did you actually say?"

Unlike Menachem, Herzl was sensitive, introverted, thoughtful. His friends knew his views, which were not radically different from those of his brother; but Herzl never made a public show of them.

Menachem was far too active in the movement to participate in the usual student pastimes. In the hostel where he lived there was a ballroom that served as social center, but it was only a nuisance to him. When he returned to his room, after an exhausting day at the office and a round of lectures, the music interfered with his studies and habit of getting to bed early. Not even the prettiest girls in town could entice him to join the other students on the dance floor. He was sought after, and his courteous manner attracted the attention of the other sex, but he could not afford to waste time on trivialities. When he did find a spare moment, he devoted it to giving private lessons as a means of increasing his meager income.

In September 1935, as a result of organizational changes in the Polish *Betar*, Begin was given a job more appropriate to his talents: head of the Propaganda Department. His big moment in that job came two years later when, in the winter of 1937, *Betar* organized a conference to celebrate its thirteenth anniversary, and held large-scale and elaborate parades all over Poland. Begin himself spoke at public meetings with the usual powerful effect, but his biggest hour was in Lodz where the scheduled speaker, Abba Ahimeir, did not arrive in time. The absence of the Revisionist hero who had been acquitted of conspiring to murder Arlosorov was embarrassing for the organizers of the meeting. But Begin stepped in and made a speech that left his audience in no doubt of his place in the first rank of the Revisionist leadership. Thousands of people listened to him with an attentiveness and emotional fervor reminiscent of Jabotinsky's appearances. Begin addressed them in three languages—Yiddish, Hebrew, and Polish—and his style was polished in all three. From time to time he was interrupted by a storm of applause, but the peak came toward the end when, in speaking of the Land of Israel, he quoted a Polish poetess: "We shall not abandon the soil that is the rock of our monument, so help us God!"

In Palestine, the clash with the British Mandate had reached a new height. In the forefront of the fight was the *Irgun Zvai Leumi* (National Military Organization), the underground organization that would later declare war on the "foreign régime." *Betar* members and Revisionists were among its founders; throughout Poland, *Betar* held demonstrations of sympathy and identification with their comrades' battle. The biggest was a mass gathering outside the British Embassy at Warsaw; and at the head of the march to the embassy walked Menachem Begin.

The Polish police apparently had advance knowledge of the demonstration. As the crowd was broken up by force, Menachem Begin was arrested and taken by two policemen to the local station. After a short interrogation he was locked in a cell. However the intervention of friends, some of whom had influence in the top echelons in Warsaw, secured his release within a few weeks.

Menachem came out of prison with his head completely shaven. He brushed aside the questions from friends waiting at the prison gate about life behind bars and insisted that they accompany him, that same evening, to the satirical theater in Warsaw, where a Jewish actor—Lupek Stokowsky—was starring.

That demonstration and the arrests that followed,

now a part of *Betar* legend, made a deep impression on youngsters in Warsaw and elsewhere in Poland. The Propaganda Department, under Menachem Begin, was succeeding in reviving both *Betar* and the Revisionist Party after the years of post-Arlosorov humiliation. At the same time the department was weaving a web of conspiratorial activity that in no way contradicted the paramilitary nature of the movement. The eyes of a handful of members, Begin among them, were focused on events in Palestine. To them the time seemed ripe to put all the emphasis on the Palestinian branch of the movement—the one that was fighting a shooting war against the British.

It was under these conditions that Menachem Begin found himself in his one and only conflict with Zeev Jabotinsky. Revisionist-written history tends to tone down the fact, and Begin himself has never mentioned it in public; yet silence cannot detract from the sharpness of the clash at the time. The stage for the conflict was the Third World Congress of *Betar,* which opened in Warsaw on September 11, 1938. Two years earlier Jabotinsky had warned the Jews of Poland about the approaching storm. With his finely honed political instincts he could sense the undercurrents in Eastern and Central European nationalism, and was aware that Polish nationalists were likely to seek cooperation with the German National Socialists. Polish Jewry might be the first victims of such a pact. While the leaders of the free world, and some of the prominent figures in Zionism, were dismissing Adolf Hitler as a demented clown, Jabotinsky took him seriously on the assumption that the mad corporal would indeed carry out his threats. He urged the Jews of Poland to pack their bags and go while there was still time—but his cry fell on deaf ears. The danger seemed so far off. Generations of Jews had learned to live under the shadow of threats, of pogroms, and of anti-Semitism, and they now assumed that they could weather this storm as they had all the others.

But on that September day in 1938, against the background of the work being done by the small group of activists, Jabotinsky's voice sounded more considered and reflective than ever before. His scheduled speech was in fact a historical review of *Betar*. Begin and the activists were demanding to know where their group stood in relation to the Palestinian branch of the movement, and events provided them with an inspiring example. The British in Palestine had executed Shlomo Ben-Yosef for underground activity. Identifying himself as belonging to Zeev Jabotinsky's movement, and subject to its discipline, Ben-Yosef went to the gallows singing *Hatikva* ("Hope")—the anthem of the Zionist movement—and the *Betar* song. In the eyes of the activists there was a certain contradiction between Jabotinsky's measured and moderate tones and the pace of events in the Holy Land. Were they to stand aside while their comrades fought alone?

Menachem Begin was the main speaker of the activist group. As a *Betar* staff officer in Poland, he was already a known and respected leader. In the previous year he had spent five months as acting *Betar* commissioner in Czechoslovakia, where he had often gone hungry and slept under the sky in public parks. This, then, was a man the delegates could not ignore.

"We can no longer wait patiently," he said. "We must strive for large-scale military activity, and to become a decisive factor in determining the fate of

Palestine. Through the fifteen years of our existence we have taught ourselves and others that *Betar* wants a large Jewish State. *Betar* seeks a full solution to the Jewish problem. But how? By what means can we achieve the objective of our lives?"

Begin went on to argue that the days were gone when the British could be relied upon to cooperate in creating a Jewish State in Palestine. Great Britain had brought her full weight and power to bear against that objective, and the League of Nations was no longer a factor in any hope of rescuing the Jews of Germany, who now stood alone against the terror of Nazi rule.

"Zionism is an eternal ideal," he continued, "but its realization will be postponed for many years if we continue to walk along our present road. We can no longer give way. We want to fight, to win or die."

A rustle passed across the hall as Jabotinsky cut into Begin's speech.

"Perhaps the gentleman would be kind enough to explain how he intends to get the soldiers of *Betar* into Palestine?"

"I want us to begin creating our military force, and it will not be subject to the grace of anyone."

"By what means?" a Jabotinsky supporter asked.

"I am suggesting an idea. The experts will say how it is to be done."

"Is the gentleman aware of the balance of forces between Jews and Arabs in Palestine?" Jabotinsky wanted to know.

"We shall be victorious because of our moral might," said Begin, and he went on to purpose an amendment to the phrase in the movement manifesto known as "The Oath." In place of: "I shall prepare my arm for the defense of my nation—and shall not bear arms except in defense," Begin wanted: "I shall prepare my arm for the defense of my nation—and the conquest of my homeland."

At the end of the Congress Begin's amendment was accepted, but not before there had been an emotional and angry response from Zeev Jabotinsky.

"Permit me to say a few sharp words to you," said the leader whose authority no one before had dared to question. "Indeed, as your teacher I must do so. Forgive me for doing it so sharply. There are all sorts of noises. There is for example a whistle. Each person relates differently to such a noise. I relate one way, somebody else another. Most of us, I imagine, are used to the screech of machines. Yet it is hard to suffer the noise of a door slamming because it is pointless. The words that we have heard from Mr. Begin represent just such a noise, and noise like that must be ruthlessly suppressed. *Betar* is not the place for that kind of chatter. Both the speech and the applause are door-slamming that serves no need and no purpose."

Not satisfied with hurling insults, Jabotinsky went on to say that acts of heroism, however deserving, could not take the place of intensive diplomatic activity. He praised the heroism of Shlomo Ben-Yosef, whose example had so enflamed the activists, but "Now, after he has died a hero's death, I give him a retroactive order to do what he has in fact done."

Many of the delegates openly took Begin's side.

"I don't hear a door slamming," observed Shimshon Yunichman. "I hear voices announcing the coming Hebrew revolution, and I see in Begin's words the background against which Shlomo Ben-Yosef offered his life."

Although the Congress resolved to accept Begin's amendment, Jabotinsky's rhetoric caused some consternation in the activist camp. His authoritative figure seemed to tower above all differences of opinion, and it put a damper on some of their enthusiasm. No one was ready to dispute that. When the discussions were over, Jabotinsky was again elected unanimously as the head of *Betar*. Menachem Begin, who chaired the election session, announced ceremoniously to Jabotinsky: "Sir, world *Betar*, in all its branches, its camps and standards, stands ready for your command."

"I undertake to serve in the spirit of the *Betar* oath," Jabotinsky responded.

Within seven months after the dispute that clouded their relationship, Begin reached a new peak in his career. In April 1939 he was appointed *Betar* commissioner in Poland. His predecessor, Aharon Zvi Propes, intended to go to Palestine—and the man slated to succeed him, Shimshon Yunichman, refused the job, believing it to be too difficult for him to handle. Begin stepped in without hesitation, and with the same devotion he had brought to all his jobs in the movement.

He moved into a rented room in the center of town, and devoted all his time to *Betar*. Although at Jabotinsky's recommendation Begin was accepted as a law clerk to do his articles in a law firm, that in no way interfered with the intensity of his activity as head of *Betar* in Poland. He toured the branches, exhorted members to be active, made speeches even to convinced opponents, tried to convert Jews who were leaning toward communism. Chronically short of funds, he stayed in the homes of local functionaries and ate whatever his hosts could provide. In one such home—

that of Zvi Arnold—he met the twin daughters of the house. A month later, on May 29, 1939, he married one of them, Aliza (Ala) Arnold. They both appeared before the rabbi dressed in the brown *Betar* uniform; then Aliza joined her husband in his rented room in Warsaw.

Jabotinsky's warning to "'eliminate the Diaspora before it eliminates you" was becoming more tangible by the day. True, the Jews of Poland could not yet imagine what would befall them; but the shadows were gathering on the horizon, and Menachem Begin's work adjusted accordingly. The primary task was now one of rescue, and Begin set about organizing convoys for a semilegal exodus from Poland. The biggest and best organized convoy of all ran into trouble a few days before the outbreak of war. Among the travelers were some of his best friends and colleagues from *Betar*. Begin himself escorted them as far as the Rumanian border, where they were going to try their luck as illegal immigrants on a ship out of Rumania. Under pressure from the British Embassy, however, the Rumanian authorities refused transit, although the Jews held valid visas. The group spent three weeks in a tent camp on the border, and some of them did manage to slip through, but the majority were forced to turn back. They returned to their homes to find draft papers for the Polish army. Some died on the battlefield, others in the German extermination camps. Very few members of that convoy are still alive today.

On September 1, days after the unlucky emigrants returned to Warsaw, the German army invaded Poland. The Jews of Poland, although perhaps unaware of the details of their futures, realized that this was a major catastrophe. Many of them thought back to the words of Jabotinsky, and most particularly to a speech made one year before the war:

For three years I have been pleading with you, the Jews of Poland, the cream of world Jewry. I have warned you again and again that the catastrophe is approaching. My hair has turned white and I have aged during these years because my heart bleeds that you, my dear brothers and sisters, cannot see the volcano which has started to spew out the fire of extermination. I see a terrible sight. Time is short, but it is still possible to be saved. I know you cannot see it because of your daily problems. But I demand faith of you. After all, you have learned that my prognoses always come true. If you think otherwise, then drive me out of the Jewish community. But if you believe me, then listen to my eleventh-hour cry. In the name of God, let each and every one save his soul while he still can. And I want to tell you one more thing. Those who succeed in getting away will be privileged to witness a moment of great Jewish rejoicing: the rebirth of a Jewish State. I do not know whether I myself will do so. My son —yes! I am as sure of this as I am that the sun will rise tomorrow morning.

In retrospect, Jabotinsky's dark prophecy was revealed to be a reality down to the last detail.

On September 5, Aliza and Menachem Begin celebrated the marriage of a friend, Natan Friedman-Yellin. The next morning they joined a long line in the courtyard of the Warsaw Commissariat in the hope of getting exit visas. That same evening, exit visas in hand, Menachem and Aliza went to the home of his sister and brother-in-law, Rachel and Yehoshua Halperin, in Moranov Square. There, by arrangement, they met Natan and his new bride Frieda whose wedding they had attended the evening before. The four crammed some clothes, toothpaste, shaving cream, towels, and a little food into three rucksacks.

Rachel and Yehoshua looked on with a little envy and much compassion. They would have liked to go too, but they could not pick up and leave home that easily. The Begins and Friedmans looked like ordinary refugees; who could tell where their road might end? But the parting was that of people who expected to see each other again soon.

At the railway station Menachem Begin stood with the two women while Natan pushed through to the window to buy tickets.

"Four to Lvov, please."

"There's no train to Lvov."

"Where is there a train to?"

"To Vilna."

"Okay."

Vilna was in the opposite direction, but Friedman was not going to waste time consulting with the others as to whether it would do. After showing their exit permits, the four shoved through onto the platform and found the cars destined for Vilna. There was no hope of getting in through the doors, but a friend who recognized them helped them in at a window. No seats were to be had, so Menachem put his rucksack on the floor for Aliza to sit on and stretched out next to her.

Although the four had boarded at dusk, the train did not move until almost midnight. They tried to sleep but the rumors passing through the packed cars were too troublesome.

"The Germans have hit the tracks."

"The Germans have blown all the bridges."

Eventually exhaustion got the better of rumor. They awoke at dawn to the sound of a prolonged shriek of the locomotive's whistle. The train ground to a halt. Somebody ran through the cars.

"German planes attacking . . . all out!"

The passengers spread out along the track. Within minutes the train was again in motion. During that day the four made their way between the packed bodies in the cars, finding numerous old acquaintances. From time to time German planes strafed the train. Occasionally they halted while repairs were done on the track ahead. On the third day of their journey air raids forced the train to stop in a small town. It gave the passengers a chance to replenish their food supply and stretch their legs. The Germans were flying overhead, but there was hope that they would be able to move on again at dusk. Then suddenly bombs were dropped, some of which exploded nearby. As they scuttled for shelter Menachem got his first glimpse of dead bodies, their blood mingling with the dust.

Toward evening, on the way back to their car, Menachem and Natan surveyed the situation. The train was probably going to stop every few hours because of air raids—and it was in any case a prime target. The roads would also be under constant air attack. If they wanted to continue, there was only one possibility: to move east across country. They left the train, each of the men shouldering a rucksack while the two women shared the third.

They had been walking for some hours when they

saw the lights of a small town. As they entered they saw that members of the civil guard, bearing white armbands, were patrolling. Among them were Jews, and one of them—a *Betar* member—recognized the travelers and invited them into his home.

"Where are you going?" their host asked.

"Who knows?" Menachem answered. "East—and where we land, we'll land."

"You probably aren't aware of it, but the Germans are already in the east. We're surrounded."

The four jumped to their feet and reached for their rucksacks.

"Where do you think you're going? I've just told you we're cut off. If you go east, you'll run into Germans. If they find you on the move, they'll shoot you and no one will even know. Better stay here. There are many Jews here. What will happen to all of us will happen to you too."

The four left nonetheless and continued east. The rustling of trees and barking of distant dogs now added an eerie note to their trek. Menachem tried to analyze what it all meant. Apparently they were surrounded. The Germans already held all of West Poland; Silesia was in their hands; the corridor to Danzig had fallen. They had declared the annexation of territories by the Third Reich.

They kept on walking, passing towns and villages, not stopping except for short rests. The women were exhausted but they were spurred by the thought that to keep in motion was their only hope. However slight the chance, they might just find a gap in the wall of Germans. From time to time planes passed overhead, but they were looking for more important targets than four refugees trudging through the darkness. By the third night the two men were worried that their wives could no longer stand the pace.

"What do you suggest?" Friedman-Yellin asked.

"Perhaps we'll find a farmer who'll agree to take us in his wagon."

They knocked on the first door that they came to. The Polish farmer was friendly. They seemed to him like brothers in distress, and the money they offered was quite substantial. Within minutes he had hitched horses to his wagon and agreed to drive them some distance. The four felt considerably relieved. At the entrance to the village they picked up a Polish cavalryman fleeing the battlefield.

At dawn the next morning the farmer woke his five passengers: "That's it."

He dropped them at a dirt road going in their direction, and the four were again on their own. The next night they reached the Warsaw-Lublin road. They stood looking on in shock and amazement at the stream of human beings, animals, and occasional vehicles pouring south—evidence of a world in ruins. Military convoys were moving the other way, toward the battlefield. Along the road were all the signs of the German *Blitzkrieg:* burned bodies, smashed vehicles, blood, piles of sooty rubble. They crossed the road quickly and pressed on eastwards.

On the eve of the Jewish New Year (September 13, 1939) the four reached Vlodava on the River Bug. It was a demographic boundary. West of the river the inhabitants were Polish. On the other side were Ukrainians. In the town itself were many friends— members of *Betar*—who competed for the privilege of entertaining the refugees at the festive table.

On New Year's Eve it is a tradition for Jews to greet

each other with a blessing for the new and fruitful year; but now the words seemed empty mockery.

"I suggest you stay with us," their host said. "There's no point in going on. The Germans are already there to the east."

But the next morning they moved on again. At the bridge across the river a Polish officer was directing traffic, and turning back some people. The two men walked over to him.

"We're Jews," Begin said. "If we fall into German hands, we're in special danger."

"Please let us cross," Friedman added. "If we get away we might perhaps be able to do something in the battle against the Germans."

The officer glanced at the two women clutching their rucksack, and smiled with understanding.

"Go—and may God be with you!"

From time to time they paid farmers to give them a lift part of the way. Then, on the road, they met three men who were veteran members of *Betar*. They fell into each other's arms.

"Where are you going?"

"We're going to try to get to the Rumanian border. If we get across, the way is open from there to Palestine. There are IZL representatives there organizing illegal immigration."

But Palestine was a very long way off. At Machov they were greeted by the most staggering news yet: the Red Army had crossed the old Polish border in order to come to the aid of the Byelorussians and the Ukrainians. Begin and Friedman were unable to draw any conclusions as to what this meant to them. They were having occasional doubts about whether it had been wise of them to leave Warsaw. True, the Germans had declared their intention of cleaning out the Jews from Europe, but that could mean that they would allow the Jews of the occupied territories to emigrate wherever they wanted—and the Soviets certainly would not let the Jews go anywhere. That was their official policy.

"What do you think?" Friedman asked.

"I don't know. I only know that we must do everything to get out of the Soviet area before they occupy it completely."

But it was clear that too much haste would not be a good idea. The roads were still exposed to danger. So the two couples decided to stay a while with friends, each couple in a different home.

Then Aliza Begin suffered a sudden attack of bronchitis, and neither doctor nor drugs were to be had in the local town. So two days after Yom Kippur Menachem and Natan rented a wagon to drive to the town of Kobol. The Soviet presence was already felt in the area, while the German threat seemed like a nightmare that had passed. The two couples stayed one day in Kobol, then continued to Lvov, where they again met *Betar* members, including emissaries from Palestine who had originally come to Poland to organize IZL cells. The company was pleasant, but time was running out for Begin. A Soviet militia was already seeking out enemies of the régime, and there was no way of knowing whether the Russians considered Zionism an enemy.

Begin was the best known of the group. He had lectured often enough all over Poland, and he assumed that there would always be someone willing to pass that information to the new Soviet masters.

Some days after they arrived in Lvov, a woman approached him.

"Sir, you owe me my money."

"What money?"

"I deposited an advance with *Betar* against the costs of illegal immigration to Palestine."

"What do you want me to do about it?"

The woman did not answer. She complained to a local militiaman and Begin was summoned for interrogation.

"This woman claims you owe her money."

"All right, if she says so—I'll pay her.'"

The woman named a sum. Begin and his friends held a short consultation and all agreed the money should be paid in order to be rid of the problem. But now it was clear that incidents like this one could happen every day. Prolonging his stay in Lvov involved considerable danger. After consulting his friends, Begin took Aliza on to the town of Drohovicz, where her parents lived. Friedman-Yellin traveled alone by train to the Rumanian border to check on the chances of crossing. When he got off the train, he was arrested for interrogation. But he was released after a few days, having promised never to show his face in the area again. As he returned to Lvov the local press was announcing an agreement between the Soviet Union and the Lithuanian Republic, under which Vilna would be returned to the Lithuanian people.

"If that's the case, I suggest we go to Vilna, then see where we can go from there," he said.

Within two days Menachem and Aliza were back in Lvov, ready to join the trek to Vilna. They arrived there on October 28, 1939, and settled quietly into a suburban house together with another *Betar* member, Dr. Yisrael Sheib.

But the comparative calm could not last. In 1940 the Soviets annexed Lithuania, Latvia, and Estonia. On September 1, 1940, Menachem Begin received an official letter containing a strange message: "You are invited to the town hall, Room 23, between the hours 9–11 A.M. in connection with your request."

Begin had made no request of the local authorities, but many ominous and disturbing things were happening. Not long before he had received news of the death of Jabotinsky, in New York, and had mourned him not only as a teacher but also as his spiritual father. Now news was seeping through about the fate of the Jews of Poland. What had happened to his parents? Were they still alive? And, if so, what were they suffering? Where was his brother, Herzl; had he got out in time? And what of his sister, Rachel; was she still living in the same Warsaw house from which Menachem had begun his own wanderings? Was there truth in the terrible stories?

After receiving the strange letter, which Begin ignored, he noticed that he was being followed. And grim-looking men were watching the house.

"Let's fix them," he said one morning to his wife. "We'll go to town by train and we'll see whether they follow—or whether they arrest us as we get on board."

They set off, with the Russian agents following quite openly. Begin could actually see them gesturing from time to time to each other to take over the surveillance. But nothing happened.

Some days later he was sitting over a chessboard with Dr. Sheib when they heard a knock on the door. Aliza opened it to find three men outside.

"Which is Begin?" asked one, his eyes fixed on the man he wanted.

"I am."

"If so, why didn't you come to the town hall?"

"I never submitted any request to the town hall."

"But you still have to come and pay. You were summoned."

"I have no business there."

"But you still have to come."

"I won't."

"You will."

"Anyway, gentlemen, who are you? Why are you wandering around outside this house? If you don't stop harassing us, I'll have to complain to the police."

Begin knew exactly who he was dealing with, but he wanted them to admit who they were.

"The police? Fine! Come with us to the police."

"Not now. I'll do it when I want."

"If you don't come with us, we'll take you by force."

"All right. Then tell me who you are. Do you represent the authorities? If you don't show your credentials, I'm not going with you."

The three whispered among themselves, then one of them produced an identification card. Begn was not surprised to find that the man was a detective.

"Okay, if you came to arrest me, why didn't you say so? Have you got a warrant for my arrest?"

"No. But we are authorized to use force if you refuse to come with us."

"Fine. I understand that you have come to arrest me. Then allow me to prepare myself."

Dr. Sheib's wife burst into tears.

"Calm down," Begin told her, "there's no need for tears." Then, turning to Dr. Sheib, he added: "I'm sorry, Yisrael, we'll have to finish the game some other time."

Explaining that he would need a few moments, Begin invited his unexpected guests to have a cup of tea, but the three men refused. He went to put on his suit, then polished his shoes and prepared a parcel of food.

"There's no need for that," said one. "We have come to arrest you, but no one intends to hold you for long. I'm sure you'll be back here very soon."

But Begin thought otherwise. Finally he picked up two books: the Bible and André Maurois's book on Disraeli translated into English—a language he had just learned to read.

"Ready?"

"Ready!"

Aliza was allowed to accompany him to the waiting car. Their neighbors lowered their eyes as Begin wished them farewell. As he stood beside the car he noticed David Yoten, a friend the Communist police had been seeking for some days, standing nearby. They exchanged a silent greeting.

"I think I'll be back," he told Aliza. "But in any event, if I don't return quickly, try not to seek pity from people."

"Don't worry. Everything's going to be all right."

"Don't forget to tell Dr. Sheib that I admit he was winning. The game was interrupted, but he did have the advantage."

"I won't forget."

She waved until the car was out of sight. It was doubtful whether Aliza Begin could have guessed how long it would be before they would meet again— nor where the next meeting would take place.

CHAPTER 5

Custody and Court

The NKVD headquarters was in what had been the district courthouse, a drab building in the center of Vilna. As Begin walked along the dimly lit winding corridors, he was reminded of a song that Communist students used to sing at the university. The last line of every verse was: "And the judges will be us."

He was worried by the feeling that he himself was about to be a guinea pig for the revolution, yet he tried to keep a straight, impassive face. His escorts brought him to a room where there was a desk and a number of chairs—then vanished into another room, leaving him alone. Menachem pulled out one of the books he had brought with him, and began to read. After a few minutes the door opened and three men entered; two of them were the detectives who had arrested him. The third, a tall man, studied him with tiny eyes. Begin noted that the man was carefully dressed in a gray suit, cut to the latest fashion, with a necktie to match.

"Good day," said the man, taking a seat on the other side of the desk. "What is your name?"

"Menachem Begin."

"What are you reading?"

"A book on Disraeli."

"Interesting?"

"Very."

"Tell me, why are you looking at me like that?"

"Me?" said Begin, trying to gain time. "How was I looking at you?"

The interrogator did not miss a thing. Although Begin had tried to keep a straight face, his eyes had apparently reflected all that he knew of the Soviet secret police. He wondered whether they would all be like this man. He needed to get his measure, and he would very much have liked to know about the man's education and outlook. There was an occasional suspicion that the man was a Jew.

"Do you know why you have been summoned?"

"Why I have been summoned?" Menachem repeated the question.

"Yes. I want to know whether you are aware of why you have been summoned."

"I have no idea. I only know that I wasn't summoned, but rather arrested."

"Who told you that? No one has arrested you. I only wanted to talk to you. I have a number of questions, and if you answer sincerely, you can go home straightaway. Incidentally, you have a wife?"

"Yes."

"How old is she?"

"Twenty."

"Hm . . . Young. She must certainly be waiting for you . . . But you have nothing to worry about. All you have to do is answer my questions, and you'll return to her immediately. You must see yourself as a free man, not as a prisoner. I want to emphasize that. You were not arrested, but summoned here for a conversation."

"Why are you trying to deceive me? I know I've been arrested, and I'm prepared to answer your questions as a prisoner."

"Who told you?"

"The men who brought me here."

"What? They said that?"

The interrogator jumped to his feet and stormed out into the corridor. Begin could hear him abusing the detectives who had brought him here. Then the man returned and sat down. The friendly expression was still on his face.

"Tell me, are you involved in politics?"

"Yes."

"Which?"

"Zionist."

"In which Zionist organization were you active?"

"*Betar.*"

"In the ranks, or did you hold a leadership position?"

"I held a position."

"What was it?"

"Head of the organization in Poland."

"Did you have many members?"

"Tens of thousands."

"Fine. Now tell me honestly—but honestly—about your activities in Vilna against the Soviet administration."

"I haven't done anything of that sort."

"You're lying!"

"Excuse me, sir, I had heard that representatives of the Soviet régime addressed citizens courteously."

"I didn't intend to insult you. I see that you are an educated and cultured man—and you must tell the truth. It's to your benefit. Apart from that, take into account that we do know everything."

That statement was not far from the truth. In all the years of *Betar* activity in Poland, information had been diligently collected about Begin, the organization, and the other people at its head. The Soviets were well aware that there were active *Betar* members at present in Vilna. Begin was himself able to judge that the interrogator was well versed in the facts. On the other hand there was no reason to hide the objectives, structure, and nature of the activity of *Betar* and its members. In telling all the details, there was only one fact that Begin withheld: that on the thirtieth day after Jabotinsky's death, a number of the *Betar* members who were in Vilna had gathered for a memorial service at the grave of a young *Betarist*. They had *Betar* flags with them. They sang the anthem, and all took an oath to remain loyal to their teacher's testament. Begin himself had told them: "We shall be privileged to fight for a Jewish State, and if we are not among the fighters, we will benefit if we are privileged to suffer for the sake of the idea. Whatever may be, we shall keep our oath."

Clearly the holding of such a memorial service would constitute a political crime according to the laws of his interrogator.

"I repeat, you must tell me what actions you have taken against the Soviet régime here in Vilna."

"And I repeat that I do not understand to what

101

crime you refer, since we have done nothing against the Soviet régime."

"I refer to the sabotage you planned."

"We have never planned anything of the sort."

"And I refer to espionage activities."

"We have never involved ourselves in anything of the sort, and have no interest in doing so."

"Listen, I will leave you alone. Here is a piece of paper and a pen. Write! Write all you have to tell us about your life and your political activities. But I warn you—write the truth! In any case we know it all. If you write the truth, you have a chance of returning to your wife."

"What language do you want me to write in?"

"Doesn't matter. We have translators for many languages. Personally I think it would be best if you wrote in Yiddish."

"You know Yiddish?"

"Yes. I'm also a Jew—and as such you can treat me with trust. Write the truth!"

He left Menachem Begin with a stack of blank paper. Begin wrote out an account of his life and, in a typical manner, interwove it with his political biography—describing succinctly how he had decided to devote his life to the movement for revival of the Jewish people, and how he had come to work for the ancient dream of a return to the Holy Land.

As he was writing in his usual illegible hand, a soldier with rifle and fixed bayonet came into the room. Begin took no notice of him, yet the change in his own status was clear. There was no longer any point in continuing the charade with his interrogator that he was not a prisoner.

The interrogator returned, still friendly and amiable.

"Finished writing? Show me what you've written."

He thumbed through the pages, then lifted his eyes again to Begin.

"Good. Are you ready to tell the truth?"

"What I have written is all the truth."

"Listen, please, don't you know that we have the means to make you tell the truth?"

Begin did not answer. What was there to say?

"Why are you silent? Haven't you considered that you can be free of the affair with that piece of paper you gave me? Let me suggest one last time—don't be obstinate!"

"Can you bring me something to drink?"

"I'll arrange a cup of tea."

The interrogator left and the armed soldier returned. Begin waited a long time for the tea. He picked up the book and went back to reading about Disraeli. The soldier said nothing. The hour came for the changing of the guard. A sergeant strode into the room, followed by a group of armed soldiers. The sentry whispered something in his ear.

"So," said the sergeant, "I hear you've been spending your time reading. Who allowed that? Where do you think you are?"

"The interrogator allowed me."

"Interrogator? The interrogator has nothing to say about anything here. We're responsible for this room, and now you'll stop reading. On your feet—and move over there!"

He moved Begin's chair to a corner of the room. Menachem sat down, but not before moving the chair to face the center.

"Not like that! Not like that! Here you sit with your face to the wall."

Begin fixed his eyes on a point on the wall. He was tired, hungry, and thirsty. Trying to take his mind off the situation, he started to think about his childhood. Suddenly he felt homesick for his parents' house in Brest Litovsk. Where were they? What had happened to them after the Nazi invasion of Poland? And Herzl and Rachel, what of them?

From time to time he dozed, only to be awakened roughly by the guard.

"It's forbidden to sleep here!"

Again he fixed his eyes on the wall and returned to his childhood memories. Every few hours the interrogator returned.

"Have you changed your mind?"

"I've told you the truth."

"You're a stubborn man!"

"Incidentally, what about the cup of tea you promised me?"

"Ah, yes. You didn't get it?"

There was a trace of mockery in the man's voice. Menachem Begin was only just beginning to become acquainted with NKVD interrogation methods. Promises were part of the game.

Some sixty hours after he had been brought to the room and assured that he would soon return home, the door again opened and a group of strangers came in. One of them told Begin to gather his belongings and come with him. He was taken out to a car in which a number of men were already sitting, none of whom he knew. One of them was complaining bitterly.

"I left a wife and baby at home, and they'll starve."

"You've nothing to worry about," the guard assured him. "Don't forget that your wife and child are in the land of the Soviets. Don't you know that no one goes short of bread here?"

The prisoner fell silent. Begin was amused at that answer, but he was too tired to think about anything else. He fell asleep in the car, awaking as the gates of Lukishki Prison opened before him. Lukishki, on the outskirts of Vilna, had housed political opponents of successive régimes for many years. The procedure inside was routine. First of all they shaved his head, then put him in a cell with a middle-aged man—a man who proved to be educated and amiable, and who had still kept his manners and sense of humor. Neither of them could quite understand what the other was doing there, but they quickly found a common language and began to instruct each other in their individual national histories.

They were joined by an aged Polish marshal, whose only crime was that he had once, long ago, served in the czarist army. His attitude to the imprisonment was one of cynical amusement. The three spent much of their time discussing the outside world and the war.

"I think that if the Germans win, we have a reasonable chance of getting out of here one day," one of the occupants of the cell observed. He then turned quickly to Menachem. "But don't worry, Mr. Begin, we'll stand by you and help you."

"I do indeed want very much to get out of here, but when I think of what my people can expect from the Germans—I prefer to stay locked up here."

Begin began to lose weight rapidly; the rations in prison were barely enough to keep a man alive. But although he was starving and worried about events on the outside, his religious faith served as a prop. He had always been religious, but prison was strengthening his faith even more. Many years later, in reconstructing his period in prison, he would testify that faith alone enabled him to hold on. His cellmates noted that he bore suffering almost with love, but to Begin it was all perfectly natural. The Jewish tradition passed down from father to son had taught him that only the coming of the Messiah would bring relief for the tribulations of this world—and that suffering can speed his coming. This belief had sustained countless generations of Jews through the worst of persecutions and pogroms. For Begin, this period was his personal "birthpangs of the Messiah."

If he counted the days in prison, it was because he wanted to observe the Jewish holidays. On the eve of Yom Kippur—the Day of Atonement—he did not hold out his bowl for the daily ration of soup.

"You can divide it between the others," he told the guard.

"What's wrong? Are you ill?"

"No. It's the Day of Atonement."

"What has that to do with food?"

"It's a day that we fast."

"Nonsense! You can eat—on my responsibility!"

"Thank you for worrying about me, but I will not eat. You can divide my share between the others."

"Crazy!"

Yom Kippur is the day on which Jews commune with their Creator, request His forgiveness for their sins, and draw up the balance sheet of their consciences, while purging their souls by abstinence from food and drink. Begin spent the day sprawled on his cot, deep in thought, his lips constantly mouthing the ancient prayers. Traditionally the day ends with the words: "—next year in Jerusalem." Would there be another good Day of Atonement? Where would he be for the next one? And his wife, family, friends, comrades from *Betar*?

Begin's interrogator in the prison was a young captain who wanted to know when Begin became a Zionist.

"As a youth."

"I see that you began your criminal activity early."

"Why criminal?"

"Because it is anti-Soviet and anti-revolutionary."

"Why anti-Soviet?"

"Hold on, I'm the one who asks questions. Who introduced you to *Betar*?"

"I went by myself. I heard Jabotinsky speak, and I liked what he said."

"Jabotinsky? Ah! He's an old acquaintance of ours. The leader of Jewish fascism."

"Jabotinsky was a liberal."

"Nonsense! We know he was an agent of British Intelligence."

"Then you should know that the British refused him entry to Palestine."

"Forget that idle gossip. We know very well who Jabotinsky was. You don't have to defend his name that ferociously."

"What would you do if someone falsely accused Lenin?"

"Don't you dare compare Lenin and Jabotinsky. Tell me, where is he now?"

"You don't know that he died?"

"Are you sure?"

"To my sorrow—yes."

"Where?"

"In America."

"He lived in America?"

"No. He went there after the outbreak of war to try to raise a Jewish army."

"Aha! To help the imperialists!"

"To fight Hitler's Germany."

"Nonsense. Only arms traders and bloodsuckers are interested in the imperialist war. Your Jabotinsky is helping them."

"He wanted to help his own people."

"Don't you tell me who he wanted to help. Did you know him well?"

"Yes."

"What did you talk about between you?"

"*Betar* matters."

"Did you talk about the Soviet Union?"

"No."

"You're lying!"

"Why should I lie? Have I denied my Zionist activity?"

"Tell me, of whom was your movement composed in Poland?"

"People of all levels, mostly youngsters."

"Mostly bourgeois?"

"No. On the contrary, the majority were poor workers."

"Ah! Then you dragged the youth away from the Communist Party!"

"We didn't drag them; they came of their own free will. Clearly anyone who came to *Betar* didn't go to the Communist Party."

"That's just it!"

Begin signed a transcript of the conversation, written by the interrogator himself. The latter had added some emphasis of his own. When Begin complained, he was told that he could raise his complaints at the trial.

"There will be a trial?" he asked disbelievingly.

"Of course. Where do you think you are? Don't you know that, in the Soviet Union, no one is imprisoned without trial?"

At Begin's request, a translator was invited to the next session. Begin's command of Russian was far from perfect, and he felt the need for precision in what he had to say. The translator, a Jew of his own age, broke off in the middle of a sentence to argue with him.

"Zionism is a comedy!"

"Listen," Begin interrupted him, "as a Jew you should be ashamed to say that. The attractions of the Land of Israel were in existence long before the world knew of communism, and—if you insist—long before the concept of the bourgeoisie was born. Over the years there have been false messiahs who have played on the homesickness. They attracted tens of thousands, who sold all they had to be ready for the return to Palestine. And you call all that a comedy. I was arrested because I am a Zionist, because I belong to *Betar*—and I'm not complaining. I'm prepared to accept all the suffering that it involves—and you insult that!"

Begin ended the rebuke with a thump on the table. The room was still.

"What does he say?" the interrogator asked.

Begin noticed that the translator started from the middle of his speech—with his words about false messiahs who had fostered the dream of return to the Land of Israel.

"True, very true, they were vain dreams," the interrogator commented.

"You didn't translate me properly," Begin said in Russian.

"I haven't finished . . ."

"Then speak Russian," the captain ordered angrily.

In broken Russian Begin repeated what he had told the translator. The interrogator flushed with anger.

"Zionism is a puppet theater. The Zionist leadership tries to whip up loyalty for a state that doesn't exist. You say the Jews in Poland were persecuted throughout the years? Correct! But why? Your mental capacity isn't enough to find the real answer. They were persecuted because the Polish capitalists wanted to throw sand in the eyes of the masses. And what do you do? You distract the Jews from the main objective and console them with some strange dream. That's a comedy. You, Begin, not only did you desert the revolution but you were among those who organized the desertion!"

Begin had to listen all that night to a lesson in Marxist-Leninist-Stalinist doctrine on the advantages inherent in the socialist régime, and on the false attraction of Zionism—which had to be uprooted because it was anti-revolutionary and anti-Soviet. From time to time he tried to interject a sentence, but was only told that his words were the idle chatter of a confirmed reactionary.

"You must know that with us you pay not only for deeds, but also for thoughts. We know what everyone thinks—and repay them accordingly."

Though the captain, supposedly an expert in Jewish and Zionist affairs, was displaying appalling ignorance, Begin could see that he had acquired some of the Zionist jargon and was using it as if to prove his familiarity.

At dawn Menachem Begin was again asked to sign the transcript, and he did so without any hesitation.

The nights of interrogation continued. On occasion they became confrontations between the ideologies of communism and Zionism, as the captain drew on his store of juicy Russian epithets to describe the Zionist leaders and their viewpoints. Begin's legal education also came to the fore as he used clauses of the Soviet Constitution to support his claim of innocence.

"Don't make me laugh!" The interrogator smiled. "Do you know under which section of the criminal code you are being charged?"

"No. I have no idea."

"Anti-revolutionary activity and treason—and that section was drafted by Vladimir Ilich Lenin in person."

"But how can that apply to things I did in Poland?"

"Menachem Zeevitch Begin, don't be a fool! That section applies to everyone anywhere in the world! Do you hear? Anywhere. The only question is whether he comes to us or whether we reach him."

That was a point that shook Begin's legal mind. While in prison he had become familiar with representatives of the Soviet régime and their concepts of justice. But he had not realized that they were quite so capable of debasing law.

"What were your connections with the Polish secret police?"

"Sir, I refuse to answer such a question."

"What do you mean, refuse? Don't you know that no one refuses to answer questions here?"

"Sir, it's an insulting question, and I do not answer insulting questions."

Begin repeated his previous statements, about his role in *Betar*, about the fact that he headed the organization in Poland, about his intention of going to Palestine and taking part in the struggle for the country's liberation.

"Aha! If that's so, then we also accuse you of plotting to leave the Soviet Union illegally."

"I have never hidden my intention of leaving the area of your jurisdiction."

They confronted him with a friend from *Betar*, who was in the same prison, and were astonished to see the two compete with each other in accepting the blame and avowing their Zionist activity. But even if these individuals ploys failed, they were slowly accumulating a long enough list of charges to ensure that Menachem Begin would be on their hands forever. And he knew it. From the moment that he had got the measure of his captors, and grasped the true nature of the Soviet system, he had resigned himself to his situation as being decreed by fate. In any case he could console himself with the thought that the outside world, in the middle of a war that spelled suffering for millions, was no better a place to be.

From time to time his interrogators moved him to different cells, and in each he became acquainted with different types of men. Most were political prisoners like himself, but in one cell he met a Jew from Warsaw who was a well-known criminal, and who had been put with the politicals by mistake. The Russians

112

had caught the man smuggling stolen goods across the border and had charged him with espionage.

Begin's anti-Soviet opinions were hardening. His acquaintance with the Soviet régime was through his experience with its most brutal representatives. It was to instill in him an everlasting disgust for the way in which they distorted the most fundamental concepts of human justice.

On April 1, 1941, after a long series of night interrogations, while he sagged physically from starvation and exhaustion yet remained strong in spirit, a jailer appeared with a few sheets of paper in hand and began to read aloud:

"The Special Committee of the Popular Commission for Internal Affairs has decided that Menachem Zeevitch Begin is a dangerous element to society, and that he is to be imprisoned in a corrective work camp for eight years . . . Please sign," the man added politely.

Begin signed, remembering the interrogator's promise that there would be a trial. By now experienced in the secrets of Soviet justice, he could feel nothing but contempt for the judges who had sentenced him *in absentia*.

CHAPTER 6

White Nights

Lukishki Prison could easily break a man's spirit. Menachem Begin watched human shadows flitting by him, moaning over the bitterness of their fate, trying to understand why they were there, hardly daring to imagine what their future would be. From time to time even the noises of the town penetrated the thick walls to mock his ears.

At midnight on January 1, 1941, Begin was shaken awake by another Polish prisoner.

"Mr. Begin, a new year is on the threshhold."

Begin tried to smile. Lukishki was the last place on earth to greet a new year but he did not want to spoil the joy of the occasion for his comrades, if they could conceive of it as joyful . . .

"To life, Mr. Begin!"

"Happy New Year!"

In the absence of liquor, they dutifully raised half mugs of coffee deliberately left over from the midday meal for the purpose. Somewhere outside, in the stillness of the night, they could hear a clock chiming the midnight hour—a distant greeting from the world at war, but free. For the men in the cell the question was not "When will we get out of here?" but rather "Will we get out?" And to that the Polish marshal, who was literally fading before their eyes, had his own answer.

"Gentlemen, you are at liberty to delude yourselves as much as you want. I have no illusions. I will not leave here alive."

In the cruel world behind prison walls a man can lose his human image unless he is capable of clinging to some kind of faith, whether in God or in his own ability to hold on to the very limits of human endurance. Begin reached those limits two weeks before sentence was passed on him, and all because of something he said to his cellmates. Menachem Begin was not blessed with a sense of humor; he took himself and the world far too seriously for that. But a warder, overhearing some snatch of conversation, was convinced that Begin had told a joke at the warder's expense. He reported it, and Menachem Begin was sentenced to seven days in solitary confinement.

His fellow prisoners were so convinced that Begin was too weak to take it that one of them asked whether he could appropriate Begin's belongings if he did not return. Begin very politely agreed. A few days earlier the prisoners had been allowed to receive parcels. Aliza and their friends had brought everything that the authorities would allow. At the end of the week, when Begin appeared in the doorway of the cell, his cellmates stared in astonishment. Begin was thin, pale, and sickly—but in good spirits. He flopped down on his cot, but the stench of his body forced him back on his feet to stumble over to the water bucket.

None of the prisoners knew where the work camp they had been assigned to was located, or what they would be doing in it. Nor could they learn about the living conditions—and there was no one to enlighten them. Nevertheless the prison was buzzing with rumors of doubtful origin. Meanwhile Begin received another parcel of underwear and handkerchiefs from Aliza. He had been hoping to find some message concealed in one of her parcels, and in this one, on one of the handkerchiefs, Aliza had embroidered the letters "OLA."

He had difficulty in deciphering the hidden meaning. At first he thought it might be her own nickname, but quickly dismissed the idea as her name would have been "ALA." He asked a friend from *Betar* who happened to be sharing the cell, but he had no suggestions. Then, after an hour's puzzling over the riddle, Menachem Begin suddenly beamed.

"I have it! She's telling me that she's on her way to Palestine."

The others in the cell could not understand what he was talking about, but to him it was so obvious that he wondered why the pieces had taken so long to fall in place. For a Jew the journey to the Holy Land was not migration but "going up"; and the Hebrew for that, in its feminine form, is *olah*. Aliza Begin was telling her husband that for her the dream was coming true.

For weeks he had been debating whether to give Aliza a divorce. "She shouldn't suffer because of me," he told a Jewish friend. "Who knows when she will see me again, if at all . . ."

"You don't need to do that."

"Why should she suffer?"

"Even that will end sometime."

"Then perhaps I should send her a conditional divorce. If I don't return within a certain number of years, she can show the document and marry someone else."

"Don't do it!"

"I have no choice."

His nights were sleepless. He thought about their first meeting, about their plans for the future, about their brief happy interlude in Warsaw. Could he divorce the woman he loved and who loved him?

He had hesitated at the last moment, and when he got the news, he was grateful that his friend had talked him out of it. Aliza was going! At least half of the dream was coming true. At least now, when he thought of the Promised Land, she would be a part of the promise—of the dream. Now he had a double reason to look forward to the great moment. Yet the joy was not unmixed. Until this point he had known that she was nearby, somewhere outside the walls. But now she was going to Palestine, while he was going he knew not where.

Two weeks before their departure the prisoners destined for labor camp were allowed a family visit, and were asked for the name and address of their nearest relative. Begin gave the name of his wife. Some days later he was escorted by a warder to the visitors' cell. The woman who sat there was very familiar to him—but she was not Aliza.

"You can speak Russian or Polish," the warder announced.

"Menachem, *shalom*, everything's okay," said Paula

117

Deiches, a graduate of *Betar*. "Aunt Ala is with Uncle Shimshon. I've already had a letter from her." Menachem was silent but his heart was pounding with joy and excitement.

This time there was no trouble in decoding the message. Shimshon could only be Yunichman, who had gone to Palestine some time ago, and arranged the illegal immigration of *Betar* members. So Aliza was already in Palestine!

"Menachem, did you hear me, Aunt Ala is . . ."

"I understood. I understood."

"There were also letters from your parents. Don't worry. They're being helped."

"I understand."

"And the brothers are well. They're also with Aunt Ala."

Menachem only had one brother, so he grasped that Paula must mean his friends.

"I understand."

"I've brought you greetings from Auntie." Then she added in Hebrew: "Letter in soap."

"No tricks," the warder intervened. "I told you only Russian or Polish."

She held out a parcel of food. The warder took it and searched it.

"There's an epidemic outside. No food allowed."

Begin's heart stood still as the warder took a knife and cut the soap in half. If he found the letter, Paula would be arrested, and they would discover that she wasn't Begin's wife. But their luck held. Begin took the two halves of soap and parted from Paul. It was the last time he would see her. Two months later, during the German invasion, Paula was killed defending Vilna.

118

Apart from confirmation of the good news, the letter also contained a bulletin from his friends: "The comrades in Palestine and the United States are working for your release. They have influence. Hold on!"

The Passover festival went by, and there was still no sign of the move to a labor camp. It was a strange Passover within prison walls. The traditional service celebrating the Exodus from Egypt, usually read by the family sitting around a festive table, ends with the words: "This year slaves—next year free men. This year here—next year in Jerusalem."

Within the walls of Lukishki the ancient words had a double meaning. Reciting the words with special emphasis, Begin wondered whether he would ever see Jerusalem.

One of the two barbers who came to the prison to shave the inmates' heads was Jewish, and did not hide the fact. Somebody persuaded Begin to ask the man whether he knew where they were going. Begin asked—and the barber shrugged. But the next time he came, he talked endlessly.

"It's not a bad place. Not bad at all!"

"What sort of place?"

"A labor camp."

"What do they do there?"

"Work!"

"How many hours a day?"

"Eight. No more than that."

"Afterwards?"

"There's a cultural club. Once a week they show a movie."

"And the food?"

"Plenty of it! The prisoners get paid for their work, and they can buy cakes in the canteen."

"Where is it exactly?"

"Somewhere up north."

Like lightning the rumor spread through the prison: We're going to a place where the conditions are human. The warders volunteered confirmation of this, commenting that Soviet labor camps always took the needs of the workingman into account.

Meanwhile Lukishki was filling up, and those prisoners slated for transfer were moved down to an underground floor, but were ordered to leave their eating utensils behind in their cells. The daily soup was now served to them in cans that had previously been used for collecting garbage.

"Can't eat from those," someone complained.

"They've been washed," a warder answered.

"You have forgotten that we're human beings."

"No alternative. There are a lot of prisoners and not enough utensils."

"Who asked you to arrest half the town?"

After two days in the cellar they were taken to the railway station and loaded like cattle into freight cars—a first indication of the "human conditions" that they could expect at their destination. The journey lasted days, some of them spent for no apparent reason standing at a remote siding. The prisoners were packed in like sardines. They were given only dry bread and inadequate water. From time to time an armed soldier opened the heavy door of the car to make a head count.

"Where are we going?"

"I don't know!"

One morning a rumor spread through the cars like wildfire: The Soviet Union is at war with Nazi Germany. Nobody knew from where it came, but they soon had evidence to support it. Through cracks in the car walls they could see troop trains moving in the opposite direction. Then, a few days later, the train halted near some earthworks, and a loud voice greeted them:

"Who's there?"

"Polish prisoners!"

"So are we. Have you heard about the war?"

"A rumor . . ."

"The Germans are moving like a knife through butter. They're already in Vilna."

There was an uproar in Begin's car. Some prisoners regretted that they had been moved to the labor camp so quickly; a few more days in Vilna, and they would have been free men. Begin lay still in his place and said nothing. He did not doubt what would have happened to him when the Gestapo took over Lukishki Prison. And he could console himself with the knowledge that his wife and friends had got out of Vilna in time.

"Not long now," observed the old marshal, who was obviously dying. "I guess we will disembark at Kotlas."

"How do you know that?"

"If I remember rightly, there was a labor camp there back in czarist times."

The marshal was taken off at Kotlas—but not alive. The train rolled on without him. One week later it finally stopped, and the prisoners descended into a frozen landscape. By their calculation it had to be midnight, yet the light was as strong as day.

"You have reached the land of white nights," an NKVD officer informed them.

They were lined up, then ordered to march.

"One step out of line, and you get a bullet!"

Alongside them walked armed soldiers with hunting dogs on a tight leash. One of them spoke to Begin.

"How long did you get?"

"Eight years."

"What for?"

"Article 58."

"Oh! That's not so good."

"They told us in Vilna that if we work well, we'll be out sooner."

"No one gets out of here."

"What does that mean? I only got eight years."

"I'm telling you—nobody leaves here!"

A few hours' marching brought them to a transit camp, a compound surrounded by barbed wire and guard towers. They lined up at the admissions building, where inmates recorded the details of the new arrivals.

"How much did you get?"

"Eight years."

"Date of release—September 20, 1948. What was the charge?"

"Article 58."

"Never mention 58 here! It's a bad article. If they ask, tell them exactly what the sentence says: dangerous element in society. That doesn't sound so bad."

A few days later the prisoners arrived at the Pecora River, and were taken by boat to Pecora Labor Camp. Begin sat on deck watching the wonders of the white night landscape.

"What have you got in that parcel?" a guard asked.

"Some clothes and boots."

"Leather boots?"

"Yes."

"They'll take them from you."

"Who?"

"You'll see."

On arrival Begin fell ill with a high fever. He traded a shirt for a bed in the camp infirmary, and it was here that he got his first taste of life in a labor camp. It was vastly different from the barber's stories in Vilna.

The first person to approach him was another prisoner, also down with a high fever.

"Tell me, weren't you *Betar* commissioner in Poland?"

"Right."

"I saw the name on your rucksack, and I thought it must be you. I'm also from *Betar*."

The young camp doctor, who was shocked by the presence of bugs in the cells, told Begin that he was in the camp because his wife had fallen in love with an NKVD man. To get rid of her husband, she had reported that he demanded his patients cross themselves and avow their religious beliefs before he would treat me.

"May God have pity on my wife, but I never preached religion—and certainly not to my patients!"

For assistance in the infirmary he had a woman, of indeterminate age, whose sole crime had been to study the English language. The NKVD had decided that this was ample evidence that she and her husband were British spies. The husband died in prison.

Another prisoner, a peasant sent straight to the camp from a commune, accused of sabotaging the communal effort, was the only one who did not complain.

"I'm happy here. At least we get bread every day."

Begin's neighbor in the next bed was a veteran Communist named Garin, who had been deputy editor of *Pravda*. Garin was a Jew, but he despised Zionism in a way that no normal Jew could.

"You are the servants of imperialism. You help the worst anti-Semites. Zionism is a nightmare!"

Begin could not understand how the man retained faith in communism after several years in the hell of a labor camp. He suffered from cardiac disease, but was allowed into the infirmary only when his temperature passed 38° C.

"Life is hard here, but we mustn't lose our sense of proportion. I want the Soviet Union to be victorious. Listen, Begin, you think you're the first with whom I've argued about Zionism? When I was a youth in Odessa, I had endless debates with youngsters who became Zionists. You know how old I was when I joined the Communist Party? Seventeen!"

Garin talked about his activity in the party, about his climb up the ladder to the senior post of deputy editor of the party's official newspaper. Then, quite by surprise, his wife—a university lecturer—was arrested and charged with Trotskyism.

"It was nonsense, of course. She wasn't a Trotskyite, but in 1937 this whole country was one big madhouse. The party had stopped running national affairs, and the NKVD had taken over. It was completely crazy. One day an investigator sent someone to prison—then next day he joined him there."

Garin's wife sent a letter to Stalin, giving a well-reasoned account of her innocence. Stalin ordered her release, but she was arrested again two months later. This time there was no one to take her letter to the all-powerful ruler of Russia. Then her husband was also summoned for questioning, and charged with Trotskyism. All his articles against Trotsky, published over many years, were of no help. He was sent for reindoctrination to a labor camp.

After a week in the infirmary Menachem Begin joined the other prisoners in the routine of a sixteen-hour day of hard labor. They unloaded iron railway sleeping cars from boats in the river, and reloaded them on railway flat cars. Each day began with a pep talk from the camp commandant.

"Remember that you are working for the Soviet homeland! Far away from us there is a war, and you must be grateful to those who defend you against the German cannibals. For this you must work with dedication to fill the quota that the government and the party have given us."

The prisoners were a cosmopolitan collection of Russians, Poles, Latvians, Estonians, Rumanians from Bessarabia, and Jews. They were divided into two groups—political and criminal. The latter worked hard, but they were also the only ones who answered back to the guards, who were afraid of them. The criminals often terrorized the political prisoners, taking their food by force or stealing their clothing. Begin himself lost all he had apart from the rags he was wearing.

The work was hard, and the pace inconsiderate of a man's ability to endure. The authorities had set a quota that took no account of illness. Begin was horrified by the sight of Garin, with his cardiac condition, laboring like the rest—and not uttering a word of complaint. Many prisoners looked for any way to earn a day off work, even to chopping off fingers with an ax. On the banks of the frozen river, in temperatures well below zero, men fell like flies. Death was a constant companion, but the labor force was constantly being replaced by fresh prisoners.

The winter nights were dark and freezing, the food bad and insufficient. None of the prisoners was properly dressed for the Arctic winter, and there was no hope of enough sleep. Begin once succeeded in getting three straight days off work. His temperature rose to about 40° and he was sent to the infirmary. On the third day, when his fever was down to 37.5°, he was ordered out to join the night shift.

"I'm still ill. I don't have the strength to move."

"You heard what I said!"

"I'm completely exhausted."

"Don't argue with me. I don't need problems because of you!"

At times he was overcome by despair at the thought of the eight years ahead. But he knew that he must not crack. All his life he had been telling others not to lose faith, to cling to the human spark that allows mere mortals to prevail over intolerable conditions. At moments of despair, he thought of Jabotinsky's poem: "Whether slave or tramp/You have been created a prince . . ." He resolved to remain human come what may. Secretly he harbored a hope of early release, but the first hint of it came quite by surprise.

"Are you Polish?" a warder asked as they marched to work.

"Jew, citizen of Poland."

"If so, you'll go free."

"Who says?" Begin felt the blood rushing through his veins. His heart beat wildly.

"I do."

"Who told you?"

"You don't want to believe, eh? I heard it on the radio. All Polish prisoners will be released to fight the Germans. Now do you believe?"

Work went on as usual and the Poles did not know whether to rejoice or not—but there was hope. A few days later the Poles were summoned for a talk with the camp commandant. Among them was a woman.

"You are also Polish?" the commandant asked her.

"Of course. I was born there."

Begin remembered her from Warsaw University. A beautiful Jewish girl who had joined the Communist Party, and waged bitter arguments with her Zionist colleagues, then dropped out of sight.

"Do you remember me?" she asked Begin.

"Of course," he said, shaken by the fact that she now looked like a sick old woman.

It turned out that she had gone to the land of her dreams, Russia, and had married a confirmed Communist like herself. The fact that he was Russian was now working against her.

"No," said the commandant, "you're not Polish. There's nothing for you here."

He told the prisoners that he had read in *Pravda* that Polish citizens were to be released to enlist in a Polish army against the Germans.

"For the time being, you go on working because I have not yet received explicit orders."

Freedom was on the horizon, but at this very moment some of the prisoners were scheduled to be sent farther north to another camp. The Poles went to the commandant.

"You can't do that to us right now!"

"I have no specific orders to release anyone, and so I can't treat you any differently from the way I treat the others. We have surplus manpower, and some of you will be transferred to another camp."

Begin found out that he was included in the group to be transferred. He was ordered to board a boat waiting in the river. A friend tried to bribe a guard on Begin's behalf, but the Russian did not want to take the risk. So the boat sailed with Begin on board. In the cramped cabins the criminal element went on the rampage, seizing what they could and threatening the other prisoners with knives. All Begin wanted was to find a corner to lay his aching body. Garin saw him and crawled over. The man was obviously ill.

"I think this is the end. I won't make it," he murmured.

Begin leaned over and listened to Garin's feeble heartbeat.

"Don't give up! You mustn't give up!"

Garin muttered something, then laid his head on Begin's chest.

"Tell me, what was that song you used to sing? I don't remember the words—only something like 'To return, to return.' "

Begin looked puzzled as Garin switched to Yiddish for the first time.

"When I was a youngster in Odessa, I remember your people singing it. You don't know it? A Zionist song?"

"Ah! You mean *Hatikvah*!"

"If that's it, I beg you sing it to me. I'm not going to leave here alive."

Begin began to sing, and was joined by the *Betar* members who had spoken to him in the camp infirmary. This was a version of what was to become the State of Israel's national anthem. Garin listened to the Hebrew words: "Our two-thousand-year hope is not lost/To return to the land of our fathers/The land of Zion, Jerusalem . . ."

"I'm finished," he said. "Maybe you'll get out. Who knows? Perhaps one day you'll find my sons. If you see them, tell them about their father. Tell them all of it."

Although his imprisonment in Vilna and in the labor camp molded Begin's distaste for communism and the Soviet Union, this conversation with Garin was a key to his later attitudes. He would refer to it often in the coming years, pointing out that Judaism and the ancient bond could even overcome the beliefs of an orthodox Communist who had denied his people and their national aspirations.

Days later Begin heard a guard call his name on the deck above. He raced up the stairs.

"Begin? Father's name?"

"Zeev."

The man read out a list of names, then told the assembled prisoners: "All those whose names I have called are to collect their belongings. An order has arrived to release Polish citizens. You are free."

Begin said farewell to Garin. As he was heading back on deck, a criminal prisoner tried to stop him.

"He's a Jew, not a Pole!"

Begin shook him loose. Within the hour he was a free, if penniless, man. He and the other released Poles began the long trek across Russia, most of it on foot, as they were thrown off trains for having no tickets. They slept in stairwells and public gardens. Then, one day, at a remote railway station somewhere in the depths of Asiatic Russia, he overheard the name

Halperin, and turned to question the woman who mentioned it.

"Excuse me, madam, the Halperin you mention is a lawyer?"

"Yes."

"From Warsaw?"

"Yes."

"And his wife's name is Rachel?"

"Yes. Do you know her?"

"She's my sister!

With the woman's help, Menachem Begin found his sister in a miserable mud hut in Dzizak, a small Uzbek town between Tashkent and Samarkand. They fell on each other's necks. They remembered the gloomy evening in September 1939 when they had separated in Warsaw, hoping to see each other again soon. They did not know that they were now all that remained of the Begin family.

There are various versions of what happened to Dov Zeev, Hasia, and Herzl Begin. Some survivors from Brest Litovsk say that they were executed by a German firing squad, together with most of the Jews of the town, immediately after the Germans arrived. Other witnesses claim that Herzl died in a concentration camp, and that Dov Zeev was led with other community leaders to the banks of the nearby river, where they were drowned after being tortured by the Gestapo. A third version claims that Menachem's father was killed by a German soldier who caught him digging a grave for a Jewish victim, and that Hasia was dragged out of hospital to her death.

Be that as it may, the prime minister of Israel is among the many Israelis who lost their families in the Holocaust, without knowing exactly what became of them. Like many of his generation, Menachem Begin marks the anniversary of their death on a day when all Israel mourns the victims of the Nazis. For him it is a day of awesome associations, and also a day of personal mourning. The destruction of Polish Jewry, and the loss of his own parents, are still there in the background of his attitude to Germany.

His stay with his sister did not last long. There were rumors that the Russians intended to arrest the Jewish citizens of Poland who had been released under the terms of the agreement between the two countries. Begin could not take the risk of the rumor being true. On the other hand he knew there was little chance of leaving Russia legally. That left only one option: enlistment in General Vladislaw Anders's Free Polish Army, which was organizing on Russian soil. He presented himself at a recruiting office, and was sent for a medical examination.

"My friend," the doctor told him, "you have a serious heart disease, and a defect in one eye. I don't see how they'll make a soldier out of you."

Begin knew that his time in prison and the labor camp had taken a toll on his health, but he had to enlist. He decided to write to the Chief of Staff of the Polish army explaining that, if he was not inducted, he would be thrown in prison a second time. The Chief of Staff summoned him for an interview. Begin made use of all his old persuasive powers.

"All right, if that's the case," said the Polish officer, "I will do something for you. I only warn you that if the division goes abroad, don't try to desert and head for Palestine!"

Begin reported once again for a medical.

"You've already been here," the doctor said angrily.

131

"Yes, but the Chief of Staff told me to come again."

Skeptically, the doctor turned aside and whispered to an officer. They fished through some files, and finally found a document that the doctor read. He then returned to examine Begin.

"Heart and lungs—fine," he announced out loud. "You seem to be slightly near-sighted, but our army will make a marksman out of you."

CHAPTER 7

"In the Flame of Revolt"

General Vladislaw Anders was captured by the Russians when, under the terms of their agreement with Germany, they occupied Eastern Poland. As a confirmed and declared anti-Communist, Anders was clapped into a Soviet prison. Confident of their new-found strength and preparation, the Wehrmacht and Luftwaffe did an about-turn and attacked the Soviet Union. Stalin made an agreement with the Polish Government-in-Exile in London, whereby all Polish citizens would be released from Soviet prisons and detention camps in order to build an army to fight the common enemy.

This was the point at which the paths of General Anders and Private Begin converged. But it was not the only thing they shared in common. Anders detested the Soviet rulers, whom he could never forgive for their opportunistic cooperation with Nazi Germany in carving up Poland. Thus he was in no mood to rely on the Kremlin. If his army was to fight, it must do so far from territory under Soviet jurisdiction. In coordination with the government to which he owed allegiance, Anders took his force through Iran and Iraq to the fords of the River Jordan. For Begin, and the other Jews in the Free Polish Army, this was the crowning moment of their lives. There, just across the river, lay the Promised Land that had captured his dreams from his earliest years.

Menachem Begin arrived in Palestine in May 1942. Once there, he had no difficulty in being reunited with his wife and friends. He moved into Aliza's one room on the ground floor of 25 Alfassi Street in Jerusalem not far from the Polish Town Marshal's Office, where he was serving as clerk and translator. On March 1, 1943, he became the father of a boy whom he named Benjamin.

It was quickly obvious to him that *Betar* was on the verge of collapse. Many of the members of its largest branch in Poland were either dead or dying in Nazi concentration camps; others had been killed resisting the Germans in various Polish towns; still others had vanished, without a trace, into the penal system of the Soviet Union. *Betar* in Palestine, which had been mostly supported by Polish immigrants, was crumbling. The few members who were active preferred to gather under the standard of the IZL, the underground army. Although IZL was committed to driving the British out of Palestine in order to create a Jewish State, its members were compelled to cooperate with their enemy, as were the other underground organizations of the Jewish community.

Though he was still wearing the uniform of the Free Polish Army, Begin was very quickly appointed *Betar* commissioner in Palestine. Somebody, however, told the British police, who were keeping a close eye on the activities of organizations associated with the underground. They had no hesitation in passing on the information to the headquarters of the Polish army. When Begin heard about it, he promptly resigned his *Betar* position.

Now pressures were brought to bear on him to desert and devote himself to the war for liberation of the nation in Palestine. Among the friends who were pressing was Dr. Yisrael Sheib, the man who had witnessed Begin's arrest by the NKVD in Vilna.

"Yisrael, do you remember that we were interrupted in the middle of a game?"

"Of course. How could I forget . . ."

"Are we ever going to finish it?"

Although Sheib had memorized the positions of the places on that chessboard in Vilna, he thought there was other business slightly more important to transact with his old friend.

"Menachem, when are you going to take that uniform off?"

"An attempt is being made to get my release."

"I doubt whether it's serious. Anyway, the *Betar* members who are supposedly trying to get your release aren't overly interested in you. They are now leading the IZL into a policy of restraint, and they don't need an activist like you."

"They did promise . . ."

"But let's assume they don't succeed."

"What do you suggest I should do?"

"Simply leave the army without any ceremony."

"Desert?"

"Yes."

"Yisrael, where's your concept of honor?"

135

"Look, you have a very simple choice: desert from the army, or desert from our war. You choose . . ."

"Yisrael, you're exaggerating. And I will not be a deserter."

"Menachem, do you really think this is the time for honor games?"

A few days later Dr. Mark Kahan, a member of IZL, called at Begin's Jerusalem apartment and found him sprawled on the bed, covered with his overcoat.

"Will you let me deal with your release?" Kahan asked.

"As far as I'm concerned you are free to try. But, if you ask me, I wouldn't count on it too much."

Begin knew what he was talking about. Only two weeks earlier Dr. Arye Altman, a Revisionist leader, had met personally with General Anders in an attempt to obtain Begin's discharge from the army. Since Altman had not succeeded, there was no reason why Kahan should.

A while later Anders's Chief of Staff, General Ukolitzky, did agree to the release of six Jewish soldiers to go to the United States on a campaign to get the Jewish community to help the remnants of European Jewry. The Chief of Staff, who was well acquainted with Dr. Kahan, invited him to his office for a drink. There were a number of senior officers present, and Kahan realized that this was a farewell party for Ukolitzky.

"I'm leaving here on a mission, and my colleagues are throwing a party—but the last document I signed was an approval of release for Menachem Begin."

Kahan did not waste a moment. He dashed straight over to the Begin apartment.

"Menachem, it's fixed! There's an order to discharge you!"

The first reaction was from Aliza—"He has no civilian clothes."

That was quickly taken care of and Begin, now dressed in a pinstripe suit, hurried off to a terminal where taxis made trips to Tel Aviv. The manager, who knew everyone in Jerusalem, came to greet him.

"I see you're a civilian now. What are you going to do?"

"Take a refresher course in law."

"I wish you success."

In Tel Aviv Begin rushed to a staff meeting of the IZL.

"Gentlemen, I am reporting for duty in civilian clothes—the IZL uniform."

In December 1943 Menachem Begin was appointed head of the IZL, with orders to build a general staff. His predecessor, Yaakov Meridor, was now his deputy. Begin assumed command at the age of thirty. The organization that he was taking over, and on which he would make more of a mark than any other man, was thirteen years old. It had originally come into being as a result of serious differences of opinion between its founders and the other commanders of *Haganah*—the secret defense arm of the official Jewish organizations in Palestine—and was then a vastly different organization from the one that Begin took over, and from what it would become under his leadership.

Since 1920, when Zeev Jabotinsky organized the first Jewish defense force in Jerusalem, the trade unions under the direction of the parties of the Zionist left had gained control over the *Haganah*. Under the conditions of the British Mandate, and because of the strong socialist pioneering flavor of the early waves of Jewish immigration, the Palestinian "General Federation of Hebrew Labor" was the major center of political power in the community. Apart from political activities, and an extensive cultural and professional function, the General Federation—or *Histadrut*—also coordinated large-scale settlement operations that would, in the final resort, determine the land borders of the State of Israel. Though *Histadrut* leaders did not actively intervene in *Haganah* operations, they did control budgets and organized its structure according to the ever-changing needs of Jewish colonization, while keeping an eye on the political indoctrination of *Haganah* members.

Early in the 1930s, as relationships between the Revisionists and the labor movement were worsening, a few *Haganah* officers in Jerusalem were under suspicion of sympathy with Jabotinsky's party and objectives. The Jerusalem commander, Avraham Tehomi, had indeed met with Jabotinsky in Europe to suggest a plan for a military-type organization, but Jabotinsky had rejected the idea. Remaining loyal to his own convictions of the time, the *Betar* leader had argued that there was no place for an illegal organization, and that the Palestinian Jewish community must put pressure on the British to permit a regular Jewish army. Tehomi's approach to Jabotinsky was actually evidence of his dissatisfaction with the way in which the *Haganah* was being run, rather than proof of his pro-Revisionist leanings. Tehomi, in fact, had expressed open reservations about colleagues who harbored such leanings.

Meanwhile Yosef Avidar, a Jerusalem *Haganah*

member, had collected evidence of Tehomi's Revisionist attitudes, including some correspondence with a friend outside the country. From this evidence it was possible to conclude that Tehomi was cooperating with the Revisionists, and did seek to create a parallel secret army. Acting on this information, some *Haganah* members in the Holy City attempted to find Tehomi's hidden arsenal of arms and ammunition. Their activities were condemned by the *Haganah* commander-in-chief, but this did not stop them in their attempts to drive Tehomi out of the organization. Finally, seizing on the opportunity presented by his brief absence abroad, they replaced him by a loyal labor movement officer.

Tehomi was not finished. He and some of his comrades next argued in favor of a nonparty defense organization; but this was interpreted as an attempt to transfer the *Haganah* from the labor movement to the Revisionist camp. When news of an impending Arab attack on the Jewish quarters of Jerusalem was received, men hurriedly drew weapons from the secret arsenal. After the crisis was past, Tehomi's followers refused to return their weapons. They set up a separate arsenal of their own—and took a major step toward a schism in the community's defense structure.

The *Haganah* leaders used all their influence and persuasive powers on Tehomi to make him realize that the hiding of weapons from the common arsenal could be construed as an extremely drastic move calling for an equally drastic reaction. Tehomi himself needed little convincing, and indeed warned his followers of the danger of appropriating for themselves supplies that belonged to the organization. The weapons were returned—but Tehomi and his friends left the *Haga-*

nah. They wrote a formal letter stating that, under the circumstances, they could not remain members, though they would always be loyal to the underlying concept. The split was now a fact, and was formally acknowledged as such by the immediate formation of "Organization B," which soon changed its name to the National Military Organization—*Irgun Zvai Leumi* (IZL).

Quite naturally Tehomi was forced to seek recruits for the new organization from among the rural and urban bourgeoisie, and from among Revisionist sympathizers who had never been desirable candidates for the *Haganah.* His efforts were unsuccessful. Anticipating what would happen, the *Histadrut* leadership convinced the Revisionist elements not to turn their backs on the *Haganah,* promising them equal representation in its high command. Tehomi then tried Jabotinsky again. But he was still resolute in his conviction that the British must be approached to approve an official Jewish army, and he had no wish to be involved with any underground organization.

Contrary to Jabotinsky's wishes and better judgment, however, there were groups of Palestinian *Betar* who responded to Tehomi's call—among them two students of the Hebrew University in Jerusalem, David Raziel and Avraham Stern. The former, known to the underground as "Ben Anat," was to become the commander of IZL; while the latter, under the code name of "Yair," would lead an extremist faction out of the IZL to form the group *Lohamei Herut Yisrael* (Israel Freedom Fighters), or as it would be more familiarly known, *Lehi* to its friends and the Stern Gang to its British enemies.

Tehomi still had hopes that his men would one day

return to the parent organization, the *Haganah*, which would no longer try to suppress factions such as theirs. He was very careful therefore not to allow Revisionists and right-wing sympathizers to gain control over the IZL, and to stay clear of any political influence. In the spring of 1933, after a number of feelers, the two organizations were reunited. It lasted less than three weeks. This time the immediate cause of dissension was the stoning of a *Betar* parade in Tel Aviv by trade unionists, for which Dov Hoz, a socialist Zionist member of the *Haganah* high command, was blamed. Tehomi tried his best to bridge the widening gap, but to no avail. The Revisionist Party and *Betar* had already gained too great an influence among his men.

The Arlosorov murder in that same year served to stoke the flames. The IZL was now openly labeled Revisionist, and Jabotinsky was ready to suggest that the organization should be brought under his party's wing. Tehomi rejected the idea, and it was finally agreed that IZL should be managed by a supervisory committee. Apart from Jabotinsky himself, a number of moderate right-wing leaders, who had traditionally been the buffer between the Zionist left and the Revisionists, were roped in to serve on the committee.

But Jabotinsky and his followers were not, at any stage, prepared to forsake their basic objective of eventually bringing the IZL under Revisionist control. Tehomi resisted, yet he was in the position of a King Canute ordering the tide to stay away from the shore. Revisionists were in the majority. In 1937 Tehomi tried once more to take the IZL back into the *Haganah;* but he no longer controlled his own creation. Most of his members considered themselves bound by

141

the discipline of Jabotinsky's *Betar* movement and Revisionist Party. Tehomi's effort did siphon a few men and weapons into the *Haganah* fold, but the majority retained their separate identity.

The existence of IZL in Palestine made an impression on the *Betar* branches in East Europe, and particularly in Poland. And, as we have seen, it supplied the background to Jabotinsky's dispute with the activists of his own movement. Though few were the *Betar* members who would even consider challenging Jabotinsky's leadership, activists such as Begin were prepared to exchange military ceremony in Poland for military action in Palestine.

Within the IZL itself these were lean years, so lean that the body almost disintegrated. When Dr. Sheib tried to talk Begin into deserting from the Polish army to cast his lot with the fighters for national liberation, Sheib was in fact a member of a group that had left IZL. He was hoping that Begin would be able to restore unity to the camp, and possibly even regain its lost members.

The turmoil in the IZL ranks was mostly the result of the organization's inability to define the objectives of its war in clear terms. Matters were further complicated by the world war in which the Jewish community, and the IZL, found themselves suddenly on the side of Great Britain. The approaching threat of the Afrika Korps, and the scope of genocide in Europe, created a trauma for underground armies that were initially formed to drive the British out of Palestine. The *Haganah,* whose original objective had been Jewish self-defense against Arab marauders and rioters, was in a less traumatic situation.

At the same time the *Betar* control over IZL had

become so strong that its commander, David Raziel, was virtually receiving his instructions directly from Jabotinsky—a situation not to the liking of his own headquarters staff who, though they did not basically disagree with Jabotinsky, did want political autonomy for the underground. Some of the staff officers were already thinking of their situation after the war, when the honeymoon with the British régime would be over.

The British were not exactly enthusiastic either about cooperating with the IZL, which they viewed as hardly representative of the Palestinian Jewish community. However they were prepared, within reason and to a limited degree, to make use of IZL provided that no one considered it close cooperation, and always on the understanding that they were not misled as to IZL military and operational strength.

The internal dispute reached its high point in the summer of 1940. While Raziel relied on the support of the Revisionist Party, his adversary, Stern, tried to influence the rank and file to revolt against their supervision, contending that the IZL must be subject solely to its own officers who were the men who would lead it into battle. Stern accused Raziel of inactivity and short-sighted politics. As a firm believer in the thesis that the end justifies the means, Stern argued that the Palestinian Jewish community must find itself allies overseas—no matter who they were—and that the IZL by a show of force must convince the British that the Jews of Palestine were equal partners in the war against the Nazis. The way to achieve that, paradoxically, was to wage a terror campaign against the institutions of British administration and economic might, on the assumption that this method would be the most persuasive. The obvious reward then would be British willingness to grant Jewish independence.

Raziel stoutly maintained that the IZL could not defy Revisionist directives and policies. Among his supporters were men who did not necessarily agree with those policies, but who believed that the only way to resolve their differences was within the framework of the party.

The conflict between the two camps of IZL deteriorated into violence. In June 1940 Jabotinsky moved decisively to put an end to the dispute. From the United States he cabled Raziel a power-of-attorney to appoint or fire whomever he wanted among his senior assistants, and at the same time he cabled instructions to Stern to obey Raziel's orders. Less than a month later Jabotinsky was dead. No supreme authority remained to prevent the final split.

The shock of Jabotinsky's death spurred the two camps into a last attempt to settle their differences, but it was too late. Within two and a half weeks after the funeral, Stern had set up *Lehi;* and after a period of regrouping and organization, his force launched a terror campaign against the British in Palestine. The IZL loyalists believed that everything must be directed toward the struggle against the common Nazi enemy.

This loyal faction, which remained with the Revisionists and retained the IZL name, was eventually compelled to cooperate further with the British. To the dislike of some of its leaders, IZL members were allowed to enlist in the British army. This was obviously difficult to accept for those who viewed their fight as being against the British.

In the spring of 1941, while the IZL was still trying to overcome the effects of the split, the organization's Intelligence officers presented to headquarters the

British command's proposal to send an Intelligence team to Iraq, where Rashid Ali el-Kilani had just led a pro-Fascist revolt. In return for their cooperation the IZL were promised a free hand in taking prisoner the Mufti of Jerusalem, Haj Amin el-Husseini, who was the militant and pro-Nazi leader of the Palestinian nationalist movement. The IZL accepted the proposal, and Raziel decided to lead the team himself. Raziel and three of his men were flown to a British base in Iraq, then proceeded to Habaniya, which was under siege by Rashid Ali's forces. They made contact with the local British headquarters that was to help them on their way into the interior of Iraq. The team planned to go to Baghdad, where they would capture the Mufti—the man responsible for the Arab riots and attacks on Jewish settlements in Palestine. The Mufti was also wanted by the British authorities on charges of cooperation with the German enemy.

While Raziel and his men waited at British headquarters, German planes bombed the camp intermittently. In one of these raids Raziel was wounded. He died before he could even begin his mission. He was buried there, though his coffin would be transferred for interment in Israel many years later. Upon his death the command passed to Yaakov Meridor.

Meanwhile opposition to the IZL was spreading, part of the reason being its way of collecting money. At first some IZL members unsuccessfully tried armed robbery; then they levied a tax on that section of the population that could be expected normally to support them. They went from house to house, in some cases using threats to back up their request for donations. On occasion they even resorted to terror tactics against those people who refused to contribute. Rumors of these techniques were rife among the entire Jewish community and aroused the anger of those who already had little enough liking for anything that reeked of revisionism. The boycott imposed on members of the Revisionist Party and *Betar* was now extended to include members of the IZL.

Furthermore Avraham Stern's faction, *Lehi*, increased its campaign of personalized terror against British police officers, on the assumption that the wear and tear on British nerves would eventually force them out. Stern's tactics aroused the Jewish community's hatred even more than had the IZL. The *Lehi* faction was seen to be sabotaging Britain's war effort against what was undoubtedly the cruelest enemy that the Jews had ever known—Nazi Germany. Stern's men were compelled to go deep underground, more from fear of the Jews than of the British. Many decent Jewish men and women would no longer hesitate to turn *Lehi* members in to the Palestine police.

Stern received reinforcements from among Polish *Betar* members who were trickling into the country. While Menachem Begin was being interrogated by the NKVD at Vilna, many of his colleagues were getting through to the Promised Land, and the majority of the newcomers belonged to *Betar*'s activist faction. Some of them had aligned themselves with Begin when he challenged Jabotinsky. Two of those who arrived in Palestine were Dr. Yisrael Sheib and Natan Friedman-Yellin*—one of whom had witnessed Begin's arrest while the other had accompanied him out of Warsaw. They both joined Avraham Stern.

By the time that Begin was on his way to Palestine

---

*Until 1948, his name was Natan Friedman-Yellin. In that year he changed it to Natan Yellin-Mor.

with General Anders's army, *Lehi* was no longer recognizable as a Revisionist Party faction. True, some of the leading figures in Stern's group still spoke the remembered jargon of *Betar;* but his new recruits included Palestinian-born youngsters who had no interest in Jabotinsky's youth movement or political party. Some of them felt a deep contempt for the exaggerated ceremonies and military structure of *Betar*. Stern himself had traveled a long way from the ideology that originally nourished him; *Lehi*'s credo now spoke of national liberation and war on imperialism.*

The two poles of political opinion had coexisted in *Lehi* almost from the beginning, but the common denominator of Stern's declared aim to oust the British from Palestine by any means served to draw in youth from all camps. So deep was their commitment to that aim that they swore an oath taken from a poem by Stern himself: "Only death liberates from our ranks."

On February 12, 1942, just weeks before Begin arrived in Palestine, British troops and police cordoned off a two-story house in Mizrahi Street, Tel Aviv. Armed detectives climbed to the attic, burst through the door, and without warning shot a man who was hiding in a clothes closet. Avraham Stern's description would no longer decorate the "wanted" posters offering a reward, dead or alive.

The death of Stern—a rare combination of fighter

---

*After 1948 and Israel's independence, thoughts such as these would take some *Lehi* members into the ranks of the extreme left. They are to be found in the Israeli Communist Party, and Natan Friedman himself is among Prime Minister Begin's bitterest critics on the outer left fringe. Dr. Sheib, on the other hand, has moved even farther to the right; he now heads a political-religious faction that although it supports Begin, demands that he should ignore the opinions of friendly countries, and must go ahead with the evacuation of all the Arabs in the occupied territories.

and intellectual—was a deep shock to *Lehi*. There could be little doubt that the British had been told where he could be found, and what applied to their leader certainly applied to all of them. They were hunted men, and no Jew in Palestine would offer them sanctuary.

The command passed to a triumvirate consisting of Natan Friedman-Yellin, Dr. Sheib, and Yitzhak Shamir. In trying to persuade Begin to desert the Polish army, Sheib was secretly hoping that the *Betar* leader would be able to mend the broken fences between IZL and *Lehi*. Sheib himself was in *Lehi* because he believed in uncompromising war on the British, regardless of any incidental circumstances such as World War II. Unlike some of his colleagues, however, he had not cut himself off from the spiritual world of the Revisionists. He still considered himself a disciple of Zeev Jabotinsky.

Sheib fervently believed that even if he did not succeed in attracting Begin into *Lehi*, there was at least a hope that his old friend would stir up things in the IZL and turn it away from its willingness to cooperate with the British army. He had very clear recollections of Begin's impassioned plea before the Polish *Betar* to support the underground war for the liberation of the Land of Israel. The one factor Sheib overlooked was Begin's commitment, first and foremost, to *Betar*. As commander of the IZL Begin would mend fences. The IZL and *Lehi* would cooperate. They would share the role of "hunted" when the *Haganah* and the *Palmach* (the socialist-oriented "official" secret army of the Jewish community) turned on them. Later Begin would take the right-wingers of *Lehi* into his political camp after the War of Independence. But he could not and would not turn his back on *Betar,* the Revisionist Party, and its military arm, the IZL.

Begin's first act as commander of the IZL was to order a temporary lull in operations and to disband the organization's concentration of force. Since many IZL members had cooperated with the British, their faces were well known. He needed a tight and secret system of operation. As well as a new spirit and leadership, he instituted a new strategy for the time when he would take over, since the eventual defeat of the Third Reich seemed only a matter of time. Clearly the days of open armed struggle against the British were not far off.

Those who were close to Begin during this first period were quick to note the change taking place in IZL. And when the rank and file were called back to duty, they also felt it immediately. Amihai Paglin would say thirty years later: "We felt that someone had arrived who brought with him an awareness of historic mission. He appeared confident of his authority and willing to accept the full responsibility."

Begin was in fact absolutely convinced that a sovereign Jewish State was not a matter for coming generations. If he had harbored doubt of ever seeing his dream come true in the period when he sat in Lukishki Prison and Soviet labor camps, as the newly installed head of the IZL he knew that it was "here and now." The conditions were right for establishment of a Jewish State in his lifetime.

Here and now, with the verses of the *Betar* anthem: "In the flame of revolt—carry the flame to kindle. . . ," resolving in his mind, Menachem Begin was ready for the underground campaign.

CHAPTER 8

"Only Thus!"

The campaign to establish a Jewish State in Palestine might well have taken a completely different course had the British not closed the country to Jewish immigration during World War II when millions were being herded into the Nazi gas chambers. The few who escaped Hitler's Europe were turned back at the very shores of the Promised Land, and all because of a document, a "White Paper" issued by the British Colonial Office, that insisted on the maintenance of a demographic balance between Jews and Arabs. For the immigrants, this was not only the Promised Land of their forefathers; it was literally their only hope of remaining alive. For them there was no other place under the sun. Back where they came from, the Germans were waiting to transport them to death camps. The neutral countries would not take them in for fear of violating their precious (and hypocritical) neutrality.

Among the Jewish community of Palestine, the

feeling of bitterness and frustration was growing beyond all endurance. All attempts to soften the callous attitude of the British government in London, with the help of the Jewish lobby, were a waste of time. Meanwhile smoke poured from chimneys at Auschwitz, Treblinka, Bergen-Belsen, Dachau, and scores of other places whose names would haunt human consciences for generations to come—the smoke of burning bodies of men, women, and children. The secret roads of illegal immigration could not cope with the flood of fleeing humanity. And the heartlessness of the British Mandate, in the face of the greatest tragedy that had ever befallen the Jewish people, seemed to the youth of Palestine to be on a par with the cruelty of Hitler's hated SS. The British had truly become "the foreign oppressor."

The steamship *Struma* left a Rumanian port carrying 675 people, among them members of *Betar* and others who had narrowly escaped the German jackboot as it marched across Europe. The *Struma* was a rickety vessel, never intended for such a purpose, and certainly not designed to carry such a big load. When she reached the shores of Palestine, she was turned back under the terms of the White Paper. She sank in the Black Sea, and no one knows to this day whether it was the result of a German submarine attack or the poor condition of the *Struma*'s hull. Whatever the cause, the impression that this tragedy left was so deep and long-lasting that Menachem Begin would refer to it in his first speech to the Knesset as prime minister of Israel, in announcing his government's decision to accept Vietnamese refugees picked up at sea by an Israeli merchantman.

When Begin assumed command of the IZL, most of

its activity was centered in Tel Aviv. He traveled down from Jerusalem on Sunday—a working day in Jewish Palestine—and returned from Tel Aviv on Friday. His neighbors were under the impression that he was serving his apprenticeship in a Tel Aviv law office, but Begin actually never found time to practice the profession he had studied at Warsaw University. He was serving his apprenticeship in a trade that the British called "terrorism." Indeed all that now remains of his legal training is a strong sense of the importance of using the right word, and a respect for laws.

In Tel Aviv Menachem Begin occupied Room 17 of the Savoy Hotel, near the waterfront. It was an ideal place for conspirators. The owner of the hotel had no idea who the man with the mustache in Room 17 really was, or what was the nature of his business with the strange visitors who came to confer in whispers with him. But he did understand that he was best off not asking questions.

At the beginning of 1944 Begin's basic assumption was a very simple one, and he made it clear to the members of his staff. As long as the British were still at war with the Germans, the IZL was not to lift a finger against any of the many British installations in Palestine. But the organization was free to discourage any idea of continuing British rule. In other words, police stations and the institutions of governmental authority were fair prey. Unlike *Lehi*, Begin ordered his men not to carry weapons except when they were needed for an operation. The campaign against the British had to be well organized in all its details, and the targets were to be picked with political objectives in mind. These ground rules were passed on down the chain of command. Begin wanted his men to know what they were fighting for, and how it would be done. For him the IZL was first and foremost a fighting force, but it also had an educational function to perform.

Begin restructured the IZL into an organization that fitted in with his concept of underground warfare. The country was divided into districts, each under a senior officer. The men were distributed into assault units, propaganda warfare teams, and recruitment and procurement agencies. All units were to take part in IZL missions in addition to their specialized functions. The propaganda warfare teams, in particular, were a typical operation of the man who now led IZL. Their job was to paste announcements on walls in towns and villages across the country. If they were caught, they could expect long prison sentences for illegal activities and for belonging to an organization that endangered the public safety, as provided for under the Emergency Defense Regulations. For Begin the use of the word, whether written on walls or broadcast by the underground radio station, was an all-powerful weapon. His posters explained the purpose of the armed struggle, and called on the youth to join the ranks in their campaign to create a Jewish State. They proclaimed IZL policy and tactics, and made sure that the public was aware of successful IZL missions against the "foreign ruler."

The new structure made it easy to control men—and allowed Menachem Begin to get his message across without revealing himself. All of a sudden it was clear to IZL members that they had a leader who knew where he was leading them, and why he was demanding of them a willingness to sacrifice their lives.

In his room in the Savoy Begin wrote a broadsheet, which was later typewritten and distributed among members of the organization and its supporters. In it he defined the objectives of the IZL's war:

> Return of the Jewish People to their Land.
>
> Creation of a free and independent Jewish State.
>
> Establishment of a society in which the individual would enjoy rights to freedom, happiness, and social justice.
>
> The aspiration to return to the homeland from blood-soaked wanderings among the nations that have risen up in every generation to destroy us has been in the heart of every Jew from the day our people went out to the debilitating Diaspora until now. This aspiration has changed form time and again, until in recent generations, under the dual influence of Hebrew tradition and the political trends among the nations, it has taken on the shape of a national movement.

The broadsheet called on the youth of Palestine to work together to create a concentration of the Jews of the world in their historic homeland—the only place where they could live without constant danger hovering over their heads, and where they could defend themselves against their enemies. "It is a historic commandment. It is also a living commandment deriving from the natural aspiration for a free, normal life for our people in their land."

He warned against compromise:

> On the route to achieving Jewish rule in the Land of Israel, we must beware of compromise. Any compromise, any agreement by the Jewish people in Palestine to a limitation of the concept of rule, or the concept of the Land of Israel, is likely to result in the loss of the entire political objective. Rule means real rule: a Jewish government, and not some religious, cultural, and municipal autonomy of a Jewish community under a foreign ruler. The Land of Israel means the territory not only within the historic frontiers, but also within the natural and strategic frontiers of this region—and not some tiny tract of land on which to build a symbolic sovereign state, which does not have the possibility of concentrating masses and becoming a strong power in the future.

Suddenly the IZL insignia had a meaning. Its design was a map of Palestine on both banks of the Jordan—encompassing what was already then the Emirate of Transjordan, which would become the Hashemite Kingdom of Jordan—and, superimposed on it, a hand with a rifle and the legend "Only Thus!"

The target was clear, and the direction well defined. But Begin also defined the means:

> In the last two generations attempts have been made to liberate our land by various means—and they have not succeeded. The attempt to purchase the soil of the homeland by "practical

work"—private or group buying of a tract of land, and the building of towns, villages, and *kibbutzim*—praiseworthy as this attempt is in itself, brought what it had to bring: an impressive enterprise that can be frozen or even destroyed with the wave of a hand at the decision of the foreign ruler. We have learned that there is no other way apart from a war of liberation. A national war of liberation is a just war, waged by an enslaved nation against a foreign power that has gained control over it and its land. Since the foreign ruler holds the land that it conquered by armed force—for otherwise its representatives could be driven out overnight—our war of liberation will also take the form of armed war, a war with weapons, weapons of freedom against the weapons of oppression. The IZL is the liberation army of the Jewish People!

The objective, the direction, and the means. Still Begin's broadsheet did not stop there. He went on to lay down the pattern of the Jewish sovereign State and society in Palestine, and his words echoed his *Betar* education and the half-conservative, half-liberal world that had shaped his own views.

At last the fighters of IZL had a clear program, and many of them memorized its words. The broadsheet became the "I believe" of the fighting underground. But even as IZL was taking its first modest steps, carrying out small and relatively unimportant operations against the institutions of British government in Palestine, they discovered a traitor (the first of three who would emerge in the course of their blood-soaked battle for national liberation).

Yaakov Hilvitz of Tel Aviv, a confirmed bachelor who spent his free hours in nightclubs and gambling houses, was never a member of IZL. In 1939, when the organization mounted a fund-raising campaign ostensibly for the Revisionist Party, Hilvitz was hired as a collector to go from door to door. Nobody quite knew how he got the job, though he was an acknowledged figure in *Betar*. At the end of 1939 he faded from the scene. He did not join IZL, though he kept up contact with his acquaintances from *Betar* and the Revisionist Party of Poland.

In the summer of 1944, while IZL was gathering new impetus, Natan Friedman-Yellin, the head of *Lehi*'s operations, sent a message to his old friend Menachem Begin: "Hilvitz is a traitor." Begin, who did not know the man, asked his aides to check the information. First they found that the information from Friedman-Yellin was not firsthand. A girl who worked as a courier in *Lehi* had heard it from her brother who, quite innocently and not knowing that she was in the underground, had mentioned seeing Hilvitz in conversation with Bill Kettling, a British CID officer. Hilvitz had allegedly handed something to the Englishman. Some days were to elapse before Begin's men discovered that the something was a list of IZL members, but fortunately not an up-to-date one. Some of the people on it were now in *Lehi*, others had become inactive, and yet others had moved to different towns.

From information that was "leaked" to the IZL, it was known that the British were hunting the previous commander of IZL, Yaakov Meridor, and that their description of him included his having an acned face. And the last time that Hilvitz had seen Meridor, he had indeed been suffering from acne.

Since the British had carried out a series of arrests based on the outdated list, Begin's staff asked him to order Hilvitz's execution.

"Certainly not. The proof against him is too weak."

"But it's obvious that he's the informer . . ."

"Purely circumstantial."

Begin was adamant. Without conclusive proof there would be no steps taken. He got his proof all too quickly, however, when Hilvitz tried to betray Begin himself.

The occasion was the first birthday of Begin's new son Benjamin. One of the few friends who knew where the Begins were living brought with her, besides a present for the child, an acquaintance whom she introduced as "Yaakov." Menachem had no idea that he was face to face with the traitor his men wanted to eliminate. Hilvitz visited a while, playing with the baby and chatting with the parents, never giving any indication that he knew the real identity of Menachem Begin.

The following day the house in Alfassi Street was surrounded by police. When Dr. Kahan arrived to tell Aliza that her husband would be back as usual on Friday, she was obviously tense and nervous as she opened the door.

"Detectives," she told Kahan in Polish.

"Does —— live here?" Kahan asked quickly, using the first name that came to mind.

"No."

"Then where do I find —— Street?" He named an address around the corner.

Aliza Begin walked out with him, ostensibly to show him the way.

Kahan rushed straight down to Tel Aviv to tell Begin: "There are detectives in your home. You can't go back there!"

IZL Intelligence officers questioned the friend who had visited them to see whom she had brought with her. Totally unaware of the implications, she told them the man had been Yaakov Hilvitz. There could no longer be any doubt. Hilvitz, who had gathered that his tip to the Palestine police had not borne fruit and assumed that the IZL must already be hunting him, had fled to Egypt. Two IZL members who were serving in the British Eighth Army were instructed to seek him out and tell him he must return immediately to Palestine for a hearing. Knowing what he could expect back home, Hilvitz informed on the two couriers to the British military authorities, who were shipped off to a detention camp in Eritrea. Begin needed no more convincing. He issued the execution order. But Hilvitz was a few steps ahead of the IZL and had obtained an entry visa to the United States from the British authorities. IZL headquarters in Tel Aviv passed the information on to their emissaries in New York. Ari Jabotinsky, Zeev's son, who was leaving Palestine for Turkey, cabled from Ankara to his Revisionist friends in America: "Azef Hilvitz is coming to you. Receive him properly." Yonah Azef was the name of an agent provocateur in the era preceding the Russian Revolution, and Ari assumed that the men in New York would understand. But they took the cable at face value, giving Hilvitz a grand reception at which he made a spirited speech about the courageous war of the underground in Palestine.

When Samuel Merlin, chairman of the League for a Free Palestine, rose to his feet to deliver a vote of thanks, and opened with the words "Our friend Azef Hilvitz," the latter blanched. He knew the significance of the name. Merlin, noting Hilvitz's sudden nervousness, then remembered that his name was Yaakov. The message was finally understood.

Hilvitz vanished immediately after the reception, but the IZL were quickly on his tail. As the League was opening a major campaign in America and already had the support of a number of United States senators, however, the importance of the campaign was judged greater than the need to execute a traitor.

Meanwhile Menachem Begin could not go home to his Jerusalem apartment, and the only alternative was to move his family to Tel Aviv. But the first problem was how to get Aliza and the baby out from under surveillance by the CID. A friend was sent to tell Aliza that she must make a habit of taking the baby each day, at a regular hour, to a local park, so the policemen would accept her daily outing as normal routine. Aliza did as she was told. Then, one day, a black taxicab appeared at the park, and two men stepped out and hurriedly ushered her and the baby inside. The cab took off at great speed for Tel Aviv. The Begins' Alfassi Street apartment with all their belongings remained under British surveillance for a long time.

Such was the secrecy of the new IZL that all contacts were severed with the Revisionist Party, and those officers who were known to the British from their brief period of cooperation were kept far away from the centers of real activity. The first overt sign of reorganization and changed tactics came in the form of a poster on the walls of Palestine's towns and cities. It was the IZL's declaration of revolt, and had been written personally by Begin. The final version was ready months before it was released, because Begin wanted to be sure that he had a well-oiled and battle-ready army under his command. The delay caused controversy within the IZL, with one faction arguing for deeds before words because the youth of Palestine were weary of empty slogans. But Begin believed in the magic power of words, and it was he who decided not to publish the declaration until February 1, 1944. That night the poster appeared on walls across the length and breadth of Palestine:

TO THE HEBREW NATION IN ZION!

We are in the final stages of this world war. Each and every nation is presently making its own national accounts. What are its victories and what are its losses? Which way must it go to attain its objectives and fulfill its destiny? Who are its friends and who its enemies? Who is a true ally and who a traitor? And who walks toward the decisive battle?

The nation of Israel must also distinguish its own road, reviewing the past and drawing conclusions for the future, for the years that have passed are the most terrible in our history; and the years to come are the most decisive in our annals.

Begin went on to enumerate what had transpired since 1939 in the relations between the Jews and the

161

other nations, emphasizing the Holocaust. He then continued:

The language of these facts is both simple and horrible. During four years of war we have lost millions of the best people in our nation; millions more are in danger of extermination. And Palestine is locked and barred because a British régime rules—a régime that implements the White Paper, and aspires to the elimination of the last hope of our nation.

Sons of Israel, Hebrew youth, we are in the last stages of the war. We stand before the historic resolution of our fate for generations.

The armistice, declared at the beginning of the war, has been broken by the British régime. The rulers of the country did not consider loyalty, concessions, or sacrifices; they carried out, and still are carrying out, their plans for the elimination of national Zionism.

Four years have passed, and all the hopes that beat in your hearts in 1939 have vanished without trace. International status has not been given to us; a Jewish army has not arisen; the gates of the Land of Israel have not been opened. The British régime has completed its disgraceful betrayal of the Hebrew nation, and there is no moral foundation for its existence in the Land of Israel.

We must draw the conclusion that there can be no more armistice between the Hebrew nation and youth and the British administration in Palestine, which hands our brothers over to Hitler. We must make war on that régime—war to the end. This war will demand many difficult sacrifices. But we shall go toward it in the recognition that we were loyal to our brothers who were and are being slaughtered; it is for their sake that we fight, and we have kept faith with the testament of their deaths.

And this is our demand:

That the rule over the Land of Israel be delivered immediately into the hands of a Provisional Hebrew Government.

The Hebrew Government of the Land of Israel (Palestine), the sole legal representative of the Hebrew nation, will proceed immediately upon its establishment to carry out these major points:

a. To establish a national Hebrew Army;

b. to negotiate with all the authorized bodies for the organization of mass evacuation of European Jewry to the Land of Israel;

c. to negotiate with the government of Russia on the question of evacuation of the refugees of Polish and other Jewry;

d. to create conditions for the absorption of sons returning to their homeland;

e. to make a treaty with the Allies for increase of the war effort against Germany;

f. to propose, in the name of the sovereign Land of Israel, on the basis of the Atlantic Charter and in recognition of common interests, a pact of mutual assistance with Great Britain, the United States of America, the renewed France, and all other free nations that will recognize the sovereignty and international rights of the Hebrew State. Honorable peace and good neighborliness will be offered to all the neighbors of the independent Land of Israel;

g. to put down roots that have the sanctity of the Bible for the life of the liberated nations in its homeland;

h. to guarantee to all citizens of the State work and social justice;

i. to declare extra-territorial status to the sites holy to Christianity and Islam;

j. to grant full and equal rights to the Arab population.

Hebrews!

The establishment of the Hebrew Government and realization of its plan is the only way to rescue our nation, to save our existence and dignity. We must go that way, for there is no other.

We will fight. Every Jew in the homeland will fight.

God of Israel, God of hosts, be our help. There is no retreat. Liberty or death!

Create a wall of iron around your fighting youth. You shall not abandon them, for cursed is the traitor and mocked is the coward.

And you too will be called on to raise the banner of civil war. You will be called on:

a. To refuse to pay taxes to the oppressor régime;

b. to demonstrate every day and every evening in the town and to demand the establishment of the Hebrew régime in the country;

c. not to obey any order of the foreign régime; but to defy them and declare, I will listen only to a Hebrew régime;

d. the working public will be called on to declare a general strike in all places of work, private and public. Be prepared for hunger and hardships but do not break the strike, for it is holy;

e. student youth will be called on to strike the schools and devote all their time and energies to this war.

Hebrews! The fighting youth will not recoil from sacrifices and hardships, blood and suffering. He will not surrender nor rest as long as our days are not restored as they once were, as long as he has not guaranteed our nation a homeland, liberty, dignity, bread, justice, and law.

And if you help us, your eyes will soon see—in our own times—the return to Zion and the resurrection of Israel.

May God permit and aid us!

The declaration of revolt electrified the IZL. Its men were more than ready for the action they had awaited so long. But the reactions from outside the IZL were disappointing to Begin, who had labored so hard in drafting the declaration.

"It's not serious," Wilkins, a British CID officer, told the press. "There's nothing to worry about."

Wilkins, a well-known and crafty man, was considered an expert on the underground organizations. He would eventually be assassinated by *Lehi* members in Jerusalem, but meanwhile his words carried weight. Many years later, when Begin surfaced and turned the full force of his rhetoric on Wilkins (then dead), it was clear he had been deeply insulted by his disparaging tone. The Zionist left and its *Haganah* were also in no mood to take the declaration seriously.

They made the point that the two renegade factions were always well known for their fancy words.

But on February 12, 1944, everyone knew that the revolt against the British had really begun. That evening three explosions rocked the cities of Jerusalem, Tel Aviv, and Haifa almost simultaneously. The targets in each case were the immigration offices—the symbol of the hated White Paper. It was here that the British kept their records of illegal immigration, and of Jews who had arrived in Palestine as tourists, then vanished without a trace. All of them faced the threat of deportation if caught. But without records, the British would be helpless. Menachem Begin decided that the first IZL operation would have symbolic meaning, both in its location and its timing.

A few days earlier the man in command of the Tel Aviv operation had appeared in the Immigration Office there to apply for a passport. He had brought with him a mass of unnecessary and irrelevant documents which, apart from annoying the clerks, gave him time to study the thickness of walls, the layout of corriders, and all the entrances and exits. His first objective was to identify the room where the precious files were stored, and that did not take long. To be on the safe side he stuck his head around the door, then apologized to an angry official inside. He had done his job well. On the evening of the operation an IZL team entered the building from the roof, laid their explosive charges by the door of the file room, and left the way they came. The files were a total loss.

In Jerusalem, two drunks attracted the attention of the policeman on duty outside the Immigration Office. They were cursing and kicking each other. He ordered them to move on, but they had not gone far when he heard one of them scream, "He's killing me!" While the policeman tried to find out what was going on, other members of the IZL team were slipping through the open windows of the building. As he returned to his station in the doorway, the building was rocked by a massive explosion.

In Haifa, another diversionary tactic was used to remove the policeman on duty. A young couple sprawled on a wall at the corner, not far from the guard's post. As he looked their way, they seemed to be in an advanced stage of lovemaking. The policeman, an Arab, was not used to seeing public demonstrations of this kind, and he was fascinated by it. While he watched open-mouthed, a number of figures flitted into the building. Within minutes the Immigration Office crashed to its foundations, a heap of rubble. The team had used more explosives than they needed.

Newspapers the following morning reported that the Arab policeman was still in a state of shock; IZL wags suggested that the cause of his state was over-excitement at the private show of copulation put on for his benefit.

Two weeks earlier nobody had believed the IZL capable of anything more than personalized terror of the kind already associated with *Lehi*. Now the British woke up to the fact that Begin's declaration was deadly serious, and the urban Jewish communities were thrust into a state of anxious doubt. The man in the street was secretly delighted at the choice of targets, whose symbolism was not lost. But the British Criminal Investigation Department knew they had no time to lose. They were looking for a short, slight, nattily dressed man who smoked heavily, and was believed to live in a one-room apartment somewhere in Jerusalem.

From time to time flying squads were dispatched to some address where their quarry appeared to be. Begin here, Begin there, Begin nowhere. The search went on. But it could not prevent the next painful blow.

CHAPTER 9

"To Die or Conquer the Mountain"

The new IZL policy of revolt called for a new deployment both politically and tactically. Menachem Begin was no expert on guerrilla warfare. In fact his military knowledge was somewhat less than that of a private in the Polish army for his time had been served, not in the line, but in Jerusalem in the Polish Town Marshal's Office as a clerk. As commander-in-chief of the IZL he granted his officers full tactical discretion, only reserving for himself the choice of targets —and it was a very careful choice politically.

In declaring the revolt Begin had stipulated one very clear condition: as long as the war with Germany continued, the revolt would be against the foreign ruler, but military targets were out of bounds. However the implication was abundantly clear: when the war was over, military targets would be fair game.

The parties of the Zionist left, which virtually controlled all the Jewish national institutions—including the *Haganah* and its striking force, the *Palmach*—still believed that, once the war was over, Britain would keep Lord Balfour's historic promise of a National Home for the Jews in Palestine. Their restraint policy favored, first and foremost, the preparation of a social and economic infrastructure ready for the moment of transfer of power from the British to the Jews. The fate of the Arab community, if the British honored their commitment, was not quite clear. Begin did not believe that the British would leave of their own accord; but at this stage he was willing to leave the question open. His principal demand centered on the granting of fredom of migration to any Jew who wanted to come, and he viewed the negation of this freedom as a British attempt to repudiate Balfour's promise. That being the case, the British must be driven out of Palestine. Meanwhile he discerned that the Arabs of Palestine had lost their political and military initiative. Before he published his declaration of revolt, the Arabs had provided the British with a convenient reason to deny Jewish independence and immigration. If the demographic balance was upset, so the British argument went, the Arabs would be provoked into open acts of hostility.

From time to time the Arabs provided a bloody reminder of their opposition to an "open door" policy. Throughout the twentieth century Arab armed gangs had at intervals attacked Jewish settlers, ambushed traffic on the roads, and rioted in urban districts where Jew and Arab lived in close proximity. But the declaration of revolt had transferred the initiative in Palestine into the hands of an organized Jewish force. With each operation of the IZL an ancient truth was evidenced: the side with sufficient military power to conquer and defend Palestine would keep hold of the land. And where the Arabs had attacked defenseless men, women, and children, Begin's military force was careful to choose strategic and tactical targets attuned to the political objectives of the organization. In effect Begin was following the principle that war is diplomacy by other means, and in so doing he was emphasizing the difference between IZL and *Lehi*. The latter, his rivals, carried weapons at all times, and considered any British soldier and policeman an enemy to be dealt with at every opportunity. Begin tried to persuade his old friend Natan Friedman-Yellin to abandon these tactics. The two men did not meet face to face, but they maintained close contact. Begin harbored a deep respect for the courage of Friedman-Yellin's men, but he considered their activity to be both counter-productive and immoral.

The conditions of Palestine called for a different concept of guerrilla warfare. There were no forests or mountains from which freedom fighters could foray out, complete their missions, then vanish back into impenetrable terrain. Begin's men operated out of their homes and offices, and thus they had to be doubly careful—especially since their next target was even more ambitious than the opening shot at the immigration offices. Indeed so ambitious was it that anyone hearing about it in advance would have burst out laughing at the sheer impudence of the thought. In all three main cities, the offices of the Palestine Police Criminal Investigation Department were well guarded. By virtue of their function, each contained a considerable arsenal of weapons. Yet Begin had not chosen the CID out of any idea of bravado, but in order to add a dramatic note to his war on the foreign oppressor. His choice of a well-fortified objective was meant to push home the lesson that nothing could stand in the way of a nation fighting for its liberty. The CID, more than any other institution, symbolized the harshness of foreign rule.

The British troops and police in Palestine tried to behave with restraint to the civilian population, and some of their officers were known for their gentlemanly conduct. As was the custom of colonial soldiers, the British abused prisoners that fell into their hands and used any means possible to locate underground suspects. But the officers and men of the CID were a different story. Their brutality and hostility toward the population were well known, and their interrogations were not at all reminiscent of the behavior for which Englishmen were famous.

In mid-March 1944 the IZL began its surveillance of CID headquarters in Jerusalem, Tel Aviv, and Haifa. Observation teams watched and noted the routines, the comings and goings, the changes of shifts and of guards, routes of access and alternatives for speedy retreat. Others went on seemingly innocuous errands to the neighboring police stations, and managed apparently inadvertently to stray down corridors normally closed to the public.

The operation was scheduled for the evening of March 23. The teams called together for the mission did not know their objective until the very last minute. All they knew was that it was a big one. Some of them had spent the day fasting in response to a call by the Chief Rabbinate for a gesture of solidarity with the Jews being slaughtered in Hitler's furnaces. That was sheer coincidence, but it would add an element of even further drama.

The Tel Aviv CID was located in a four-story building on a main thoroughfare between Tel Aviv and Jaffa. Apart from the CID it housed living quarters, police staff offices, and an armory. The building was surrounded by barbed wire and under constant guard. At first the planners of the operation considered digging a tunnel under the street. They talked to a shopkeeper who agreed to let them have the use of his premises, which were opposite the police building. The initial stage simply involved bringing sacks in which to cart away the rubble from their excavations, but on the day they were to begin digging the shopkeeper had second thoughts. He had realized the danger to himself. IZL headquarters came to the conclusion that, since there was no way around the guards, they would have to break their way in by force.

Early on the evening of March 23 a porter staggered through the narrow streets of Tel Aviv carrying fruit and vegetable crates in a shoulder harness. Routine police patrols paid him no special attention. It was a normal scene for the city, and at most aroused pity from some of the passers-by, which amused a young, well-dressed girl who kept the porter in view, although from a distance. The man stumbling along was actually powerfully built under his porter's smock, and well able to tote far bigger loads.

"How's your back, Haim?" she asked, when both had reached their destination—a small, neglected apartment in the southern part of the city.

"Don't laugh, Ruth. That was quite a weight."

"Okay, you two," the operation commander interrupted. "Was anyone overly curious at his load?"

"I was behind him all the way. Who would want to pay any attention to such a miserable-looking lout?"

173

"As if anyone paid any attention to you!" The porter in disguise had the last word.

The four demolition experts who were to carry out the mission now made their way to the IZL weapons cache. They were in British army uniforms, with standard-issue rucksacks slung over their shoulders. On their way back the rucksacks were loaded with 30 kilograms of explosives. They hailed a cab, looking for all the world like servicemen leaving a nearby bar, and ordered the driver to take them to Jaffa. They were in the middle of an off-color soldiers' song when the cab was stopped at a police checkpoint. But the police only needed a glance inside to reassure themselves. They waved the driver on. Then, on a street that ran downhill to their objective, they saw a British armored car. According to their briefing the street should have been deserted at that hour. But again there was nothing to worry about. The machinegunner in the turret of the vehicle bent down to examine the occupants of the cab, but made no attempt to stop them.

Meanwhile IZL backup forces had arrived and taken up their positions. To their consternation the police guard on the building had been reinforced, and armored cars were racing out in the direction of the city. Later they learned that *Lehi* had shot two policemen in retaliation for the wounding of some of their men. The British had declared a state of emergency. It looked as if *Lehi* had inadvertently upset the IZL plan. The officer in charge was ready to call it off; but the four demolition experts were already on their way to the target and there was no possibility of recalling them.

The four descended from their taxi and strode

down the street past the police post into a side turning, threading their way through armed police.

"Hello, George," a drowsy Arab constable greeted them.

They raised a hand in greeting and kept on walking toward the side entrance of the building. The guard on the gate did not bat an eyelid as they passed him and entered the building. Once inside they unloaded their rucksacks and set the delayed-action detonators. Nobody paid any attention to them as they strolled back to the street and through the police cordon.

While the detonators were ticking off the minutes, police patrols—made nervous by the *Lehi* attack in broad daylight—were combing the streets around Tel Aviv's police stations. A flashlight in the hand of a member of one such patrol came to rest on the faces of three of the IZL backup unit, who were lying on the ground clutching their weapons. A fourth, who was still in the shadows, aimed his pistol and fired. The policeman carrying the flashlight dropped to the ground. In the ensuing fight one of the IZL men was wounded but the unit got away, carrying the injured man with them. Just as they were leaving him in hospital, the police building exploded in rubble and smoke.

The next morning, while the inhabitants of Tel Aviv flocked to gape at the wrecked building, the police posted a guard on the injured IZL man. They interrogated him, but he insisted that he had never met any of his comrades before the night of the operation, and knew them only by code names.

That same evening of March 23 the Haifa operation was in full swing. There, the explosives were brought to the site by two British soldiers—but real ones, unlike the fake Tel Aviv variety. They had enlisted in the Jewish Brigade of the British army under the orders of IZL, and were now on leave in Palestine. In a courtyard close to the police building they handed their loads over to a team that had been waiting in a darkened stairwell. Two demolition men then crept through the barbed-wire fences into the yard of the police station, making expert use of the darkness and the slackness of the guards on duty.

The Haifa charge might not have been detonated but for the coolness of a young girl—a courier who brought a bottle of vital acid from Tel Aviv. Her bus was stopped en route at a police barricade, and the passengers were searched. When a policewoman approached her, she hissed: "Don't you dare touch me!" Whether because of some premonition, or simply an understanding between women, the policewoman only glanced at the girl, and then passed on down the bus.

It was not the only hitch that threatened to disrupt the Haifa operation. While the explosives experts were placing their charges, the voice of an Arab coffee vendor was heard on the street leading to the building. As he moved through the darkness toward the concealed backup team, someone called out from a nearby garage: "Hey, you with the coffee! Here!" As the vendor turned, the mechanic came out to meet him. They stood 3 feet away from the IZL team's hiding place; their faces icy with sweat, the team lay petrified. If one of the Arabs noticed them and called out, the British police would come running—and would be on the alert for their two companions. But the car mechanic was only interested in a cup of coffee and, like all good Arabs, he wanted to sip it slowly. The minutes crawled by. Finally he finished it, paid the vendor, and vanished back into his workshop. As the vendor moved on, the team could already see their two companions wriggling through the fence around the police building. They prepared their weapons and kept a keen eye on the line of retreat. But all was well. As soon as the sappers were out of sight around a corner, the backup team slipped away through the shadows. They reconvened in a stairwell near the municipal vegetable market. Elsewhere in the city a young girl was placing a call from a public phone box to police headquarters.

"This is the *Irgun Zvai Leumi*. In a few minutes from now an explosive charge will detonate in the CID offices. You must evacuate the place immediately."

"Hello . . . Who are you? Where are you speaking from?"

But the girl had replaced the receiver.

In the stairwell rendezvous the IZL team waited for an armorer to collect their weapons. Very soon an explosion would rock the city built on the slopes of Mount Carmel, and by then each member of the team must be safely in his own home. The British would certainly comb the city and make mass arrests. But the armorer had not arrived and the men were nervous. And he still had not come when they heard the sound of a massive explosion—ahead of time. Had the two demolition men made a mistake?

One of the backup men volunteered to take the weapons home with him. He stashed them under the floor of his bathroom. As he went to bed, he could already hear British armored cars and police patrols in the street outside, on their way to seal off all the exits from the city.

The following morning the IZL men learned that four British policemen were dead and three wounded; the entire CID archives, with its mountain of information on the underground and the Jewish community, had gone up in flames.

The Jerusalem assignment was the most difficult of all. The local CID, which served as countrywide headquarters, was on the second floor of the police staff building in the center of the city. It was a well-guarded fortress, difficult to approach unobserved. The team leaders made a number of reconnaissances.

On the evening of March 23 the IZL men selected for the mission convened in a cellar. As yet none of them knew why they had been called, and only the veterans among them recognized the officer who briefed them as the IZL commander in Jerusalem. He told them, "Tonight you will take part in a daring mission. This operation will shake down the foreign ruler and prove that we will rule the country. Tonight the IZL will break into CID offices in three large cities. You will carry out the mission in Jerusalem. Be strong and brave!" At that point the supply officer for the Jerusalem district, Asher Benziman, who answered to the code name of "Avshalom," took the officer aside.

"Look, I'm a veteran member of IZL, and I'm entitled to go on this one."

"I decide who goes."

"How can you send newcomers? I'm a veteran."

"I don't have anyone as good as you in Jerusalem for handling and hiding weapons."

"So what?"

"The organization needs you in your present job."

"I'm asking you . . . just this once!"

"All right, if you're going to be obstinate about it . . . But look after yourself!"

The team moved out at an hour when the citizens of Jerusalem were pouring out of movie houses in the city center. The first to go was the squad entrusted with the job of breaking into the police building. They went singly or in pairs, mingling with the crowd in the streets. The next to go were four men dressed as British police; their caps were not quite regulation police issue, but they relied on darkness to conceal the fact.

A house painter's ladder had already been placed in a building next to police headquarters, and the explosives were stashed nearby, having been carried through the streets of Jerusalem by two men who risked search at every corner. The assault team arrived and the four disguised as policemen went straight into action. Striding confidently forward they approached the entrance, where they quickly overcame the two guards, who were dragged back to the neighboring building and warned to sit quietly if they valued their lives. Two of the team then took their places in the gateway, while their companions crouched in nearby shrubbery. Within minutes a two-man British patrol returned from the city streets and approached the gate.

"Good evening."

"Good evening," replied the IZL men, drawing their pistols.

While the two Englishmen remained rooted to the spot, taken completely by surprise, the other IZL pair emerged from the shrubbery, rammed their guns into the backs of the prisoners, and led them off to the next building. They came back carrying the ladder, which they placed against the wall inside the gate at a carefully chosen spot. They were quickly followed by four more IZL members, one pair to act as the backup unit and the other carrying a heavy load. The first two scrambled up the ladder to the second floor, then signaled a third to follow them. They lowered a rope to which the fourth member of the team attached the package of explosives.

Meanwhile one of the guards on the gate hissed a warning.

"What is it?"

"Somebody's moving around in the courtyard. Keep your eyes open!"

A British officer was taking a stroll around the courtyard with his girlfriend. If he sensed anything, the game would be up. One shout or shot, and the entire team would be in a trap from which their support squad would be unable to rescue them.

The last of the packages had already been hoisted to the second floor when two figures were seen approaching. A burst of gunfire rent the night air. In response the support squad raked the street outside with rapid fire, sending a number of policemen who had come out of a nearby café to investigate the noise scuttling back inside. On the second floor of police headquarters a pitched battle was now in progress, as each side sought cover behind the pillars that supported the roof over a long open walkway.

"I'm wounded," Avshalom said as he fired at two of the enemy who were retreating, hitting one.

Two boxes of explosives were still down below, and the question now was whether to haul them up or to beat a hasty retreat. The commander of the team decided that the three boxes in position would have to do. The team scrambled down the ladder,

Avshalom among them, and ran along the withdrawal route with the support squad still covering them. Then the whole team took off down a nearby alleyway.

Avshalom fell. His comrades lifted him and raced on to the rendezvous, where three young girls collected their weapons and replaced them in the IZL hiding place. Avshalom was laid on a bed, groaning with pain. Only hours before he had argued with his commander for the right to participate in the operation. Now he was in desperate need of an IZL doctor. While Jerusalem was ravaged by explosions Avshalom fought for his life; but by dawn he was dead. The following morning, along with a communiqué on the successful demolition of all three CID offices, the IZL published its first announcement of mourning for the death of a member killed in action on a mission to fulfill the declaration of revolt.

The three-pronged strike achieved its desired effect. For the second time since its published pronouncement of war on foreign rule, the IZL had shown the Jewish community and the British authorities alike that there was an underground army capable of planning and executing coordinated, countrywide military operations. A great many Jews, including some who had never been sympathetic to IZL and its parent organizations, experienced a new pride in these boys who could defy the forces that denied a national right to the Jewish people.

Yet the hatred of the ideology and politics that had given birth to the IZL was still stronger than any national sentiment. The official agencies of Palestinian Jewry, almost exclusively controlled by the Zionist left wing, which still believed that the way to independence lay in cooperation with the British, issued a sharp condemnation of the operation. The National Council of Palestinian Jewry added to it a call on the community not to support efforts to collect funds for the "hotheads." The Chief Rabbinate issued a plea to cease and desist from actions that were likely to bring holocaust down on the heads of the entire Jewish community. Eliahu Golomb, a *Haganah* leader, at a Tel Aviv press conference said: "The road that they follow can result in civil war in the Jewish community, and that can only be a tragedy for all."

The British proclaimed a curfew in Tel Aviv and in the Jewish districts of Jerusalem and Haifa. Reinforced patrols searched for suspects and weapon caches, and the government reinstated the law imposing the death sentence on anyone who possessed or used firearms.

The next date chosen by the IZL was May 17—the fifth anniversary of publication of the White Paper that formally locked the gates of Palestine—and the target was the Palestine Radio Transmitting Station at Ramallah. The object of the exercise was to interrupt regular broadcasts and replace them by an IZL announcement. An IZL team took over the station without resistance and the broadcasts were stopped; but Menachem Begin, sitting in his room with his ear to a radio set, did not hear the voice of the organization that he headed. Only later did the team discover that the entire station lacked a single serviceable sound studio; the sound studios were all in Jerusalem. They spent about an hour and a half there and were able to make their escape without serious opposition.

Some weeks later the IZL in Jerusalem was scheduled to make another attack on CID headquarters, which had meanwhile been repaired, and at the same time to stage attacks on other police posts in the city. Again Begin chose a date with symbolic significance. While he had still been *Betar* commissioner for Poland, the British had executed Shlomo Ben-Yosef, whose name was associated with the termination of the policy of restraint in the face of Arab attacks. Ben-Yosef and his comrades had thrown a hand grenade at an Arab bus in northern Palestine. Though no one had been hurt, Ben-Yosef was caught, tried, and sentenced to death by hanging. On the eve of his execution he carved in the walls of his cell the words of Jabotinsky's *Betar* anthem: "To Die or Conquer the Mountain."

Begin selected the anniversary of Ben-Yosef's death, but the operation never took place. It was an innocent Jerusalem woman who inadvertently upset his plan. She noticed some shadowy figures in the courtyard of her house; unaware that the IZL were storing their explosives behind the garbage cans, she screamed: "Thieves!" While the team were trying to decide what to do—whether to tell the woman the truth—a neighbor phoned the police. The IZL team got away at the last minute, but the police discovered enough explosives to blow the entire police headquarters sky-high.

Begin, once more waiting in his hiding place for a report on the completion of the mission, could not understand why there was no word. Only later did he discover that the Jerusalem housewife had in fact saved a great many IZL lives. The British by now were wise to Menachem Begin and his inclination to the dramatic. Knowing full well the propaganda value of Ben-Yosef's anniversary, they had put all police posts and army camps on full alert. The IZL would have walked into a deadly trap.

In the fall of the same year, 1944, the tension in the Jewish community reached a new height. Before Yom Kippur, the most sacred of Jewish holy days, the IZL published a series of handbills in Hebrew and English, warning the British authorities not to interfere with Jews praying at the Western Wall inside the Old City.

According to tradition, the fast of Yom Kippur ends with the blowing of the *shofar*—a ram's horn—the tones of which are designed to break a way through the heavens, so the prayers can reach their destination. A similar tradition brought the Jews of Jerusalem to the Western Wall, the last remaining vestige of the Second Temple, to pray and terminate the fast. The British forbade the blowing of the *shofar* at the wall for reasons they never successfully explained to the Jews, yet which were clearly designed to give the Arabs *de facto* control over the holy area, which also included two mosques. The Mosque of Omar was in fact built on the site of the Second Temple, which had been destroyed 2,000 years earlier by the Romans, but the British did not care much for the historic rights of the Jews. They would not give them even a foothold in their most sacred place.

In the dozen or so years since *shofar* blowing had been forbidden, there had always been some *Betar* volunteer who was willing to carry a concealed *shofar* into the Old City and raise it to his lips at the end of the fast, while the congregation recited: "Next year in a rebuilt Jerusalem."

Each year the scene was repeated. British police and soldiers waded into the crowd, lashing out to right and left, arrested the horn-blower, and carted him off to prison. But this year Begin was determined to end the ban once and for all. On the eve of Yom Kippur a poster appeared on Jerusalem walls:

> Any British policeman who dares, in violation of the laws of cultured humanity, to break in on the Day of Atonement and interfere with the crowd in prayer at the Western Wall, thereby desecrating the sanctity of prayer, will be considered and recorded by Hebrew youth as a criminal.

Although the Jewish institutions warned against the shedding of blood on Yom Kippur, and the Chief Rabbinate publicly condemned the IZL proclamation, Begin was adamant. In reality he had no intention of turning the Western Wall into a bloodbath, but the police could not be sure of that. Thus, at the end of the sacred day, a relatively small force of police stationed themselves at some distance from the wall. They were not wearing the usual insignia with their identity numbers and, when the horn was blown, none of them made any attempt to approach the offender.

Expecting the British to preserve their prestige at any price, Begin had prepared to retaliate with a punitive mission far from the Western Wall—at four police stations. After sundown (the Jewish day, and hence the Jewish holy day, is timed from sunset to sunset) heavy gunfire was concentrated on the four buildings. Although the British had not interfered with the prayer at the Wall, IZL headquarters decided to go ahead anyway. Now it would be considered simply another stage of the revolt.

In an underground pamphlet, Begin wrote:

> We are not bragging about our achievement. We did our duty. We defended the nation's dignity and sanctity. We are not exaggerating the value of our action. Nothing decisive has changed in the country. The oppressive régime exists. The slavery of the nation in the Diaspora and the homeland continues. But the achievement is important and perhaps also historic. The will of the oppressor has been broken. The rulers have learned that they face proud free men. The Jewish community, which has become used to capitulating under protest to every decree and restriction, saw with its own eyes the route that leads to true liberty. . . .

But the British were not prepared to give in easily to a band of fighters that still numbered no more than 400. They prepared for a counteroffensive that included a full-scale hunt for the IZL leaders—and the posting of a price of $15,000 on Menachem Begin's head.

CHAPTER 10

Hide-and-Seek

At first the British CID had no idea of Begin's actual status in the IZL leadership, though they gathered that he was not a soldier and was anything but an expert on terrorism. The Free Polish Army records left no doubt of that. Despite or maybe because of this, he was acquiring a public image. Responsible newspapers across the world were publishing mostly fictitious accounts of the man who led the IZL, and rumors were circulating that perhaps he was a Soviet agent planted to undermine the British in Palestine.

Begin himself, when he emerged from the underground, told Western journalists who knew nothing about him, with an ironic smile: "In my country they say I'm a Jewish Fascist. You say I'm a Communist. I wish you would make up your minds. Communist Fascist—or Fascist Communist?"

The British had never met him, but they were putting together a fairly accurate picture based on the style of IZL operations and proclamations. That they never caught him was a matter of pure luck. Often enough he was separated from them only by the thickness of a door.

Begin was registered at the Savoy Hotel as Menachem Ben-Zeev. The hotel owner was unaware of the true identity of the man who rarely left his room —although Aliza did go out at infrequent intervals to do her shopping, leaving young Benjamin in his father's care. However, being conversant with Palestinian affairs and the men involved in them, the owner was well aware of the identity of Begin's occasional visitors, and he had a pretty shrewd idea what they were up to. One thing was eminently clear to him: it was best not to speak about this Ben-Zeev.

Begin might easily have remained in Room 17 at the Savoy, but something happened one night that could have ended his IZL career. A search team of British police arrived, after curfew, to check the occupants of the hotel. They went down corridors, hauling the occupants out of their rooms, checking papers, and taking away with them anyone who seemed suspicious. Room 17 was on the second floor and the entrance was via a balcony, so it did not open directly off the corridor. Menachem Begin awoke to sounds he recognized immediately. As his wife and son slept on undisturbed, he had to make a quick decision. If the police came to his door, there was no question but that they would identify him. Even those members of IZL who carried fake identification papers were finding them little protection against the British CID. He was beginning to regret having asked his comrades to bring Aliza and Benjamin down from Jerusalem. Had they remained at home in Alfassi Street, no one could have proved anything against

188

Aliza; but now she would be suspected of helping her husband in his activities. And then what would become of the child?

Meanwhile there were footsteps in the corridor outside. Begin held his breath as he heard the British ordering guests out of the neighboring rooms, telling them to dress and get down to the reception desk in the hotel lobby. He lay wondering what he would do if they knocked on his door. Should he ask "Who's there?" in all innocence, or perhaps tell them, "Gentlemen, I have been waiting and am ready to go with you"? Did he have any choice? The building must certainly be cordoned off, and he could not escape—even if he could overcome the searching party.

As the steps approached his fear suddenly passed, to be replaced by gnawing depression. This time he knew what to expect, and it wasn't a labor camp in the Arctic Circle, serving time on trumped-up charges. This time it would be a prison in Palestine, charged with very clear violations of the British law.

The footfalls now seemed to be right outside the door. Begin stole a glance at his wife and son. They would soon be forced to part from him, although perhaps the British would insist on taking Aliza along. What would happen to Benjamin? Was he to blame because his father had decided to raise the banner of revolt?

Then, as swiftly as they had come, the steps receded. The voices in the lobby below died down. The hotel went back to sleep, but not Begin. He remained awake till dawn. In the morning he met the hotel owner in the corridor.

"Good morning, Mr. Ben-Zeev. Did you hear what happened during the night?"

189

Begin decided to keep a straight face, though it was obvious to the hotelier that his guest must know what he was talking about.

"I didn't want to wake you. A number of policemen were here, searching for suspects. A good many people were hauled off for interrogation, but have already returned. I thought it would be a pity to bother you with all that."

Begin wanted to ask how the British had been kept away from Room 17, but he held his tongue. It would not do to appear overconcerned. At a much later date the hotel owner told him that when he had brought the police down to the end of the corridor and the doorway to the balcony, he had told them: "That's it. No more rooms." The British moved on to the next floor.

That same day IZL headquarters decided to remove Begin from the Savoy. Until they could find a safe hideout, they suggested that he should start to leave the room more often so as not to arouse suspicion. Then, a few days later, he, Meridor, and their families went off to Safad near the Sea of Galilee for a "holiday." Their car was likely to be stopped on the roads, but they assumed that the presence of women and children would help allay any doubts. The journey took four hours and they passed through three police roadblocks, but the policemen merely glanced at the faces of the occupants and waved them on.

The following day they were seated in the dining room of the Hotel Herzlia in Safad, discussing the menu, when the blood in their veins almost froze. The men being shown to the next table were the commandant of the Tel Aviv police, his deputy, and two other officers of his staff. They were, it turned out, also on a brief holiday in Galilee. Meridor, who recognized them, trod hard on Begin's toes under the table. Begin glanced around and understood immediately. The conversation flowed at their table, and to all appearances the two families had no cares in the world apart from the caliber of the food served for lunch. The occupants of the next table threw studied glances in their direction. Eventually two of the officers got up, and moving to a table behind Begin and Meridor, asked two men from there to come with them into the corridor, where they were told to identify themselves and submitted to a body search.

Even though the two IZL men had aroused no suspicion, the very presence of police top brass was enough to send them back to Tel Aviv immediately. Begin now knew that he could no longer trust to luck. Two close shaves were enough. On the way back, however, they risked stopping off at Ben-Yosef's grave in Rosh Pina Cemetery near Safad. Not yet having anywhere else to go, Begin returned to Room 17 at the Savoy, where he settled down to the next operation.

Soon afterwards an apartment was found for Begin in the Mahane Yehuda District of Petach Tikva—an area inhabited by Yemenite Jews. It was small, neglected, windswept, and isolated, but Begin could console himself with the thought that he was sleeping in sheets originally intended for the British High Commissioner MacMichael, whom the IZL had once planned to kidnap. Some wag had decided that their prisoner should be comfortable, so they had bought a set of sheets for his bed. The operation never took place, and all that remained of it were two bedsheets.

But the IZL were not happy with his new quarters. In the first place, its isolation from neighbors was enough to attract attention; secondly, Begin was the only European Jew in a predominantly Yemenite area, and among their dark skins he would stick out a mile. Begin himself was having difficulty explaining to his neighbors what exactly he was doing in their district, and why instead of going to work early each morning, as they did, he spent the whole day indoors. Paradoxically the inhabitants were sympathetic to the IZL, and some of its best fighters were drawn from among them.

Begin was quickly moved again, this time to the Hassidof Quarter at the other end of Petach Tikva, where he was known as Yisrael Halperin and carried identification papers made out in that name. Hassidof was a workers' district surrounded by orange groves. Its inhabitants left early and returned late each evening. Few of them had any inclination to delve into the affairs of others, or any interest in this Halperin who spent his days at home and only strolled out into the nearby orange groves in the evenings. But they were intrigued by the frequent visitors who walked with him deep in whispered conversation.

On the very first evening there was almost a mishap. As Begin began his stroll he was greeted with a friendly "*Shalom*" by a neighbor.

"How do you do," he replied, "my name is Halperin. Yisrael Halperin."

"Halperin? I thought you were someone else . . ."

From the way it was said, Begin knew that his neighbor had identified him, yet would say nothing about it. It was Aliza who spread their cover story through the neighborhood. They were refugees from

Poland, and her husband—who had studied law—was now preparing for his examinations in Palestine.

"How do you live?" a woman asked.

"Oh, we have some help from the Joint," Aliza replied, referring to a Jewish welfare fund. She reflected on the irony of it: Begin's allowance was even smaller than the pittance usually given to refugees.

Their landlord Mr. Michaeli, an ardent supporter of the IZL, believed that "Yisrael Halperin" was the organization's legal counselor. Consequently he assumed that the frequent IZL visitors were in fact consulting his tenant about upcoming court cases involving other IZL men taken by the British.

Begin has always been friendly and outgoing. As Yisrael Halperin, even though he was a hunted man with a price on his head, he still kept open house for his neighbors. They found him a pleasant man and a good conversationalist, and he never lacked for visitors or for return invitations. This social contact with his neighbors brought him his first job as a lawyer— even though he had never really practiced his profession. As a cover, his new home was full of legal volumes, but he rarely opened them. However one persistent neighbor talked him into writing a petition to the Petach Tikva Council regarding an illegal outhouse on his property, which the council wanted to destroy. Much as Begin disliked it, he had little choice. He worked hard, not over the text, but over making his handwriting legible, then finally signed it "Yisrael Halperin, attorney."

Occasionally, by the light of a kerosene lamp, Begin conducted meetings of the IZL high command, while Aliza sat at the door ready to intercept any unwanted visitor. With their neighbors so friendly, on more than one occasion Menachem had to take his colleagues out into the orange grove to complete a session.

On Saturdays he joined his neighbors in the small synagogue. It is a tradition among Jews to honor a man by calling him up to the pulpit to read the weekly portion of the Torah, and Begin was called on by the rabbi, who summoned him under his borrowed name: "Yisrael, son of Dov Zeev." Begin felt uneasy about deceiving his God with an assumed name, yet consoled himself with the thought that the deception was being perpetrated in the name of Divine Providence.

While Begin was in the Hassidof Quarter, the British police extended their search to the Petach Tikva District. One morning as he left his house, he saw that the entire area was cordoned off by troops. In the distance he could hear police loudspeakers telling the inhabitants to stay indoors. He did not doubt that they would soon be at his door; there would be questions to answer, and the risk that one of them might recognize him.

The neighbor who had greeted him on that first night came up to him.

"Mr. Halperin, I suggest that you get out of here through the groves."

Begin thought about it a moment, then rejected the idea. The orchards would be full of traps, and if he ran, he could never come back to Hassidof. There would certainly be someone who owed allegiance perhaps to the *Haganah*, who would not hesitate to inform the British. But meanwhile the voices were approaching.

"What's going to happen?" a neighboring woman wailed.

"There's nothing to worry about. This will also pass," Aliza calmed her.

"You've got nothing to worry about, Mrs. Halperin, but I've got an army issue blanket in the house. What if they find it?"

Aliza chuckled to herself but said nothing.

Begin's luck was still with him. The British turned Petach Tikva upside down, searched every house, dug into every corner—except the Hassidof Quarter. The search was over, the curfew lifted, and the danger past. But it left a tragedy for the Begins. Aliza's brother-in-law (who was also her cousin), Dr. Arnold, lived in Tel Aviv. He and Begin were close friends. Arnold knew about the curfew and search in Petach Tikva; he also knew where the Begins were hiding, and he feared for them. He was one of the Jews who had not left Poland in time. When the Nazis came, he and his family had been among the first sent to an extermination camp. He had watched his only son being torn from his wife's arms and consigned to the ovens. His wife committed suicide. Arnold himself reached Palestine alone and broken. Now, thinking that he was about to lose his remaining loved ones, his overtaxed heart finally collapsed.

Aliza and Menachem could not even go to the funeral. Some friends went in their place and, at the cemetery, noted alien eyes. The British knew of the family link and were waiting for Menachem and Aliza Begin to appear at the graveside. Begin was at that moment in the small Hassidof Quarter synagogue reciting *Kaddish*—the prayer for the dead. He returned in the evening, depressed, to a home in mourning.

Shortly thereafter the ground was again burning under Begin's feet. IZL Intelligence reported that someone in Hassidof apparently knew too much about the Halperins, and the danger was now greater than ever before. The CID offices had been blown up; the leaders of Palestinian Jewry were publicly declaring disassociation from the IZL and calling for boycott. If someone in the neighborhood was in the know, the Begins must get out of there fast. Yisrael Halperin vanished as suddenly as he had appeared, to be replaced by a bearded orthodox Jew named Yisrael Sassover, whose sole interest was in the Holy Books. (Begin had begun to grow the beard while still in Hassidof, explaining to his neighbors that he was in mourning. The custom forbade religious Jews to shave or cut their hair for thirty days after a death in the family.)

When Menachem Begin, alias Yisrael Sassover, arrived in Yehoshua Bin Nun Street in Tel Aviv, he was already to all appearances a devoutly orthodox Jew who, in keeping with the practices of *Hassidim*— the followers of a great rabbi—wore a black trilby and long black coat.

On his very first day in the new home the usher of the local synagogue came to call.

"I heard that a religious Jew had moved in, and I'm happy to invite you to services in our synagogue."

Sassover immediately accepted the invitation. From then on he was a regular fixture at Shalom Temple. At first he attracted no attention, but then the whispers began as his neighbors wondered why Sassover did not go to work, instead of spending his days bent over the Holy Books. Of course, normally that was not particularly unusual behavior for a religious Jew of Sassover's ilk. There were many *Hassidim* who spent their time studying the Torah and the Talmud, their livelihood being provided by the charity of orthodox Jews; but they mostly lived in a community of their own kind. Yehoshua Bin Nun Street was not that kind of community. The inhabitants did go to synagogue, but they pursued a normal working life outside its doors. Moreover some of the more observant noticed various strange habits of Yisrael Sassover that were not in keeping with his cover. Begin tried very hard to play the game, but it was not always possible. His neighbors could only conclude that he was odd, perhaps naïve, and certainly no great success in life. "Such a pity for Mrs. Sassover. She's the one who has to take care of all the household affairs . . ."

Here and there Sassover encountered problems. One of them was on a Saturday, when members of the synagogue congregation were gathered around the rabbi to hear a lesson on the holy writings. The rabbi mentioned Queen Helena, a Jewess who had enlarged and helped decorate the Second Temple during the Hellenistic era. Helena is not a Jewish name. One of the congregants asked the rabbi about that but, being learned in the Bible but weak on history, he could not answer.

"It's very simple," said Sassover. "It's a Greek name like many that were given our people during those times."

All eyes turned on him. These were simple, not particularly learned people, and his knowledge was worthy of attention—perhaps speculation.

"How did you know that?"

"I heard it from somebody."

From then on Begin was careful to keep his knowledge to himself.

Their second child, a daughter, was born at Yehoshua Bin Nun Street, and Begin named her Hasia after his mother. Hasia Begin was an illegal child in more ways than one. He could not call her Begin, nor was he eager to register the birth under his assumed name, for there was no good reason to record with the public registrar the existence of one Yisrael Sassover of Yehoshua Bin Nun Street. He did not even go to the hospital to bring home his wife and daughter. An IZL member by the name of Yisrael Epstein stood in for him. In fact, Epstein lent his name to mother and daughter—and that too was to have its own entertaining consequences. On the day that Hasia was born, another expectant mother named Epstein gave birth to a son in the same hospital.

"*Mazel Tov,* Mr. Epstein, you have a son," a nurse greeted him.

She was surprised to see the proud father turn on his heel, and without pausing to see either wife or baby, run out of the hospital. She could not know that Epstein was rushing to give the good news to the real father.

"You have a son!'"

Begin was astounded when Epstein returned later to correct the misunderstanding.

"You have a daughter—and Aliza and the child are both doing well!"

The neighbors in Yehoshua Bin Nun Street did not trouble the Sassovers. Only once did Begin have to summon all his persuasive powers to get out of a situation that could have spelled trouble.

"Mr. Sassover," the usher of the synagogue greeted him one day, "I need your help."

"What with?"

"Our butcher—you know him—has troubles. Somebody has spread a terrible libel that he sells non-kosher meat. Of course you know it isn't true."

"Of course. I eat his meat myself."

"Excellent. Then you must come with me to the Chief Rabbinate to give evidence that you know the butcher shop, and it is kosher."

"Why me?"

"Look, Mr. Sassover, you're an observant Jew. They'll believe you."

"But I can't go!"

"You must do this favor for a poor unfortunate Jew."

"There's no way that I can."

"Why?"

"I have a terrible stomach ache. The doctor has forbidden me to go out."

"Then I'll have to find somebody else."

All Begin needed was to appear before the Chief Rabbinate—rabbis being known for their pedantic efforts to confirm the identity of their witnesses. But then Begin really fell ill. He was having dizzy spells and intestinal problems.

"You must call a doctor," Haim Landau, the IZL Chief of Staff, told him.

"Certainly not."

But Landau was obstinate and brought in a doctor himself.

"Mr. Sassover, you need fresh air. You must take a stroll every afternoon. I have the impression that you don't go out often, isn't that so?"

"What can I do, doctor? I spend most of the day over my books."

Next, Begin faced the danger of another British search, this time because of a dog. Roxie had belonged to the previous owners of the apartment, and now she wandered around the neighborhood but always returned to the Begins' door. One night the British set up a roadblock by their house, and began to check all passers-by. Roxie decided she was going to get rid of them and began barking loudly. Through the slats of a blind Begin watched a British officer walk over and try to calm the dog—without success. The Englishman turned toward the house, obviously with the intention of asking the owners to call their dog off. One more moment and he would be ringing the doorbell.

Suddenly the barking stopped. The British had given up and were moving their checkpoint somewhere quieter. For the present the danger had passed.

While Begin divided his days between IZL meetings and synagogue services, the British intensified their manhunt, in the certainty that Begin's capture would spell the end of IZL operations. But this time they had help: the official bodies of Palestinian Jewry, including the unions and the *Haganah*. The war between left and right was about to acquire a new dimension as the *Haganah* assigned a special unit to surveillance of IZL members—with the specific intention of turning them in to the British.

CHAPTER 11

Hunting Season

When Ezer Weizman became Defense Minister to Menachem Begin's government in 1977, a silver-haired colonel on the reserve list moved out of an office in the ministry in Tel Aviv. Colonel (Res) Shimon Avidan left without any farewell parties, and almost in secret. The daily press, busy as it was with details of the negotiations for Middle East peace through the agency of the United States, devoted little space to the resignation of the Comptroller of the Ministry of Defense, although when Avidan was appointed to that post by Weizman's predecessor, Shimon Peres, the story had been worth columns of type. Avidan was a part of Israeli history—the officer whose brigade had stopped the Egyptian offensive in 1948 a mere 20 miles from Tel Aviv.

With Weizman at the head of the defense establishment, however, there could be no room in it for the man who had commanded the *Haganah* campaign to break the IZL that took place from November 1944 until September 1945. Weizman himself had never been a member of the IZL, and had only joined Begin's political party in the late 1960s after a distinguished military career culminating in the command of the Israel air force. But his deputy in the ministry, Mordechai Zipori, was an IZL veteran, and he could not tolerate the presence of Colonel Shimon Avidan.

For the voters who brought Begin to power in May 1977, the incident was meaningless. Most of them had not even been in the country during "Operation Season," and some were not even born then. But the hatreds of warfare between brothers die very slowly.

By the mid-1940s the conditions were ripe for an open clash between the military arm of the official Jewish community and the two dissenting groups—the IZL and *Lehi*. The pot had been a long time in coming to the boil, the flame having been lit and fanned by confrontation after confrontation between the Zionist left and Jabotinsky's movement. Toward the end of World War II hope was growing among the leaders of the community that the British would indeed keep their promise, even to the extent of granting Jewish independence in the National Home mentioned in Lord Balfour's historic declaration. And the hope was based on information leaked from London to the effect that Prime Minister Winston Churchill favored partition of Palestine, including Transjordan, between Jews and Arabs. It was reinforced by an assumption that, following a war that had claimed 6 million Jewish lives, and under the pressure of public opinion both in Britain and the United States, the British were hardly likely to be hardhearted about the comparative handful of survivors of the Holocaust whose only hope of sanctuary was Palestine.

In the meantime the common enemy was Nazi Germany and, not unlike Jabotinsky during World War I, the community wanted a Jewish Brigade in the British army on the assumption that it would eventually serve as the foundation on which to build an independent army. A Jewish Brigade was finally established in September 1944, and it went to the European theater of operations in February 1945—two months before the capitulation of the Third Reich. Its value was therefore only symbolic in military terms, and quickly proved negligible in political terms. True, the men of the Brigade acquired training that was to be invaluable to the army of Israel in the 1948 war; but in 1945 the British had not the slightest intention of letting these men become the nucleus of Jewish independence.

The British authorities in Palestine were deeply troubled by the IZL and *Lehi* guerrilla warfare. The attention that it attracted internationally was hardly designed to allow them a free hand within the country, and in fact the government in London was forced to hint, if somewhat vaguely, at the possibility of giving the Jews of Palestine the right of self-determination. But, in return, its leaders asked that the Jewish organizations restrain their hotheaded brothers.

Lehi was caught up in a dynamic of terror, and the torture of some comrades who were thrown into British prisons only served to intensify the tactic of blind violence. Some of the prisoners escaped and returned to *Lehi* operations with a renewed determination—and an absolute conviction that the British would never leave of their own free will. Because they remained deep underground, and completely cut off from the political establishment, they could not know that progress was in fact being made toward independence.

Begin's assessment was little different to that of *Lehi*. His intelligence officers gave him their evaluation of the diplomatic maneuvers, yet he could not visualize any British willingness to leave the country. So, holding true to his own fervent belief that the only way to independence lay in a demonstration of real force, he was not prepared to disband the IZL, or retire it from the field of battle, for the sake of what he considered to be empty words. He was however prepared to make a gesture with far-reaching consequences. He stated that he would be willing to put the IZL at the disposal, and under the command of the military, semi-underground *Haganah*—but only if *Haganah* was willing to join the war on the foreign régime.

Apart from making waves internationally, the operations of the two dissenting organizations had had the effect of undermining morale in the ranks of the *Haganah*. Within its élite *Palmach* striking force, commanded by Yitzhak Sedeh and Yigal Allon, there were loud murmurs about the inactivity of their high command. Many of its youngsters were fed up with repeated training to no purpose, while others of their age group were involved in adventures that spurred the imagination. Some even left the *Palmach* to join IZL and *Lehi*. Clearly the representative leadership of the Palestinian Jewish community needed some dramatic action to rein in the dissidents.

The first salvo of the war among brothers, afterwards called Operation Season, was fired by Eliahu

Golomb, a very senior *Haganah* officer, when he told a Tel Aviv press conference: "The dissident organizations are causing untold damage to the Zionist diplomacy. Thus it is no longer possible simply to condemn terrorism. Information and education will no longer do the job, neither will the articles written in the daily press. If there is no alternative, we will have to fight against these crazy and damaging actions."

The *Haganah* leaders started out from the assumption that they did in fact represent the opinion of the organized community as expressed through its elected institutions—to which it was subservient. Wherever Menachem Begin was, he clearly rejected the leadership and its authority. In fact Begin was prepared to assume that his adversaries did represent a majority of the Jewish public—though he would have argued the point—but for him this was not at issue. The war for liberation, as a revolutionary stage in the history of the nation, was not a game to be played by the rules of majority and minority.

Early in April 1944 the Executive of the Jewish Agency for Palestine decided to launch a propaganda campaign against the dissidents. "If there is to be no alternative, we shall face force with force," said David Ben-Gurion. "It will be a tragedy, but a smaller tragedy than the danger inherent in a small group gaining control over the entire Jewish community."

That was a far-reaching declaration, and each party to the dispute interpreted it as they chose. For Ben-Gurion and his colleagues it was absolutely vital to bring the dissidents back under the national jurisdiction and authority; and if Begin and Friedman-Yellin, leader of *Lehi*, lived by force, then force it would be.

Begin and his men, at least in hindsight, viewed this as stage one in the battle for control over the still unborn State of Israel—an attempt to smash IZL political power as a means of ensuring left-wing hegemony once independence had arrived. And this, again in hindsight, was precisely what Operation Season did. The public image of Begin and his followers was brought to such a low ebb that they were to spend years outside the camp as outcasts among their fellow Jews. Indeed, during the course of his years as prime minister, David Ben-Gurion would at one time or another invite all the political parties of Israel to join his government, with two exceptions: the anti-Zionist Communist Party and Menachem Begin's *Herut*.

Along with the intensive propaganda campaign, Ben-Gurion did try to establish contact with the head of IZL. On October 8, 1944, he sent Dr. Moshe Sneh —the Jewish Agency's supervisor of the *Haganah*— to meet Begin in a rented apartment in Tel-Aviv. It was an ironic occasion in Israeli history. Dr. Sneh, who came as the representative of official Zionism's military power, would in years to come abandon the Zionist ethic to join the Communist Party, thereby earning Ben-Gurion's derision. In the last years of his life Sneh returned to the Zionist fold, while Begin —a man hated by Ben-Gurion—would end up occupying the "Old Man's chair" in the prime minister's office.

Begin and Sneh were old acquaintances. Both were born in Poland, and they remembered each other from Warsaw—a fact exploited by each man in a very frank exchange of views. In his report to Ben-Gurion and the Jewish Agency Executive, Sneh wrote: "Begin made a pathetic impression. He is incapable of framing his thoughts without resorting to rhetorical riddles. And when he uses rhetoric, he tends to become emotional." Sneh's impression was that, despite anything Begin might have said to the contrary, he was not prepared to disband the IZL or make it subservient to the elected assemblies of the Palestinian Jewish community, and that he intended to use it, when the time came, as a political tool in the struggle for control over the Jewish State. As the conversation dragged on past midnight—it lasted a full five hours—both men were striving to gain the trust of the other.

"Objectively," Sneh said, "we cannot but value your deeds. I know you, and I have no doubt that you want to serve our common cause to the best of your abilities. You declared war on England . . ."

"I didn't declare war on England. England isn't our enemy, and therefore I didn't declare war on her. I declared war on the oppressive rule of the English in the Land of Israel."

"Are you at all aware of the English plans for us? How can you be capable of waging war while you're cut off from the most vital political information? Your war becomes bereft of political purpose," said Sneh.

"Let's assume that you're right," Begin countered. "How do you assess the situation?"

"I'll tell you frankly, none of us knows exactly what the future will bring. It may be this way or that. We must be prepared for any eventuality. It does seem to us that the Jewish community will have a fight, come what may. If a negative situation shapes up, there is no doubt that it will bring a clash. We may have to arrange illegal immigration. We may have to organize illegal settlements, and defend them by the force of arms. The decision is not far off—but it must be subject to political objectives."

Sneh persistently tried to flatter his adversary in the hope of gaining his trust and assessing his intentions. He also tried to convince Begin that the international situation was not appropriate for terror tactics against the British in Palestine: "Zionism is also dependent on international elements and cannot ignore them. Apart from that you must understand that the Arabs are in the picture too—and Arabs were killed in your strikes against the British police. The Arabs can wake up and ask themselves: Wait a minute, what's going on here? They're likely to rebel. And your actions might stimulate their rebellion. Who needs it?"

Begin's responses were muted. This, after all, was his first face-to-face meeting with someone from the other side—and someone who was prepared to explain his views and discuss them frankly.

Dr. Sneh also presented tactical arguments: "You are accustoming the British administration to suppress every Jewish rebellion, and giving them a good reason to prepare for the future. From that viewpoint your actions are similar to an internal putsch at the height of a greater revolution."

From there he proceeded to the home front: "They must also result in internal clashes and direct the terror inward. I'm sure you don't want that, just as I'm sure you know that I don't, and that no decent Jew does—but these things have their own dynamics. It must turn in that direction. There are already signs. In one place you demand money, and threaten violence; in another you demand shelter; somewhere else you demand of a Jew that he keeps his mouth shut. These things develop dangerously. If you expand your activities, you will have to gain control over the public; otherwise you won't be able to function on a large scale. We have control over that public, and we have purchased that control by democratic methods. That public elected us. If you see the danger, you must draw the necessary conclusions. I assume that you don't want an internal war. I have come to ask you what you think. Do you want to manage your operations as you are doing—for if so, you must necessarily bring the damage that I have told you about. If you don't want to cause damage, then you must tell me the alternative. You must propose ways in which to place your organization under the sole leadership of the Zionist movement."

Begin answered at length and in some detail. He concluded by saying that the British "did us an injustice. They closed the gates of the country against the background of the extermination of the Jews of Europe, and so—in my opinion—they deserve the whip that we are brandishing over them."

"Look, I didn't ask whether they deserve the whip or not," Sneh interjected angrily, "nor whether war on them is just or not. I asked you whether it serves a purpose. What are you? A judge appointed by the Almighty? Do you want to achieve a purpose or to do justice?"

"It's also the purpose. Our actions must influence the British. We have had a number of successes, and it's undermining their prestige in their own eyes and in Arab eyes. If we augment our activities against them, they won't be able to swallow it any more. They will be forced to negotiate with us. The Americans are interested in things being quiet here. When

Europe is quiet, the war will continue in the Far East. The Land of Israel is an important crossroads on the way to the Far East. The Americans will want quiet here. Their public opinion will take our side and help the British change their attitude."

Begin argued that his actions were also influencing Arab attitudes, in that the IZL was doing them no harm; indeed, they could see that the IZL was capable of hurting the British and would have second thoughts about inviting a clash with a force of such determination. "And, perhaps most important of all, our actions have an influence on the Jewish community. What did they do when the Jews of Europe were led to the slaughter? Nothing. At most they shut their shops for a few hours of protest. Perhaps they even donated a little money for rescue work. Then, suddenly, a fighting youth arises. Suddenly there are youngsters willing to make the supreme sacrifice. The British impose collective punishments on the settlements, make searches, proclaim curfews. It makes them hated. You say that most of the community is opposed to us? Maybe. But they are beginning to despise this régime. They are slowly beginning to see that there is no other way but to fight them. And so our axiom is action. We don't complain that you condemn us. You can utilize our actions for your own tactics. You should have told the English: 'You caused this—so give us something in order that it will stop.' I'll tell you something else: I'm happy that you say we're such a small group. If such a group can fight like this, just imagine what it will be like when the entire Jewish community of the Land of Israel rises in rebellion!"

"But military action divorced from political strategy is inconceivable . . ."

"You're right. Military action must be subject to the political leadership and objective. I tell you frankly, we have no political aspirations. I'm prepared to say that in the form of a binding declaration: the IZL has no aspirations to rule the community in the Land of Israel. Moreover since Jabotinsky's death we are prepared to view Ben-Gurion as the leader of the community. We see him as the man who must manage the political and military war, and we are prepared to report to him for his orders. But on one condition —that he should begin the war on the foreign ruler. I don't doubt that you are stronger than us, better organized than us, and have a far greater hold on the community. You wage the war! If you will only do that, we are at your disposal and command. If you don't do it, then we'll go our own way. Maybe we won't succeed alone; maybe we'll all be killed. But we must try. We must go to the very end. If we don't succeed, if we are all killed, we will have made our contribution to Jewish history—in that a part of Jewish youth did rise up because it would not accept defeat, did go to the very end, did do everything, did fight. Perhaps from that some day redemption will come."

Begin was already in possession of information indicating that the *Haganah* might take the field against his men. Jerusalem IZL reported that its members were being tailed. The press was full of incitement against IZL, and it seemed like extensive groundwork for future action. So he was prepared to tell Sneh: "If you try to act against us, we shall defend ourselves. We will not be the first to raise our guns against you;

211

but if you raise yours, we won't keep our hands in our pockets. My colleagues and I have closed our accounts with the world. Take me, for example. I have been in the hands of the NKVD, and nothing can scare me any more. I ask you in the name of the friendly relations between us, don't try to threaten us."

Sneh then told Begin that if he really respected the power of the *Haganah* and was willing to operate under its leadership, he must stop all his own operations immediately so that they could be examined and approved or disapproved. But Begin reiterated that he would not stop his operations, nor would he accept the authority of the *Haganah* until it began to act as a fighting leadership. "First fight," he said; "then I'll recognize you."

Begin did not hide his bitterness over the boycott of IZL by the organized community, and over the campaign being waged against his fighters. He reminded Sneh of the ideological clash between the Revisionists and the left wing over the murder of Arlosorov, and added: "You always say that you alone are building the country. You say that you have settlements and power, that you control the community—as if you were the only ones existing here."

"We were elected democratically, you know."

At the close of the meeting, Begin had one last question.

"I have heard that you are going to fight us . . ."

"I came to talk to you in order to prevent that."

"Yes, but I can't accept your opinions. At any rate, if you are thinking of fighting us, you must know that we will also be serious about it. I ask you to inform us of it, as we did the British before we began the war. We declared war openly. We are gentlemen, and I ask you to observe the rules of fair play."

On October 31, 1944, with the help of mediators, another meeting was arranged between the two sides. This time Sneh was accompanied by Eliahu Golomb, and Begin was joined by Eliahu Lankin, a member of his high command. Golomb repeated Sneh's arguments from the earlier meeting, emphasizing that the IZL was driving away the community's friends in the British government, and that the Zionist diplomacy was encountering growing obstacles. And he had something new to add: "As you know, the *Haganah* has a great many caches of weapons; we also have workshops producing arms in secret. Your operations are endangering our stockpiles. After each operation the British search ostensibly for terrorists. We cannot allow you to endanger those stocks of weapons."

Unlike Sneh, Golomb made no attempt to find friendly words: "Even if we assume that you are right, you must accept that we are the elected leadership of the entire Jewish community. The responsibility is ours. We were chosen. Who chose you? You are a product of the Revisionist Party, which for years has been pursuing a separatist course. Even if we could tolerate that in the past, from now on we cannot tolerate it. The situation is too critical to permit such a state of affairs. There are men among us who are demanding vigorous action against you. If we have no choice we will be forced to do it. The British CID cannot eliminate you, but the Jewish community can do so far faster than you imagine. So we are demanding that you immediately cease all activity and put yourselves under the discipline of the selected institutions. Afterwards you will not be able to accuse

213

us of starting a war between brothers because it is not at all important who began it. All that is only propaganda. We have to put an end to your operations at all costs—one way or the other."

Although Moshe Sneh tried to soften the impact of Golomb's words, he admitted that when it was put to a vote, he supported taking vigorous action against Begin in the event that he still refused to listen to them.

Begin recapitulated the arguments originally presented to Sneh, again noting his agreement to Ben-Gurion's leadership of the Jewish community in Palestine, with the condition that it must be a fighting leadership: "Since the death of Jabotinsky, we have no aspirations for leadership. Were Jabotinsky still alive, we would undoubtedly consider him the leader of the community. Jabotinsky is no longer with us. We are willing to accept Ben-Gurion. But we do have conditions. As for the struggle against the British, we value your public mission, but we cannot agree that you have a monopoly in the political field. We also have political objectives, and they are no less legitimate than yours. In any event we cannot accept the rulings of your leadership as political axioms that may not be appealed."

The die was cast, and the final decision met the approval of both the national institutions and the trades unions. The *Haganah* was instructed accordingly, and assigned 170 men of its crack *Palmach* to the war on the dissidents. *Haganah* Intelligence was ordered to collect all possible data on the IZL; at the same time *Lehi* was warned not to undertake any independent action. Actually *Lehi* was in sore straits at that time. Most of Friedman-Yellin's men were either in prison or deep underground, and he was in no position to offer active opposition to the *Haganah*. But by a stroke of irony, they would be the ones who inadvertently gave the signal to start Operation Season.

While the *Haganah* leaders were making their threats very clear to the IZL, the two dissenting groups (IZL and *Lehi*) were discussing a merger. But the talks broke off on the evening of November 6, when some shocking news arrived from Egypt: two *Lehi* members had assassinated the resident British minister in the Middle East, Lord Moyne. It was done without IZL knowledge, and the IZL command promptly broke off the talks. The two assassins were caught, brought to trial, and executed. Ironically, their performance in court served as inspiration for Egyptian youth in shaping their own nationalist movement and aspirations to rid themselves of British rule. As far as the Jews were concerned, the historical record would show that Moyne had been an enemy who had rebuffed a plan to rescue Jews from Hitler's Europe.

Be that as it may, the assassination represented the slamming of the last door—even though the IZL had nothing to do with it.

The surveillance of IZL members, which had already been in progress for some months, now proved its efficacy. IZL men were abducted, some of them in broad daylight, by a standard technique: surveillance, ambush, and conveyance by taxi to a predetermined destination. Some were held in caves, others in kibbutzim. They were interrogated on their activities in the organization, on the identities of their officers, on the missions they had carried out or were scheduled to perform. On occasion the *Haganah* Intelligence officers resorted to violence and torture. At first the

Haganah was resolved to hold its own prisoners; but hiding places were in short supply and it was eventually decided to turn them over to the British. Finally the *Haganah* stopped the abductions, and simply gave their information directly to the CID, who then did the job themselves. At this point the ferment inside the *Haganah,* primarily among the men involved in Operation Season, reached a dangerous point. Although the men were trained for their task, including political indoctrination to intensify their disgust at everything connected with the Revisionists and the IZL, they were finding it too hard to stomach cooperation with the British in trapping Jews who were sacrificing themselves to fight the British oppressors—even if it was a political necessity that could not be avoided.

Operation Season then changed its focus to the entrapment of IZL leaders. On February 27, 1945, Dr. Eli Tavin, a senior IZL Intelligence officer, was seized in Ben Yehuda Street in Jerusalem and thrown into a taxi. His captors tied his hands, covered his head, delivered him to Kibbutz Givat Hashloshah and from there to Ein Harod. He was interrogated at length—but would say nothing. His captors declared themselves a field court-martial and condemned him to death. That same night he was taken to a nearby forest, where he was blindfolded. They suggested that he might want to confess before being executed, but his response was a string of curses. In the darkness he could hear the click of a rifle bolt, but he still kept his silence. The macabre performance was a failure.

Tavi was then taken back to the kibbutz hayloft and chained to an iron bed. Here he was to remain for more than six months, with an occasional change

Dov Zeev Begin, father of Menachem Begin.

Begin when a university student in Poland.

Zeev Jabotinsky (lower right), founder of *Betar*, with a group of his Polish followers in the 1930s.
Begin is at lower left.

Menachem and Aliza Begin,
the day after their wedding, May 1939.

Begin when he was a soldier in the Polish Army, in exile, and his wife—1942.

Menachem Begin with his wife and children,
Benjamin and Hesia, during their days in hiding.

Rabbi Israel Sassover, one of Begin's disguises
when he was hiding from the British.

Begin inspecting a unit of *Irgun* soldiers in 1948, just after they had come out of hiding.

An election campaign in the early 1950s.

A *Herut* demonstration against accepting
reparations from Germany—1953.

As head of the opposition, Begin addresses the Knesset.
David Ben-Gurion and Golda Meir are in the foreground.

With generals Ariel Sharon and Avraham Yoffe on
the eve of the Six-Day War, June 1967.

Menachem and Aliza Begin at the polls on election day,
May 17, 1977.

Changing of the guard—former Prime Minister Yitzhak Rabin welcoming his successor.

Playing with his grandchildren.

The historic meeting at Ben-Gurion International Airport,
near Tel Aviv, on November 19, 1977
—President Anwar el-Sadat and
Prime Minister Menachem Begin.

Sadat and Begin during a "working dinner" at the King David Hotel in Jerusalem on November 20, 1977. *(Credit: UPI)*

Begin with President Jimmy Carter at the time of their first meeting in 1977. *(Credit: UPI)*

Begin and Sadat during their Christmas 1977 summit talks at Ismailia, Egypt. *(Credit: UPI)*

in routine when he was hung by his arms from a beam until he fainted. The tortures stopped when he went on a hunger strike; but Tavin was only released in September 1945 when relations between the established authority and the IZL improved.

Tavin was not the only one. During Operation Season, 20 IZL members were held prisoner, 91 were interrogated and released, and some 700 names of people and institutions—including activists, supporters, and contributors—were given to the British police. Based on this list, some 300 men were detained. At the same time anyone suspected of sympathy with Menachem Begin's organization was subjected to discrimination and persecution. Headmasters of secondary schools were instructed to expel any youth related to IZL members or suspected of IZL sympathies. Offices and shops dismissed IZL sympathizers and Revisionist Party members. It was total war and, like all civil wars, it split families in two, turned neighbors into enemies, and fanned all the old flames of hatred on both sides. To this day Operation Season still lies heavy on the hearts of some and the consciences of others. For both camps it was the darkest hour in Israel's battle for independence.

The moral stature of Menachem Begin himself was revealed in full during this dark time. The man who had declared war to the bitter end on the British régime refused point blank to permit his men to retaliate against the *Haganah* and the community it represented. When Operation Season reached its peak, it really seemed as if Begin's restraint must break. Had it done so, the community's war of liberation might have been soaked in the blood of civil war. That he wanted to prevent at all costs. He knew that the British, with their policy of "Divide and Conquer," would have been delighted, and he opted to accept the painful consequences rather than give his enemies that satisfaction.

While IZL men were being abducted, beaten up, turned over to the British—while their supporters were being thrown out of schools and work—a new IZL proclamation appeared on the walls of Palestine. Begin wrote it in a state of deep emotion, and every word bore witness to the fact:

WE SHALL REPAY YOU, CAIN . . .

You rampage, Cain, in the streets of Jerusalem, in the city of Tel Aviv, in the towns and villages where your hundreds and thousands of emissaries roam. They have been brought in not to protect but to inform; not to work but to spy; not to war for freedom but for war of brother against brother.

You have used your might, Cain, but you did not use it when millions of our brothers perished as they turned their eyes to Zion—a Zion of closed doors, a Zion enslaved by an evil government; you did not display it when the survivors of the sword were deported; you did not unsheath it to break down the gates locked by the White Paper. . . .

You mobilized the money of the nation, Cain, but you did not spend it for rescue, to help the families of soldiers, nor to organize free immigration from the countries of extermination. You embezzle the nation's monies, tens of thousands of pounds, to finance detectives, kidnappers, gangs of informers. You chose yourself an ally, Cain: the oppressive régime in the homeland and the Nazi-British CID are your allies. You serve them day and night. To them you give brothers —into hands stained with the blood of millions thrown back from the doors of the homeland into the ovens of Maidanek. Your ears are blocked against the groan of spilled Hebrew blood; yet they are open to catch any suspicious conversation. Your eyes are closed to the tragedy of the nation and its causes; but they are open wide to see the "suspect" movement. And upon hearing such conversations and seeing such movements you run to report them to your enslaving master. Cars chase cars; telephones ring; signals are given and detectives appear. The tommyguns are lifted. "Halt!"—the foreign rulers command. "Out of the cars," the enslavers order. "Which one?" the detectives, your allies, ask. And you, Cain, walk over, raise your hand, and point: "That's him. Take him!" Then once again the "Holy band" celebrates its victory.

You abduct, Cain. In the depths of night you break into Hebrew homes. Ten against one— you thrash till the blood pours. Of what interest are toddlers to you? What is human dignity that you should protect it? By trickery and deceit, in the name of the police, and always with brutality, you weed out your "suspects," taking them off in unknown directions, torturing them with Gestapo methods in the shadows of orange groves, and finally handing them over to your ally, the Nazi-British CID, for further tortures, for exile in Eritrea. . . .

Your mouth is full of socialist declarations, Cain, but you are an exploiter. An exploiter of workers who give their sweat for you, for the bureaucratic caste you have imposed upon them; you lash at them with the whip of hunger and choke them with economic terror. . . .

You incite, inform, betray, abduct, and hand men over, Cain. But these are not your primary crimes nor your only sins. Those are too many to count and too heavy to bear. In the Diaspora and in Zion you sedated the nation with false optimism; you conceded Transjordan to the East and two-thirds of Transjordan to the West; you handed over the chance of free immigration and a Hebrew State, an independent homeland; you accepted and continue to accept the decimation of the nation abroad, and slavery and the ghetto in the land of the Hebrews. Then the storm came, the tragedy happened. And when those charged with the extermination and breaking up of our nation are brought to judgment, before Him will pass in judgment the German murderer, the English betrayer—and you, Cain. . . .

And we, the soldiers of Zion, are commanded not to repay you, for even though blood boils, it is blood that is totally dedicated to the nation and homeland. Our eyes are directed, even today —particularly today!—to love of our brothers, to redemption of the nation, to peace internally and war externally. And we know it is not the incited youth who are to blame. They are our brothers in blood, and potentially our brothers in arms; and we will still march together against the enslavers. It is you who are guilty, you who are the inciter.

But remember, Cain, the day of judgment will still come. And it is not far off. The nation will arise, the anger will burst forth. And for your treachery and crimes, for your informing and libels, in the name of the maligned nation, in the name of the enslaved homeland, in the name of its martyrs, in the name of our imprisoned brothers, in the name of our bereaved mothers and deserted children, in the name of our sacred war, and in the name of our spilled blood—we shall repay you, Cain!

The IZL was hard hit by Operation Season. All its senior officers, including Lankin who had led the negotiation with the *Haganah,* were arrested. But all attempts to trap Begin himself were a failure. He remained in hiding—and still in control. His main task now was to prevent open civil war. Years later his operations officer, Amihai Paglin, would say: "We had difficulty in understanding his position. The best of our comrades were arrested, kidnapped, and beaten up, and we were ordered to sit with our arms crossed. At a certain stage I thought—enough! I can't take any more. We can organize a few boys and retaliate against the *Haganah*. Finally we accepted his decision, and now I know how right he was in historic terms."

Begin was indeed taking the long view. He was probably more infuriated by Operation Season than anybody else, but he held his feelings in check, for he knew that lack of restraint could mean full-scale civil war. And civil war, apart from giving the British the satisfaction he wanted to deny them, would in all probability destroy the unity that would be needed when the entire community had to face up to the British régime.

CHAPTER 12

Their Finest Hour

Begin's restraint during Operation Season created the
image of a leader with a genuine consciousness of
national responsibility. The hostility of the left-wing
parties, which was not to die down after the establishment of the State of Israel, was tempered by the fact
that even his most extreme adversaries—who detested
everything he was and represented—at least knew that
he was a patriot who could put himself above narrow,
sectarian interests. It was a trait that would remain
with him throughout his leadership of the underground and the main opposition party in Israel's
Knesset.

In May 1977, while his supporters were celebrating
their election victory, Begin offered his beaten adversaries a place in a national coalition government.
Among them were men who had been intimately
connected with Operation Season. Yitzhak Rabin,
the outgoing prime minister, was a major figure in
the *Palmach* from which *Haganah* had drawn the

force for Operation Season. Yigal Allon, his Foreign Minister, had been deputy commander of the *Palmach* responsible for Operation Season—until he asked to be relieved of that duty. Even though most of the men who initiated Operation Season were no longer alive, many of those who took part were in key positions in government and public life. Yet, despite the operation and other scars of the intervening years, Begin extended his hand to his traditional opponents. The pragmatic leaders of the Labor alignment were unimpressed by the courtesy of the gesture. They praised Begin's attitude but turned down his offer, saying that they did not want to share responsibility for political views and actions contrary to their own beliefs.

Begin had made a pretty shrewd assessment of the *Haganah* in 1945. His policy of restraint was based on the assumption that some time in the future, the *Haganah* forces would finally join the fight against the British. He was well aware of *Haganah*'s resources in terms of the caches of illegal weapons and the trained manpower, with a discipline born of faith in an unspoken ideal, that was dispersed throughout the country and on call in every town and settlement. Many of its officers were products of British army training, and its strategists and tacticians were busily adopting conventional concepts of warfare to the demographic and topographic conditions of Palestine. It was no wonder that this force would supply the infrastructure for the Israel Defense Forces. But at this stage Menachem Begin was thinking of the more immediate problem of the British. And his assumption that the *Haganah* and the other underground armies would soon be cooperating was on its way to coming true—as a result of events far away in the capital of the British Empire.

In July 1945, shortly after the capitulation of Germany, a general election took place in Great Britain. The Labor Party's massive landslide, which came as a major surprise, aroused a brief hope that the Jews of Palestine would become independent without a battle. Palestinian ears attuned to the election campaign had heard Labor's promises to keep, at long last, Balfour's declared intention of giving the Jewish people a National Home. Like many other politicians, the leaders of the Palestinian community did not really expect the Conservative Party—led by Winston Churchill, who had captained his nation to their great victory over Germany—to lose the election. When the unexpected happened, their joy was unbounded; not because of the defeat of Churchill, a faithful friend of Zionism, but because Labor as a party had won against the Conservatives. British labor was a traditional friend of the Zionist cause. The General Federation of Jewish Labor in Palestine sent a congratulatory telegram to the victors, not forgetting to insert the hope that the new government would know how to keep its campaign promises.

From his hiding place Begin watched the public rejoicing in Tel Aviv, but he did not share in it. He roundly detested anything that smacked of socialism, and was not inclined to place his faith in promises. He looked forward to the day when the Jewish Agency Executive would admit their disappointment in the Attlee-Bevin government in London—and he did not have long to wait.

The hunt for IZL members continued. In mid-May 1945 the *Haganah* had caught a team of three men and one girl who were trying to blow up the oil pipeline in Haifa Bay. It was a military target—one that the IZL had avoided while the war with Nazi Germany was still on; but that was over now and there were no more self-imposed limitations. The team were traveling in a small car, loaded down with explosives, when arrested by the *Haganah*. They were taken to Kibbutz Yagur for interrogation, and were thoroughly beaten before being delivered to the British.

Faced with a severe lack of resources the IZL members were compelled to change their tactics. They began to place mortars with delayed firing mechanisms in locations opposite government and police buildings, and distributed leaflets warning the civilians to stay away at certain hours. But the technique was counterproductive, for the leaflets led to the discovery and defusing of the mortars before they could do any damage. The IZL finally appeared to be helpless. Funds were running out, hidden weapons were impounded and—worst of all—most of its senior officers were behind bars. Operation Season had smashed the organizational structure. The key figures handed over to the British were deported to detention camps in Africa. Some managed to escape and find their way back to Palestine; others got to Europe, where they organized illegal immigration, tried to convince governments to lend support to their cause, or worked among Jews of the Revisionist movement to get them active on behalf of IZL in Europe. But the majority, including battle-tried officers, watched their comrades' struggle from behind barbed wire, unable to assist. They would only return to an independent Israel after May 1948.

This was also a low point for *Lehi*, which as a

group was much more isolated than the IZL. Its policy of treating every British soldier and policeman as an enemy to be shot down had earned it the hatred not only of the British garrison and the despised CID, but also of the entire Jewish community. To many Jews *Lehi* members were terrorists, and therefore fair game for conscientious informers.

With this background both underground organizations reached the almost simultaneous conclusion that they should unite, or at least coordinate operations. Both sides remembered their common origins in the Revisionist Party. Even though a residue of bitterness remained from their split, they were prepared to rise above such differences. And the deep and long-established friendship between Menachem Begin, on the one side, and Natan Friedman-Yellin and Yisrael Sheib, on the other, was of unquestionable help. All three cherished memories of *Betar* in Warsaw, and all three had shared the experience of Vilna during their flight from the Nazis—a flight in which Friedman-Yellin and Begin had walked together across vast expanses of Poland, and which concluded with Sheib as eyewitness to Begin's arrest by the NKVD. The three friends now attempted to bring out into the open the disputed points so as to find the common denominators.

In the spring of 1944 a meeting was arranged in the home of a man who had left the IZL for *Lehi*, then returned to the fold after the death of Avraham Stern. Dr. Sheib was unable to take part in the discussions—he was an unwilling guest of the British police—but Friedman-Yellin brought Yitzhak Shamir in his place. Begin opened by immediately suggesting unification under a common command. Friedman-

Yellin and Shamir readily agreed in principle, but Friedman-Yellin had one reservation.

"In my opinion," he maintained, "it's still early to talk of complete union, although there's no doubt we must increase our cooperation. Eventually full union will happen by itself."

"In that case," said Begin, "you'll have to give up some of the concepts you use so often."

"Such as?"

"Such as referring to the British as a 'foreign régime' and as 'British imperialism.' "

"What do you suggest instead?" Friedman-Yellin asked.

"The oppressor régime."

"We can't agree to that." Friedman-Yellin was annoyed. "An oppressor régime needn't necessarily be a foreign one. A foreign régime can also be liberal—yet there's still an obligation to fight against it because it's foreign. If you ask the man in the street, I doubt whether he'll agree with you that this is an oppressive régime. The British police here or there indulge in provocation, but all told people are alive and making money. Some have even got rich. You think they would call it oppressive? I doubt it. Aside from that, what do you have against 'British imperialism'?"

"We have nothing against Britain. We are fighting against the British régime in the Land of Israel. If London realizes that this administration is bankrupt, they're likely to replace it by another pro-Zionist one."

Friedman-Yellin felt that Begin was splitting hairs but he had known him too long to believe that his opinions could be easily changed by any argument; Begin was too convinced of his own position for that.

228

Paradoxically Begin was propounding an argument seemingly more similar to that of the *Haganah*. He did not have any high hopes for a sudden change in the British stance toward the Jewish national aspirations. Contrary to the *Haganah*, Begin thought the Jews should pressure Britain by means of their fighting force. But he too, like the *Haganah*, thought the change would come from London.

Since the split, *Lehi* had undergone a radical change in political orientation—a change that had emanated from the ranks as a result of circumstances. Unlike its leadership, *Lehi*'s rank and file were mostly Palestinian born and educated, and lacking in any pro-*Betar* sentiments or devotion to Jabotinsky's spiritual and political heritage. The leadership itself was less doctrinaire than Begin, and certainly did not see the Revisionist line as something to be held eternally sacred. Conditions and circumstances had changed, and they considered themselves to be functioning in the context of reality. Consequently *Lehi* had taken a clearly anti-imperialist line in the belief that their struggle was a part of the struggle of all Middle Eastern peoples for national independence and liberation from the British imperialist yoke.*

After this bizarre dialogue on the semantics of revolt, Friedman-Yellin tried to find out on what basis they could cooperate. Begin told him there was only one condition—*Lehi* must recognize Jabotinsky as the mentor of the present generation.

*It is not surprising that after Israel achieved independence, *Lehi* split up, some of its members (including Sheib and Shamir) returning to the political camp led by Menachem Begin, and others heading in the opposite direction to the extreme left. Sheib set up an ideological group that was even more extreme than Begin, while Friedman-Yellin ended up so far left that he today cooperates with the Communist Party.

Although Friedman-Yellin had respected Jabotinsky, he believed that the late Revisionist leader had been operating in different circumstances, and with radically different aims, and he thought this a stupid condition. Again, Friedman-Yellin knew Begin well enough to understand what he was up to. For Begin's ultimatum was more than an example of his flair for the dramatic; it also showed his tactical talents. The placing of Jabotinsky's credo as the oracle of the fighting underground would give the IZL a clear advantage in the partnership, for who other than Begin could be considered the authoritative interpreter of the dead leader?

"What will happen," Friedman-Yellin asked, "if there are differences of opinion between the two organizations? Who will resolve them?"

"I will," answered Begin without a moment's hesitation.

Friedman-Yellin was astounded. He had not expected that answer. Clearly it left no room for co-operation and no way for a possible union. However the two men promised to keep contact so as not to interfere inadvertently with each other's plans. Friedman-Yellin had achieved one thing: Begin's agreement that the Arabs were best left as neutrals in the clash with the British, thereby depriving Great Britain of the potential argument that her forces were remaining in Palestine to keep the peace between Jew and Arab.

Shortly after the meeting IZL published a handbill to the Arab population, in which it offered a hand in friendship and stressed that its battle was only for liberation from the British conqueror.

Meanwhile the hopes of the *Haganah* chiefs for a

turning point in British policy were rapidly deteriorating into despondency. On November 13, 1945, the new British Foreign Minister, Ernest Bevin, appeared before Parliament to acknowledge that the world war had indeed created a Jewish problem; but then he went on to appeal to the nations of the world to open their doors to the refugees—since Palestine could only absorb a tiny fraction of them. Bevin added that the problem of the Arabs of Palestine was proving to be of concern to the entire Arab world, and that His Majesty's Government could not ignore the fact.

While Bevin was speaking in the House of Commons, the first feelers were put out in Tel Aviv to see whether the leaders of the three underground Jewish armies could combine their efforts in a revolt in Palestine. The *Haganah* high command had already lost patience with the ways of fruitless diplomacy, and realized that there could be no avoiding decisive armed action—even though there were still hesitant voices among the elected representatives of the community. For the latter it was too early to buy hopes of a political solution, but they were now in the minority. Dr. Moshe Sneh and Yisrael Galili were instructed to initiate contacts with IZL and *Lehi*.

The *Haganah* commanders recognized that any military activity against the British must be both subject to the Jewish civil authority and coordinated with IZL and *Lehi*. However, following Operation Season, it was thought that the chance of such cooperation was virtually nonexistent. But that was reckoning without Menachem Begin's sense of national responsibility. Despite all the bitterness and the opposition of colleagues who had argued for retaliation against the

Haganah, Begin now agreed to extend his hand to the bitter opponents of yesterday.

Meanwhile the IZL and *Lehi* decided to coordinate their responses to the *Haganah* proposals. Friedman-Yellin's position was that under certain conditions he would not object to his people joining the *Haganah* as a unit, while Begin agreed that his group too was prepared to fight alongside them. But he said they were not ready to disband under the cloak of union. *Haganah* would be accepting orders from the Jewish Agency, and the Agency could change its mind overnight. Then what would happen?

Begin repeated his point of view to Sneh and Galili, with the suggestion that they cooperate on a trial basis. The *Haganah* delegation did not disagree in principle, but they asked for time to consult their colleagues. A few days later they returned to say that Begin's view was acceptable. Friedman-Yellin had already agreed.

For Begin it was a very important landmark in his political career. Up to this point he had been the leader of an underground army detested by a large section of the Jewish public, many of whom objected not only to his tactics but also to his strategy and ideology—a package which, to their minds, represented terrorism for its own sake. At the other extreme, *Lehi* considered the IZL's operations as purposeless showmanship. The Palestinian Jewish daily papers treated Begin as a Revisionist demagogue. And now he was being recognized by his adversaries.

From this point on the heads of the three underground organizations were to meet once every two weeks to determine policy and select targets. For the most part the *Haganah* representatives brought with them clear and well-defined plans that were already approved by the political leadership. The IZL guaranteed to carry out any assignment—and pushed hard to be given meaningful activity.

Meanwhile the operations officers of all three formed a team to plan operational details. Here again, it was the *Haganah* and *Palmach* delegation that set the tone.

The combined revolt lasted from November 1945 until September 1946. Throughout, each organization operated alone, yet in coordination and subject—if indirectly—to the authority of the elected Jewish institutions. The IZL were permitted to carry out independent procurement operations and they attacked British army units and "confiscated" their arsenals of weapons and ammunition. It was an operation of this sort that almost caused the combined effort to run aground before it got under way. A few days before, on October 11, 1946, the IZL staged a daring raid on a British camp in Rehovot and seized a few hundred rifles and submachine guns. It was a bigger raid than had been agreed upon and the *Haganah* illegal radio station condemned it in sharp language. Sneh and Galili demanded explanations and even *Lehi* complained that the IZL command had not shared the secret of its plan.

Begin was compelled to apologize. He did so haltingly; concealing his embarrassment with difficulty. He could not tell them the truth—that the operation had been carried out without the prior knowledge of the IZL command, but on the initiative of two local, junior officers. They were summoned to Begin, who sat behind a screen to preserve the secrecy of his identity, and submitted to a tongue lashing. Years later Menachem Begin admitted: "In my heart I could understand them, though I couldn't justify them. They were brave boys, but the organization could not tolerate breaches of discipline."

On the night of November 1, the new combine faced the prospect of internal dissent. An IZL team was on its way to a sabotage mission, in coordination with the other organizations, at Lydda railway junction, on the main Tel Aviv-Jerusalem line, when a series of exposions were heard along the tracks—and all British troops in the area were fully alerted. Only later did it come out that the *Haganah* headquarters that had approved the IZL mission had neglected to inform them that *Haganah* units were to blow up the tracks that same night. Despite the unforeseen obstacles, the IZL carried out the mission to perfection. But when the following morning they arrived back at the base where they were to hand over their weapons to armorers, there was no one there to meet them. The armorer, having heard the explosions, took for granted that the timetable had been moved forward. They waited till dawn, then assumed that the operation commander must have taken his men elsewhere. In fact, the IZL mission and withdrawal had been delayed long behind schedule.

At his secret hiding place Begin paced the floor nervously. His men should have returned to base before dawn. When he finally found out what had happened, he was furious. But he managed to contain his anger at the next coordination session.

"It is incomprehensible," he complained, "if we inform you of every operation, and coordinate everything in advance based on targets that you select, that you should tell us nothing of your plans. I don't want to tell you what to do—but I must protect the lives of my men."

His counterparts promised that it would not happen again. The promise was not to be kept. The next incident came as the *Haganah* was launching a full-scale offensive to attack army camps and the radar stations that tracked illegal immigrant ships and coastal patrol boats. IZL Intelligence had been collecting data about a police station in central Palestine that housed a large armory. When the coordinating committee decided on an integrated attack on British police stations, the IZL representatives asked for—and received—permission to take on this particular police station, making no bones about their reasons. A few days later Yisrael Galili notified Begin that the permission was rescinded for special reasons which he could not reveal. Begin asked for a meeting with Galili, hoping to convince him to let them go ahead; but Galili simply told him they had a very good reason for the decision to cancel the attack on that particular police post.

Begin left he meeting thoroughly discouraged, for he knew full well the rules of Intelligence operations under which Galili was bound not to reveal his reasons, and could only assume that the *Haganah* must have a large cache of weapons of its own too close for comfort. An assault on the police station would almost certainly provoke a thorough British search of the area. Yet a few days later, when the *Haganah* staged simultaneous attacks on a number of police posts, the one coveted by IZL was among them. Associates of Begin's in IZL headquarters urged him to demand an explanation; but as on other occasions, he felt the combined war on the common enemy was too valuable to be sacrificed in sterile argument.

The next time that Begin met Galili and Sneh, he asked very tactfully about the *Haganah*'s strange behavior. The men talked all around the point without really coming to cases. Begin was beginning to suspect that the *Haganah* leaders were out to prevent the IZL from laying its hands on large quantities of arms and demolition materials. Indeed he still is convinced of that, even though no proof has ever been offered.

In one *Haganah* attack on a police station, four of its men were killed as the result of faulty coordination between backup units. A great many civilians, fearing this was the beginning of more killings, expressed their disapproval. In Tel Aviv voices were raised in condemnation of the *Haganah*. Once again Begin showed his national consciousness and generosity, coming to the rescue with a handbill that praised the *Haganah* and its accomplishments: "The *Irgun Zvai Leumi* lowers its flag in memory of the *Haganah* heroes who gave their lives."

In those days, any IZL man who died in action did so as an "unknown soldier," and was buried as such. There were many who were bitter that no one was present to perform the last rites at the graveside.

The operations of the three organizations showed clear differences. *Lehi,* for example, staged a raid on the railroad workshops in Haifa Bay; despite its final success, many *Lehi* lives were lost. The IZL continued to attack agreed targets, with a better than average score of successes. But both groups were still fighting small-scale war, and were unlikely to achieve any significant strategic objective. The youngsters of the

Haganah, now they were off the leash, ached to prove themselves and were only too well aware that the dissidents were setting the standards. But their operations were on a country-wide scale that was to reach its peak in the adventure later referred to as "the night of the bridges." Simultaneously, crack *Haganah* echelons assaulted all eleven bridges linking the country with its neighbors to the north and east. In one encounter between the attacking and defending forces, a tracer bullet struck a pack of explosives. The death toll totaled fourteen—but the mission was completed as planned. The eleven bridges were a pointed reminder to the British that, if they continued to close the sea frontiers to Jewish migration, then they would find their land frontiers closed to them.

IZL operations were no less daring. Indeed the IZL men showed themselves even readier to enter the jaws of the British lion. In February 1946 the IZL and *Lehi* raided three military airfields, setting fire to forty aircraft. These were complex missions, requiring a thorough knowledge of the airfield routines and guard procedures, and detailed planning to enable pentration and the placing of demolition charges on each individual plane. Some very pointed questions were raised afterwards in the House of Commons in London. For Begin himself it was vindication of the IZL's status in the new partnership. He had proved to his colleagues in the revolt movement that the IZL could perform to perfection any task.

Proud as he was of the IZL's achievements, Begin never actually sought the victor's laurels. And indeed, there were occasions when the IZL decided not to claim credit for its actions. But the people could quite accurately deduce who performed the operation from the methods and daring of the fighters.

By now the combined forces of revolt were operating in high gear. No one believed they were capable of overcoming the mighty British Empire, but astute timing and choice of targets was making up for inferiority of numbers and equipment—and proving a considerable public embarrassment to the British government. It looked as if the revolt movement was beginning to undermine the foundations of the British régime in Palestine.

The Jewish Agency's political activity was in no way lessened by the decision to exploit the military option. To all intents and purposes, the Agency was functioning on the diplomatic scene with all the efficiency and forcefulness associated with sovereign states—so much so that the British were forced to call on all their own diplomatic resources to withstand the assault. In Palestine itself, the mandatory government made use of Emergency Defense Regulations, originally promulgated in 1937 to tackle Arab rioting, to impose the death penalty on anyone found guilty of a number of offenses—including the carrying of firearms—and life imprisonment for masquerading as a British soldier. The latter ruling did not deter the IZL from sending a unit of "RAF personnel" into a base camp where they appropriated 600 submachine guns and a large quantity of ammunition.

The British took one other step unprecedented in its scale. On Friday, June 29, 1946, under the code name of "Operation Broadside," they issued orders that would cause the following day to go down in history as "Black Saturday." A countrywide curfew was imposed, and 2,700 people were arrested, including almost all the leaders of the Jewish community and members of the Jewish Agency Executive. The few who were not arrested had to run for cover. Sneh went into hiding. Galili cut his hair and used make-up to change his facial features. While 17,000 British troops turned the country inside out, David Ben-Gurion was in Paris on Jewish Agency business. As for Begin, the man whom the British considered "terrorist number one," his identity as Yisrael Sassover still protected him from suspicion. In fact, behind the garb and beard of an orthodox Jew, Begin had no problems in going through the streets of Tel Aviv to his meetings with the *Haganah*.

Meanwhile the extreme left wing of the socialist Zionist camp was growing increasingly uneasy about cooperation with the dissidents. Apart from the traditional detestation of the Revisionist faction, with which Begin was no longer directly connected, the socialists believed that London was more amendable to political pressures than to terrorism. Naturally their opposition was based more on their hate of the IZL than on real political assessment. However the full force of their argument was brought to bear by a man who had never identified himself with the left-wing camp—Dr. Haim Weizmann, the liberal and moderate president of the World Zionist Organization. Weizmann pressed for a slowdown in the pace of the military war against the British in the firm belief that sustained diplomacy was the way to independence. Underlying his belief was a trust in the gentlemanly instincts of the British, which must eventually result —in his opinion—in a move to honor the promise inherent in the Balfour Declaration.

The activists in the Jewish Agency Executive, who

had tried to steer Weizmann away from involvement in the military struggle—a field that was in any case of little interest to him—attempted to persuade him to leave them freedom of action. But Weizmann's response was a threat to resign, and this was something the Zionist Organization could not allow itself. Their president was an experienced politician acceptable to London circles, not without influence in the British government. So the activists were forced to capitulate. To Begin's disgust, armed action slowed almost to a standstill.

It is difficult to know how matters might have developed but for one single operation, still disputed thirty years later. Unfortunately for all concerned, the dispute began too late, after the operation was over. The target was the King David Hotel in Jerusalem. And the consequences of the King David operation would turn the wheel all the way back to a state of bitter controversy between the IZL and *Haganah*.

CHAPTER 13

Death in Milk Churns

The IZL had had its eye on the King David Hotel some time before it began to cooperate with the other two groups. The southern wing of the six-story luxury hotel housed the headquarters of the British administration in Palestine. The IZL had already taken its toll of that administration: the CID, the Immigration Office, countless army camps and strategic objectives had all been dealt with. It now seemed logical that the time had come for all three underground armies to strike a coordinated blow at the nerve center of "the foreign régime." And "Black Saturday" appeared to the IZL to be the right starting point for a new major offensive.

Begin assumed that the *Haganah* would approve his plan for the King David Hotel precisely because British headquarters there contained Intelligence files crammed full of documents seized during the British searches of Jewish Agency offices and institutions—documents that included records on the diplomatic compaign and on the agreements between *Haganah*, IZL, and *Lehi*.

Sneh and Galili listened attentively to Begin's proposal. As usual he concentrated only on the political and propaganda value of the mission, leaving operational aspects to others. This could obviously be the biggest blow yet struck against the British. The *Haganah* representatives said they would submit the idea to their comrades, and indeed it was brought before a body known as the "X Committee," the members of which were drawn from both the political and military echelons. Begin, of course, knew nothing about the decision-making process of his partners in the revolt. He was just being true to his obligation of full coordination with *Lehi*. A few days later a typewritten note, signed "M" (the first letter in Sneh's surname) appeared in the regular drop agreed upon for transmission of messages between the *Haganah* and the IZL:

You are to carry out as soon as possible the hotel and the house of "the Messiah's servant." Inform us of timing. Best do both simultaneously. Don't publicize identity of the force used, not even in hints. We are also preparing something, and will inform you in due course. Don't do anything in Tel Aviv area, so as not to give them reason to strike at the center of the Jewish community. They have no important objectives in Tel Aviv.

To the happy Begin the message was clear. The IZL members were free to carry out their most ambitious project to date, together with another target, a neighboring building that carried the name of its

242

builders, the David Brothers—hence the biblical reference to the Messiah (David) and his servant's house.

Yisrael Levi, at eighteen one of the commanders of IZL's operational unit in Jerusalem, was instructed to prepare all the necessary materials and collect Intelligence data on the King David Hotel. Levi, who had joined IZL at the age of fourteen, already had considerable combat experience, including the raid on the Jerusalem CID. Saying nothing to his men, he took his deputy and two girls to La Regence Café at the King David—a regular meeting place for Jerusalem high society, including senior British officials and officers. The four young people appeared a little out of place, but the police guards on the hotel door asked no questions. Levi paid no attention to what was going on around them. When he asked his girl to dance, it was only to get a better perspective on the surroundings and on the approaches to the kitchen. By the time they left the café, his head spinning slightly from unaccustomed strong drink, Levi already knew in general terms how the job would be done. The next stage in the preparations was to detail a number of youngsters to keep an eye on all movements in and out, and to record times in order to establish a pattern of routines. His main interest was in the service entrance to the café, beneath the British administrative offices. The only alternative to that would be a frontal assault on the guards at the main entrance, who could easily summon reinforcements from a nearby army camp and police station.

Meanwhile IZL Operations Officer Amihai Paglin was meeting with his *Haganah* counterparts. He told Yitzhak Sadeh, the commander of the *Palmach*, the general conception of the operation, and asked for approval. Sadeh was particularly insistent that there should be no loss of life. Paglin promised that the IZL would do its utmost to comply.

"From our experience, the British very quickly abandon any place after notification that explosives have been planted."

"How much time do you need from planting the charges to the explosion, including evacuation of the building?"

"Forty-five minutes, allowing for discrepancies in our timing mechanisms."

"Too much," said Sadeh. "The British will have time to remove documents as well as people."

Sadeh suggested fifteen minutes from placing the charges to detonation. Finally they compromised on half an hour.

When it seemed that everything was ready, the *Lehi,* who had been assigned the David Brothers Building, asked for a delay to complete their preparations. A few days later another delay was requested, this time by the *Haganah,* who were encountering problems in moving their weapon stores out of Jerusalem away from the methodical British searches that had been in progress since "Black Saturday." An operation on the scale of the King David could only result in intensified British efforts—and the loss of valuable guns and ammunition. Again the IZL agreed, but with marked unwillingness. Begin ordered his men to be ready for action on July 22. But on the evening of July 21, the *Lehi* members announced that their aspect of the operation was proving to be beyond their capabilities. Accustomed to personalized terror, they were inexperienced in the coordination of large forces. The IZL was unwilling to wait any longer.

On the morning of July 22, the IZL forces assigned to the mission convened in a remote Jerusalem synagogue for a briefing. None of them as yet knew the target, but the presence of Amihai Paglin was ample indication that it was a big one. Paglin's identity was a close secret, but something told the assembled men that he was a member of the high command. Paglin's briefing was short and to the point. The assault force would gain entry to the ground-floor café via the service entrance, disguised as Arabs bringing the daily delivery of milk churns. Once inside, they would overcome the kitchen staff and hold them under guard while they opened the door to let their comrades in. The café itself was expected to be empty at lunch hour; if not, then its occupants would be forced to join the kitchen staff. Meanwhile the milk churns full of explosives would be rolled 150 feet into the hotel basement, and placed next to the main pillars that supported the upper stories. The churns contained a double mechanism, one to detonate the charges and the other to prevent rendering them harmless in the event of discovery. Pagli himself had designed the mechanisms, and he now insisted that the demolition team must place warning signs alongside the churns, so that no one would make the mistake of trying to dismantle them.

Levi, the mission commander, completed the briefing, totally unaware that his own deputy—German-born Heinrich Reinhold—had in fact been planted in the IZL by the British CID, or enlisted by them after he joined. When the briefing was over, Reinhold asked permission to leave for a few minutes. This was absolutely contrary to regular discipline, and Paglin refused, not because he suspected Reinhold but because it would set a bad example to his juniors. Reinhold was obviously upset and nervous. He asked if he could at least phone his girl, but was told that no one was allowed to leave for any reason before Zero Hour. His nervousness was assumed to be the fear that all of them felt before a major opeartion.

Close to midday the milk churns were brought to the service entrance of La Regence Café by men in Arab dress, who looked to all the world like members of the hotel staff. They knocked on the outer door, announced the milk delivery, and were promptly admitted. Within seconds fifteen Arab waiters, cooks, and cleaners found themselves in a side room under guard, while the demolition team moved the churns into place. As they were at work, two armed British officers, having heard a suspicious noise, came down to investigate—and immediately grasped what was happening. A machinegun burst killed one and seriously wounded the other. Meanwhile an exchange of shots was heard between the IZL backup team and British soldiers, who had not the slightest idea what was going on under their noses. Their work finished, the commander set the detonators for thirty minutes and ordered withdrawal. The Arab employees were released and told to get out fast.

At the same time the backup team detonated a charge designed to make noise and smoke on the roadway outside the hotel, as a means of drawing attention away from the route of retreat. By 12:10 there were no IZL men in the vicinity. One IZL member, wounded by an Arab soldier during the escape, was transferred by a waiting taxi to a first-aid post in the Old City, where he died before the police could get to him.

The mission commander passed by a predetermined point and waved what appeared to be a casual greeting to three IZL girls. Each then went separately to public phones to deliver messages to the King David Hotel, the nearby French Consulate, and the editorial offices of the Palestine *Post*. All three were told that the hotel would be blown sky-high within half an hour. The newspaper and the consulate phoned the British at the King David. Nobody yet knew who had placed the explosives, or where they were located. In accordance with the prior agreement, the girls did not identify themselves as belonging to IZL. The British, contrary to their usual cautious practice, ignored the warning. Sir John Shaw, the Secretary to the Palestine government, who received the message in plenty of time, was confident in the ability of the heavy guard on the building to prevent anything from happening. Indeed an enquiry held into the entire affair would later reveal that Secretary Shaw, when told of the warning, responded to a police officer: "I don't accept orders from these Jews. I give the orders here!"

At 12:37 a massive explosion was heard through Jerusalem. As passers-by scuttled for cover, the southern wing of the hotel collapsed like a house of cards. There were 200 casualties, half of them fatal, resulting either directly from the explosion or from falling debris—among them 15 Jews who were British officials. While rescue teams went to work at the scene, a massive manhunt was set in motion. The IZL team had vanished back into the anonymity of the Jerusalem crowd. Paglin had left the city to report to his chief in Yehoshua Bin Nun Street, Tel Aviv.

When Begin opened the door to Paglin, he already knew the scale of damage and death from radio bulletins. Clearly something had gone wrong, but there was as yet no way he could know that the British Secretary had refused to evacuate the hotel. Now he hastened to assure Paglin that, whatever the outcome, the IZL would stand behind him or his men.

Yisrael Levi, the mission commander, told his mother that he had to go to Tel Aviv for a few days. She asked no questions. Though she had no precise idea of her son's occupation, she had already gathered that it was something best not talked about. First Levi headed for a mental hospital in the Romema Quarter of Jerusalem, where his men were supposed to assemble for debriefing. By early evening twelve men had arrived, and were promptly hustled out of the city to a hiding place. Levi and another man, named Avni, waited impatiently for Reinhold. Suddenly they heard the engine of a British armored car. The hospital director, an IZL sympathizer, peered out of the window and saw the vehicle stop at the main gate.

He told the two men to follow him and led them swiftly into the maximum security ward, where he made them change their clothes, then ruffled their hair and daubed them with remnants of food.

"You don't look too bad as madmen," he said, leaving them to open the gate to his British visitors. The police searched every corner and potential hiding place, finally arriving at the maximum security ward. The two men who greeted them stuck out their tongues, made obscene gestures, and screamed indistinct insults, while saliva dripped from their mouths. The British retreated in digust.

"You're both suited to this place," the director observed. "I suggest that you stay here till morning."

They stayed, but Levi was already having some unpleasant thoughts about Reinhold—the only member of the team who had not come to the rendezvous. Could he have been the one who directed the British to the hospital? Had he been taken prisoner and forced to talk?

The following day IZL men were sent to Reinhold's apartment. His landlady was surprised by the visit. She mentioned that, only minutes earlier, her tenant had packed a few things and told her he must leave. No, she did not know where he had gone. In trying to trace him, they found out that Reinhold had been having a love affair with a married woman—so they visited her, and threatened to tell her husband if she did not reveal the wanted man's whereabouts. She promised to find out, but apparently opted to warn Reinhold. When it became clear that he had left the country, instructions were forwarded to the IZL in Europe to find him and eliminate him. He was discovered in Belgium. Two IZL men whisked him off the street, but a bystander called the police, who promptly arrested the IZL men. Again the traitor vanished. After Israel's independence Begin received a report that Reinhold had been spotted, but he refused IZL veterans permission to pay the old accounts, claiming: "That's in the past. Let it be."

The damage done by Reinhold was considerable. Within twelve hours of the explosion all the IZL's meeting places, and the homes of its members, were known to the Jerusalem police. Levi, who had decided not to go to Tel Aviv after all, on the assumption that he might be needed in Jerusalem, returned to his parents' home. On the second night the CID came knocking on the door asking for a youngster named "Gideon." Now there could be no doubt in Levi's mind: "Gideon" was his underground code name, and Reinhold had known no other.

"There's no Gideon here," said Levi Senior. "Only my son Yisrael."

The police inspected Levi's identification papers, then turned to go.

"Wait a moment," said Yisrael. "I believe the son of our neighbors across the street is called Gideon."

The policemen crossed the street and knocked on a door, only to find that Gideon was five and a half years old. Next morning Yisrael Levi rose early, crossed the fields to a nearby Arab village, and caught a bus to Tel Aviv. By then the public debate over the King David affair was in full spate.

It is quite possible that the Jewish Agency Executive knew nothing of the advance coordination between IZL and *Haganah* concerning the hotel, and the arguments on that point still continue. Be that as it may, on the day following the operation the Executive published a sharp condemnation, couched in the old familiar terminology of uninhibited dissidents whose acts of murder reflected on the purity of the Jewish community's struggle for self-determination. The daily press raked up every conceivable epithet to join in the chorus. Begin and his men were astounded. They were sorry about the needless deaths but they blamed it on the arrogance of the British in refusing to evacuate the hotel. Begin had not expected a vote of thanks for a mission well done, but he certainly did not expect a denial of the prior coordination. Galili was quick to calm Begin's temper.

"The members of the Executive weren't informed. You must understand that most of our people are in detention camps, and we don't have regular contact with the few on the outside. The people who condemned you weren't aware that it was done with our knowledge and concurrence."

Although he kept the thought to himself, Begin still considered this gross ingratitude on the part of the *Haganah*. The debris of the King David had buried stacks of documents confiscated during "Black Saturday," which could have revealed all the secrets of the *Haganah* and the Jewish Agency had the British been allowed the time to study them. The operation itself could easily be considered the community's response to "Black Saturday." Begin was insulted and depressed by a demand from his erstwhile partners that the IZL should accept public responsibility for the King David affair. He complied, but hardly with good feeling.

For a while it seemed as if history was repeating itself to the point where Operation Season would recur; but Begin begged his counterparts in revolt not to let relations decline to their previous low point.

"According to reports in our hands, your men deviated from the plan," Galili said when they met.

"My men did not deviate," objected Begin. "They carried out every detail as we agreed."

"Yitzhak Sedeh told me that you didn't take into account that the café might be full."

"The café was not full. We only found the staff there."

"Sedeh says that he agreed with Paglin to time the operation for the afternoon."

"I can't accept that. Paglin reported the details of his agreement with Sedeh, and he didn't say a word about disagreement over timing. However, even though I have complete faith in Paglin, I'm prepared to arrange a confrontation between him and Sedeh."

The two men then met in the presence of their respective commanders, and each repeated his own version.

"We agreed," said Sedeh, "that the operation should take place in the afternoon when the place would be empty."

"I never said a word about that," rejoined Paglin.

The argument lasted a long time, and the dispute was never resolved. Begin came away with the feeling that, but for the dead, the *Haganah* would have been delighted to share in the victory; now, they wanted to wash their hands of the affair. On the other hand he had heard Galili express reservations about the anti-IZL propaganda campaign. With a fair amount of justification he was prepared to put the whole thing down to differences of opinion with the *Haganah* and the political leadership, between the activists and the proponents of restraint. The King David bloodbath undoubtedly strengthened the hands of those who preferred restraint and diplomacy.

Then the wheel turned back in the IZL's favor, partly because of an evil and senseless order issued by the British commander-in-chief to his troops, copies of which fell into IZL hands. Begin made sure that it got wide publicity.

. . . I am determined that they [the Jewish terrorists] shall suffer punishment and be made aware of the contempt and loathing with which we regard their conduct. We must not allow ourselves to be deceived by the hypocritical sympathy shown by their leaders and representative bodies, or by their protests that they are in no way responsible for these acts. I repeat that if the Jewish public really wanted to stop these crimes, they could do so by acting in cooperation with us.

Consequently I have decided that effective on receipt of this letter you will put out of bounds to all ranks all Jewish establishments, restaurants, shops, and private dwellings. No British soldier is to have any social intercourse with any Jew, and any intercourse in the way of duty should be as brief as possible and kept strictly to the business in hand.

I appreciate that these measures will inflict some hardship on the troops, yet I am certain that if my reasons are fully explained to them they will understand their property and will be punishing the Jews in a way the race dislikes as much as any, by striking at their pockets and showing our contempt for them.

The effect of this letter to the British officers—coming as it did only months after the end of World War II and the Holocaust—was to provoke a storm of anger. Barker's overt anti-Semitism, evident in the last sentence of the letter, and his misunderstanding of the Jewish mood following the Holocaust and the

British refusal to allow entry to the pitifully few survivors, now turned Palestinian minds away from internal dispute to center on the enemy on the outside. The Jews of Palestine were reminded of the common cause. But the British had some plans of their own. In August 1946 two infantry and armored divisions, supported by the Palestine police, moved in on Tel Aviv to stage the greatest of all manhunts —and their three most wanted men were Menachem Begin, Moshe Sneh, and Natan Friedman-Yellin.

Begin now felt less secure than ever before, despite his disguise as Yisrael Sassover. The British were no longer prepared to be deceived by a beard and a black coat. Begin sat at home, convinced that the net was closing around him, and remembering—as he would later note—scenes from Lukishki Prison and the Arctic Circle.

IZL Intelligence warned headquarters of an impending curfew one day before it happened. Begin gave instructions to pass the news on to *Lehi,* but his own men did not take the message seriously enough to get out of Tel Aviv as they should have done.

At dawn the next day, some of them awoke to the clatter of tank tracks. Within minutes Tel Aviv was a besieged and isolated city, split into sectors by barbed wire behind which armed troops and police progressed from house to house, street by street. Clearly the British were using not only their best forces and efforts, but also masses of Intelligence data. In some streets they headed straight for a particular house, although they did not always find what they were looking for because their information was not always up to date.

During the curfew, which lasted a few days, arguments and traditional hostilities between the Tel Avivians were forgotten as they all became citizens under the heel of a conquering army, which dealt with them the way any conqueror did at the first sign of disobedience. Some people tried to avoid curfew by identifying themselves as members of the *Haganah,* and were unable to understand why this resulted in immediate arrest. This time the CID wanted everyone—not just the dissidents. The Jewish community was learning that, to the British, all were equal.

Begin was woken before dawn that first morning by the barking of Roxie in the yard outside. He could hear the tanks in the distance and they sounded menacing. A few hours later British voices could be heard in the street. He peered through the venetian blinds with a growing premonition that his luck had finally run out. Of all places in Tel Aviv to place the search headquarters, the British had chosen the courtyard of the Sassover home. Begin regretted not taking yesterday's warning seriously. He could have been well away from Tel Aviv.

A hiding place had been prepared against just such an eventuality in the boarded-up ceiling of the lavatory. There was barely room to lie flat and it would be stifling, but Aliza insisted that there was no choice. The British were near enough for him to hear almost every word, and sooner or later they were bound to enter the house. He was barely inside the ceiling compartment when there came a knock on the door. The soldiers took a quick look around the room where the two "Sassover" children were still sleeping.

"You alone?" they asked Aliza.

"Yes."

"Where's your husband?"

"Gone to Jerusalem."

"Then you'll have to come with us to the identification post."

Aliza woke the two children and took them with her. As a policeman began to question her, she decided she was better off not knowing English, so she replied in Hebrew that she could not understand. A Jewish policeman was summoned to act as interpreter.

"Where's your husband?" he asked.

"He went to Jerusalem."

The policeman studied the small, frail, bespectacled woman, who seemed unlikely to be interested in anything beyond the walls of her kitchen. Then, turning to the interpreter, he said: "Tell her she can go home."

Back in the house, without attracting the children's attention, Aliza announced in a loud voice: "It's okay." But until the British left the area, it was not safe for Begin to leave his hiding place. From time to time a British soldier would knock on the door to ask Aliza for a glass of water. Hearing this, Begin became infuriated. Here he was parched from thirst while they drank his water. He was even afraid of losing consciousness from the heat and lack of water.

After two days without food or drink Begin was beginning to think that the foreign prison had been infinitely preferable to this jail within his own home. At least in Lukishki Prison there had been water to drink. He could go without food for days—but water!

On the evening of the third day, after countless British soldiers had dropped in for a drink and a respite from the Tel Aviv summer heat, and as his own strength was dwindling away, he heard a commotion outside. Tank engines were starting up, both nearby and in the distance. Then the noise slowly receded. Aliza tapped on the wooden boards.

"That's it. It's over. You can come out!"

Begin jumped down, exhausted and pale. Aliza was sure he was going to collapse at her feet.

The first thing he did was immerse his head in a bowl of water.

Dr. Kahan, the Begins' faithful friend, was on his way to their house. In the street he heard people exchanging notes on the curfew, and a rumor that the head of IZL had been captured. He paled and quickened his pace. He knocked at their door, waited anxiously for it to open, then caught his breath. Menachem was stitting calmly in an armchair, sipping a glass of water and answering his son's questions,

"Daddy, where were you all the time?"

"In Jerusalem."

"What did you bring me?"

"I brought, hm . . ."

"Daddy brought a big wagon," Aliza interjected, "but he left it with an uncle."

The members of IZL headquarters staff began to appear, one by one, each with his own story of the curfew. Only one was missing—IZL Chief of Staff Haim Landau. Begin began to worry; Landau had become his close friend.

"I think someone should go and look for him."

He had barely finished the sentence when Landau appeared in the doorway. He explained that he had been held up because he wanted to collect all the information he could from bystanders, friends, and IZL colleagues. Only one IZL man had been taken.

Natan Friedman-Yellin of *Lehi* had been brought in for questioning, but no one had identified him, so he was released. Yitzhak Shamir was not so lucky, and was now being held by the CID.

Begin did not learn until much later that, in a small synagogue in the Jewish Quarter of the Old City of Jerusalem, elderly orthodox Jews had been maintaining a long watch devoted to psalm reading and prayers for the head of the IZL, who they knew to be somewhere inside the besieged city of Tel Aviv. None of them had ever met Begin, and few even knew his name, but many of them had sons in the ranks of the IZL.

By next day the curfew was simply a bad memory. In the cafés of Tel Aviv stories were told of the ineptness of the British troops. A few hundred faces were missing—*Haganah* men and those of many others who had never had the slightest connection but were unlucky enough to arouse police suspicion. Far from the bright lights of the cafés, the headquarters staff of the IZL convened to plan their next blows against the nerve centers of British rule.

CHAPTER 14

The Shadow of the Gallows Tree

Some while after assuming the premiership of Israel, Begin—who was both ill and loaded down with work —found time to attend a funeral in Rosh Pina, far from Jerusalem. He barely knew the dead man, a Polish *Betar* veteran named Avraham Amikam; but the significance of the funeral was doubly symbolic for him.

Amikam had been one of Shlomo Ben-Yosef's two young partners in his attack on the Arab bus. All three had been caught and sentenced to death, but the two youngsters were treated lightly in view of their ages. Begin, who was then still a *Betar* leader in Poland, had forwarded Amikam's birth certificate to Palestine to prove that he was a minor. To Begin, Amikam was a close friend—though they did not really know each other—both because Amikam's name was connected with the history of armed struggle for the homeland, and because he asked to be buried next to Ben-Yosef. In the jargon of IZL veterans Ben-

Yosef was one of the *harugei hamalchut,* which translated literally means "martyrs of the kingdom," and which to Israelis carries an association that goes back into their historical heritage. Its origins lie far back in Jewish history when Jews preferred to choose death rather than submit to Roman slavery or heathen gods.

The period of the Crusades is for Europeans one of the romantic chapters of their history, but for Jews it was a time of suffering and humiliation. Out of this era have come stories of famous rabbis and simple members of their congregations who went to the gallows murmuring the words of ancient prayers. The Bible is a document by which all Jews must live. Like all monotheistic religions, Judaism believes in the immortality of the spirit and in the life beyond the grave; yet it does not worship death. The Bible forbids a man to take his own life, and teaches him to do everything possible to remain alive. In only three cases are there exceptions where a Jew is at liberty to choose death: if life means renouncing his faith, killing another man, or having sexual intercourse within his immediate family.

Faced with repeated attempts at coerced conversion to Christianity, multitudes of Jews throughout the generations have chosen death, and their sacrifice has been traditionally recognized as sanctification of the name of God. Hence the term "martyrs of the kingdom (of heaven)." In recent times a fourth exception has been made to the sanctity of life: death in war for the national independence. Not that men willingly looked for death, but Shlomo Ben-Yosef, who to the British was a common criminal, to most of the Jewish community of Palestine—including opponents of *Betar*—represented a martyr for the cause of liberty.

260

At Amikam's graveside, Menachem Begin had some words to add to the historical record:

"You asked to be buried next to your friend, Shlomo Ben-Yosef. We, your friends, are today fulfilling your wish. Shlomo Ben-Yosef said before he died that the rocky peak cannot be conquered without a grave on the slopes. Tell him that we conquered the rocky peak—and oh how numerous are the graves on the slopes."

Begin's voice trembled. He is used to sorrow, and seems to be more prone to emotion in his speeches than most people, but he is never more emotional than when he speaks of "the martyrs of the kingdom." Apart from all the historic associations, Begin feels a deep personal affinity with them.

But of the many hundreds of letters that have aroused Begin's emotions, few can compare with a brief message from a man he never met. It was scribbled on scraps of paper, and smuggled out of the condemned cell at Acre Prison. The writer's name was Dov Gruner, and he addressed Begin in the third person (for reasons of clarity, the translation is given in second person):

> Sir,
>
> I thank you from my heart for the great encouragement I have received from you in these fateful days. You may be certain that, whatever happens, I shall not forget the doctrine imbibed from you—the doctrine of pride, generosity, and stringency. And I shall know how to maintain my honor—the honor of a fighting Jewish soldier. Obviously I want to live. Who doesn't? But if I regret that I am about to end my life, it is be-

cause I did not manage to do enough. I could have looked after my personal future, perhaps left the country and gone to the United States. But that would have given me no satisfaction as a Jew—and certainly none as a Zionist. . . . The correct way to my mind is that of the IZL, which does not negate the political effort without giving up a piece of our land—for our land it is. If the political effort doesn't bring results, the IZL is ready to fight for our land and our freedom, for they guarantee the existence of our nation whatever happens. And this must be the way for the People of Israel in these times of ours: taking a stand for our opinions, and being prepared to make sacrifices, even if in isolated cases it leads to the gallows. A country is redeemed by blood. I am writing these lines forty-eight hours before our overseers are to carry out their murder. In hours like these a man cannot lie. I swear to you, sir, that were I given the possibility of starting again, I would choose the same road, without considering the possible consequences to myself. Your faithful soldier,
Dov.

On a spring day in 1946 the IZL staff convened in Amihai Paglin's apartment in south Tel Aviv. During the meeting Paglin's mother came in to tell him that two men from Jerusalem were asking for him. Not knowing what to expect, Paglin rushed into the next room, only to recognize Menachem Begin and IZL Chief of Staff Haim Landau in their disguises as Hassidic Jews. They joined the meeting, and Paglin continued with his discussion of the critical weapon situation. Their ammunition was running out and they would not be able to continue unless they could get a new supply.

Begin felt that if only the population would contribute funds—or weapons—the cost in blood would be lower. His counterparts in the revolt could hardly object if the IZL raided British armories, although that type of operation required large forces, and his partners were hesitant when it came to such decisions. In any case the relations between the three organizations were strained, and the old hostilities were again building up in the *Haganah*.

A few days later Paglin brought to Begin a plan for a raid on Ramat Gan police station. Relying on his subordinate's operative judgment, Begin merely approved the timing—though he did ask Paglin whether the operation was not too daring, to which Paglin responded that they had experience of the kind.

A few weeks before the Ramat Gan mission Dov Gruner, a Hungarian-born ex-*Betar* member just demobilized from the British army, had joined IZL. Given his background it was a natural step, and even more so as a result of his experiences in war-torn Europe. He had seen the last wisps of smoke from the ovens of extermination camps and had met the penniless, homeless, and unwanted refugees roaming the roads of Europe. He returned to Palestine determined to fight for the liberation of the one country that remained viable for Jews. Gruner's British army training immediately became an asset, and his superiors decided to assign him to the next operation. The evening before his first battle, Gruner and his girlfriend sat on a bench on Rothschild Boulevard, Tel Aviv, and he told her:

"You will certainly be reading something in tomorrow's papers."

"What do you mean?"

"I can't tell you. You'll hear about it."

Gruner's name was indeed in the headlines, but not in the way he had anticipated.

On the morning of April 23, 1946, the desk sergeant at Ramat Gan police station paid no special attention to a bunch of red-bereted paratroopers who were hauling Arab prisoners off a military vehicle and kicking them in the direction of the station.

"Sergeant, these 'gentlemen' were caught stealing from Tel Litwinsky Camp. We were told to bring them to you," a paratroop noncom announced.

"Okay, we'll give them what they deserve!"

The policeman told the soldiers to take their prisoners through to the inner pen in the courtyard of the police station. As he and another policeman opened the pen, they were astonished to see the Arabs draw guns from under their robes. The paratroopers had also turned their weapons on the policemen. With the guardians of the law secure in their own pen, the IZL visitors searched unsuccessfully through the ground-floor offices for keys to the armory. The mission commander had a tough choice: either to blow the door of the armory off its hinges with explosives, and alert every policeman in the station, or to leave empty-handed. He chose the first option, with the inevitable result. While a radio operator summoned reinforcements from all the stations in the area, heavy fire was opened on the IZL team now loading up the precious weapons. Two police squads were on their way, but one was blocked by a Jewish bus driver who, gathering what was happening, engineered a gigantic traffic foul-up.

Meanwhile the team was in trouble. Three men were already mortally wounded. When the loading had been completed and not a single weapon left in the armory, they reverted to their previous roles of paratroopers and Arabs, and drove away. No one who watched the military vehicle on its way through Ramat Gan could have imagined them to be anything but what they seemed— nor could anyone know that the driver was summoning up his last reserves of strength as the blood seeped from his body.

The truck stopped in an orange grove outside Petach Tikva. A quick head count was taken: apart from the three men who had been shot, the new man, Dov Gruner, was missing.

Shortly after the battle the British found Gruner lying in a pool of his own blood in a trench near the police station. At first they thought he was dead. His jaw was twisted out of recognition. As a British officer approached, Gruner lifted up and aimed his revolver, and the officer shot him. He was brought to hospital in critical condition, and a heavy guard was posted around the operating theater. His Jewish doctors tried to prolong treatment as long as possible, in the assumption that the IZL would attempt to rescue. There were indeed plans afoot, and Gruner was told of them by the medical staff—but he managed to send back a message: "The IZL has more important things to do!"

On the doctors' recommendation Gruner was transferred to the Jerusalem Government Hospital. Dr.

Albert Shalit, who treated him, found time on occasion to chat with his patient as he recovered.

"I shall always be disabled, never able to talk or eat like a human being. People won't want to look at me," Gruner observed sadly.

"You have nothing to worry about. Give it a couple of months, and you'll have no more than a scar as a souvenir—and you can always hide that with a beard if you want."

"If I ever get out of prison . . ."

"You will. After all they'll probably take your injury and British army service into consideration."

"I don't think so. I think they'll sentence me to death. But we will win in the end."

Begin, who was following every detail as if Gruner was his own son, learned that he was transferred, still having difficulty eating and talking, to Latrun detention camp, where he waited to be brought to trial. Again he received word that his comrades were still ready to try and get him out, but he refused. There were others who had been in detention longer than he. If IZL wanted to break anyone out, then it should be by seniority. Gruner would live through the hardest days of his life without forsaking all he had been taught in *Betar* about facing tribulation with pride.

Gruner was brought to trial before a military court in Jerusalem in January 1947, charged with two capital offenses: Placing explosives with intent to kill men in His Majesty's Service, and using firearms against policemen. Asked how he pleaded, Gruner remained seated without answering. When he did rise to his feet, it was to read a declaration:

I do not recognize your authority to judge me. This court has no basis in law since it is appointed by an alien régime without basis in law. When there is no legal régime, and its replacement is a régime of oppression and tyranny, it is the right, and even the duty, of the citizens to fight that régime and to overthrow it.

Gruner's declaration was received in absolute silence, and his judges appeared at a loss. Finally the president of the court announced that the trial would continue, and that the accused's statement was his opinion alone. Gruner then asked to speak.

"I know that a death sentence awaits me, yet I shall not defend myself before this court. From now on until the end of deliberations I shall take no part in the proceedings, and there is therefore no need to translate witnesses' statements into Hebrew."

The witnesses were heard without cross-examination. Toward the end it occasionally seemed that the military prosecutor was moved to act as defense attorney. He mentioned Gruner's outstanding record with the British army, but the prisoner paid no attention, his eyes fixed on some distant spot in space. From the prosecutor's tone it was obvious that he harbored sympathy for the young man in the dock. After a short consultation the three judges returned to give their verdict, a verdict that would reverberate around the world: "Dov Gruner, this court has found you guilty of the two offenses as charged. For the first offense, you are sentenced to be hung by the neck till you are dead. The Court reserves the right to determine sentence for the second offense."

Gruner stood up, and in a clear cool voice quoted

from a poem he learned as a boy in *Betar:* "In blood and fire Judea fell. In blood and fire shall Judea arise."

That same day Dov Gruner was taken to Jerusalem Central Prison, and issued the red garb of the condemned. Now began a public campaign to save his life. Letters and cables flowed in from Jews and non-Jews alike all over the world. It seemed that the only person who had accepted the inevitability of death was Gruner himself.

On January 24, 1947, General Evelyn Barker confirmed the sentence and set the date for 08:00 hours on the morning of January 28. Gruner accepted the news with the same calm that he had shown throughout the trial. To the prison governor's formal statement that he could appeal sentence to the king's Privy Council, he responded that he did not recognize any legal jurisdiction of a foreign régime. Though Gruner was not willing to appeal, attempts were made on his behalf. His sister enlisted the aid of several United States senators. An uncle lodged a formal appeal in London. A stay of sentence was granted while the appeals were heard, but Begin was not impressed with the chances—and said as much to his staff.

"We must do something for this boy, and fast, before it's too late."

IZL operations proposed, and Begin approved, the taking of hostages from among British officers. On January 26, a British Intelligence officer was abducted, and the next day, the president of the Tel Aviv District Court. The two kidnappings caused a stir in Palestine. Representatives of the *Haganah* and the Jewish Agency, concerned about a possible escalation of hostilities, asked Begin to order the immediate release of his prisoners. The *Haganah* threatened a full-scale search. Although the combined revolt was now inactive, as a result of an escalation by the IZL while the other two organizations ceased activities, relationships were fairly stable. The different commanders did not entirely trust each other, but they had learned a great deal about each other's motivations and personalities. Begin's response did not leave room for any doubt. "For this specific cause, we shall go all the way," he said.

The Conservative opposition in the House of Commons, led by Winston Churchill, now threw its weight in against the Labor government, insisting that decisions taken by the authorities could not be shunted aside to suit terrorists; in other words, Dov Gruner should be executed, for as long as he remained alive the IZL would keep trying for his release. General Barker had meanwhile granted an indefinite stay of execution to allow the appeal process to run its course, and so the two kidnapped Englishmen were released.

The general feeling was that Gruner's sentence would be commuted if only he would request the king's mercy. But he remained adamant. Claiming that the walk to the gallows was easy if a man knew why he was dying, he refused to ask pardon of a régime that he maintained had never had the right to try his case. Eventually an attorney appointed by his family got him to agree to submit the request in order to spare the community a major bloodbath. But within twenty-four hours Gruner revoked the power-of-attorney, stating that his decision was final.

In Palestine, the optimism of the previous day again gave way to pessimism. In London, Winston Churchill demanded to know why sentence was not being carried out. From America came Gruner's sister to make one last effort to convince her brother. Their meeting quickly turned into a last farewell; she was no more able to budge him than all her predecessors had been. One simply did not ask favors of a régime that one did not recognize as legally existing!

It was at this stage that Dov Gruner wrote his famous letter to Menachem Begin. By now he had three cellmates, all in the red uniforms, and all arrested on the night of December 11, 1946—a night that is recorded in history as "the night of the floggings." A few days earlier two young IZL members had been picked up by a routine police patrol for carrying firearms. Under the Emergency Defense Regulations they were sentenced to eighteen years in prison—plus eighteen lashes each, an unusual ruling in a world that had virtually rejected corporal punishment, but quite common in British colonies.

Begin was furious. The whip was a reminder of Poland, where police and hooligans had used it on Jews. He told his staff that lashings of IZL members would not be tolerated. Since his word was law in the organization, this statement was accepted as indication that the IZL would retaliate. It was Begin himself who chose the form action would take.

"We will grab British officers, and whip them—but I repeat, not soldiers, only officers!"

He was aware that the significance of the whip was not the pain but the humiliation. So he insisted that a warning be issued: You whip our men, we whip yours. He drafted a derisive handbill telling the British officers exactly what to expect if the sentence was carried out. The ink was hardly dry before one of the IZL prisoners was lashed. Less than twenty-four hours later the IZL seized a major and three sergeants and meted out the same punishment. The message was delivered, accompanied by mockery and laughter all over the world. The British postponed the second flogging, which aroused the ire of Winston Churchill, who was furious that the British Empire should give in to a bunch of terrorists. Meanwhile an IZL unit, carrying whips, was caught at a police roadblock and given a thrashing. One of them died from the beating, and three of the others were sentenced to death by hanging—and placed in a condemned cell along with Dov Gruner.

Now that the hangings were only a matter of time, IZL headquarters instructed its Jerusalem command to plan a break into the central prison to release the condemned men. While the operation was still being planned, the four men awaiting the hangman were transferred to Acre—the fortress where Jabotinsky had served his prison sentence. They were hung before dawn on April 16, 1947.

Dov Gruner's letter reached the commander of IZL a few days later. Begin read it through many times. With each reading his emotion and his helpless anger increased. He ordered his men to intensify their campaign against the centers of British power. A wave of hostilities swept Palestine.

This was perhaps Begin's hardest hour in the IZL. He sat at home, hounded by thoughts of the colossal responsibility he bore—for the lives of youngsters willing to make the supreme sacrifice against a much stronger enemy, for the deaths of men led to the gallows. Begin himself treasured human life. Before each mission he asked countless times about the possi-

271

bility of a safe return, and he would not approve any action if this aspect was not all but assured.

He had not believed that the British would delay execution forever, but while the prisoners were alive there was hope. The execution was carried out without prior public notice, and during a twenty-four-hour countrywide curfew. Within hours the four men had become a part of the legend of the underground, an example to be held up before the youngsters in training. Their names were Dov Gruner, Yehiel Dresner, Mordechai Elkodi, and Eliezer Kashani. From now on Begin would mention them at every opportunity, and remind his listeners that the four had gone to the gallows singing *Hatikvah,* the anthem of Jewish nationalism and Zionism. He still speaks of them whenever mention is made of the struggle to establish Israel.

They were not the first IZL men to be sentenced to hang. In March 1946 an IZL unit of thirty men hijacked a British army truck carrying military travel documents, and proceeded to take it to Sarafand Base Camp, the biggest British installation in the country and the best protected. The sentries at the gate had no reason to suspect anything untoward, even though a closer check would have revealed that some of the men on the truck looked distinctly un-English, and could barely speak their adopted "native" language. Some of the passengers dropped off the truck by the gate and stood at the roadside, ostensibly waiting for a lift to a destination inside the sprawling complex. The remainder went with the truck to the central arms depot. The unarmed British storekeeper was taken prisoner. Most of the other occupants of the camp were in the chow lines at the main mess hall, so there was no one to notice a truck loading up at the weapons store. The few soldiers and officers who did pass by and show undue interest were escorted inside as prisoners of the IZL. Some of them thought at first that it was a practical joke, or perhaps an exercise; they were quickly disillusioned.

The IZL might have got away with it had not one of them had the idea of removing a heavy machine gun from the turret of a nearby tank. A soldier noticed the gun being dismantled and came to investigate. Realizing what was happening, he opened fire. The armory quickly became a battleground. Boarding their truck, the IZL detachment beat a speedy retreat to the main gate, where their comrades had already overcome the sentries and taken their places. An officer who screamed at the guards to close the crash barrier was astonished to see them jump aboard the truck he expected them to stop.

Two of the men, Michael Ashbel and Yosef Simhon, were urgently in need of medical attention. Two IZL nurses accompanied them to Tel Aviv, but ran into a police ambush. Noticing bloodstains, the police searched the vehicle and found the two wounded men. Though they were no longer in British uniforms there could be no doubt about their identities. They were brought to trial, refused to accept the court's jurisdiction or to ask for mercy—and were sentenced to death by hanging. From prison Ashbel wrote: "I am waiting for the gallows in the hope that I will not disappoint my commanders. I have been told that the revolt movement has threatened bloody reprisals if sentence is carried out. If my death can cause a fighting unity in the community, I forego any pardon." Ashbel was a poet whose verses had become the songs of the underground. (One such song—"Climb the Barricades"—is still sung at every meeting of Begin and the veterans of IZL.)

IZL headquarters resolved that the men would not hang. Its secret radio station broadcast a message to the British: "Do not hang our captive soldiers! We swear to God that we will break the posts of your gallows. We will answer gallows with gallows!"

On June 18, an IZL squad broke into the Yarkon Hotel in Tel Aviv and grabbed three British officers. On the way out they encountered two air force officers and took them along as well. The abduction achieved international headlines and considerable concern in London about their safety. Pressure was brought to bear on the Jewish Agency's Political Department to work for the release of the IZL's prisoners. But Begin had no such intention.

In the meantime the IZL learned that British search teams were very close to discovering the place where two of the officers were hidden. That being the case, the headquarters staff decided to release the pair as a gesture of goodwill. They were delivered back to the Yarkon Hotel, while the IZL radio stressed that it was hoped the gesture would be a prelude to commutation of the sentence on its own men. And indeed on July 3 the High Commissioner for Palestine commuted the sentence to life imprisonment. The remaining three British officers were released on July 4, and deposited in the middle of Tel Aviv—inside a large packing case, from which they emerged to the amusement of the bystanders, the country, and the international press.

The IZL had saved its men from the gallows, but its victory was only temporary. Within a few months

Begin would be faced with the dilemma of how to save Dov Gruner, and this time his audacity would be of no help. Begin could not have known that Ashbel's reprieve from the gallows had in fact only granted him a few more months of life.

Today Begin occasionally makes a pilgrimage from Tel Aviv to Ramat Gan, where stands a sculpture of a small lion fighting a large lion. It is a memorial to Don Gruner, and it bears an inscription from Jabotinsky's *Betar* anthem: "Carry the flame . . ." The statue stands in front of a police station. The buildings, the comings and goings of uniformed men and the street scenes, are almost unchanged; the statue is perhaps the only reminder that the men wearing the uniform have changed.

CHAPTER 15

And the Walls Came Tumbling . . .

When Begin's government took over in Israel, his Health Minister, Eliezer Shostak's, first order of business was in a maximum security mental hospital for virtually hopeless cases. Though Israel is short of hospital space, the minister ordered this one cleared because it happened to be in a building that, more than any other place, symbolized IZL's war—the Turkish-built fortress of Acre within the old walled city. It was built on the firm foundations of a Crusader fortress. Since Saladin drove the Crusaders out, Acre has been virtually impregnable. Napoleon Bonaparte besieged the city but could not enter, and he was not the only skilled general to win elsewhere but fail at Acre. With the advent of the British it was turned into a prison, on the assumption that the walls that had kept enemies out could just as easily hold them in. And one wing of the fortress-prison contains the gallows used to execute Dov Gruner and his comrades.

The IZL veterans, accompanied by their families, frequently visited this shrine, yet they always had to brave the crazed stares of the occupants of the other wing. Time and again they asked whether the building could not be vacated by the mental institution, but the growing need for hospital beds was hardly conducive to decisions based on historical sentiment alone. They were compelled to make do with access to the execution room, while the hospital quarters remained out of bounds—until Begin's ascendancy to the premiership.

In the second half of April 1947 the atmosphere of the building was completely different. Some of the IZL and *Lehi*'s best men were inside Acre. The rebellion was virtually at a standstill and Begin was pushing for more activity. He sat at home listening to the BBC and Radio Moscow, becoming ever more convinced that the British régime's days were numbered. The official leadership of the community was insisting on immediate cessation of terrorism. A delegation had met with British Foreign Secretary Ernest Bevin, who had suggested partition of Palestine and transfer of supervision of immigration to the central government. The Jewish leaders responded that partition would be a minimal demand. Meanwhile the British authorities were deporting illegal immigrants brought to Palestinian shores in ships chartered by the *Haganah*. Assuming that a combination of terror and international pressure would compel the British to leave in the foreseeable future, Begin wanted to speed their departure with all the means at his disposal—and some of those means, notably, fifty-six members of IZL and twenty-four of *Lehi*, were detained at His Majesty's pleasure in Acre Prison, all

of them for relatively long terms. A proposal by Amihai Paglin that they should break into Acre and
release the prisoners was approved by Begin as serving
both the immediate need and the longer term strategy.
It would bring home to the British the realization
that they were not secure—even behind their thickest
walls.

Paglin did not need extensive reconnaissance to
support his planning. On the route from the Arab
marketplace of the city was an old and deserted
Turkish bath, the roof of which was adjacent to the
outer wall of the cell block that housed the IZL and
Lehi prisoners. The prisoners themselves were in
constant contact by means of letters smuggled in and
out by an Arab medical orderly from Haifa. A few
days before the planned assault they were warned to
remain alert. Eitan Livni—now a member of the
Knesset—as the senior man inside, was instructed to
select some forty prisoners for the escape, it being
assumed that the rescue party would be unable to
transport and shelter more than that number. The
remaining men would also have to cover their escaping colleagues from the inside. Livni later admitted
that the selection was the hardest and most unpleasant
function ever required of him in the underground.

At noon on May 4, 1947, a British military convoy
pulled out of Binyamina, on the coastal strip south of
Haifa, and headed northward led by a stern-faced
major in a jeep. In all, the convoy comprised one
large and two smaller trucks, with twenty-three armed
and steel-helmeted "British soldiers." The major's
travel documents recorded that he was taking his men
from a combat engineers unit to a training course in
Beirut. On their way north they passed southbound

convoys, and waved a greeting. On the outskirts of Haifa the engine of one of the smaller trucks conked out. While some of the men tried to repair it, a British military police jeep pulled up and two sergeants stepped out. Seeing the major, they saluted.

"Need any help, sir?"

"No, thank you. We're managing."

His uniform, manner, and speech were exactly what they should be, for Dov Cohen had spent enough years in the British army to know what was expected. With the military police safely out of sight, his men completed the repair and the convoy was again on its way.

As they approached Acre, the convoy split up. One truck turned toward the walls of the old city. Three machinegunners took positions alongside the road, while the truck moved on to drop another squad on the far stretch of the city wall by the sea. The second truck passed Acre railway depot and turned to the east gate of the old city, but the accompanying large trucks could not enter because the heavy wood and iron door was only half open. The men tried to swing it round, but the hinges had rusted into place. There was nothing for it but to continue with the smaller truck alone.

"Major" Dov Cohen remained with his jeep at a gasoline station outside the city. He waited until the others were out of sight, then entered the station and drew a gun on the Arab pump attendant.

"If you sit quietly, nothing will happen to you."

Two IZL men, meanwhile, pumped gasoline onto the road as a means of creating a fire barricade if British reinforcements tried to get through, then placed a couple of landmines as an extra precaution.

They had barely finished when they heard a loud explosion from the area of the fortress.

As the convoy had approached the outskirts of Acre, a game of volleyball was in progress in the prison courtyard. Among the audience, each rooting for his own team, were a number of prisoners with homemade hand grenades, hastily constructed with explosives smuggled into the prison in a double-thickness jam jar. Others were in their cells preparing mattresses to use as barriers against bullets fired at their escaping comrades. Teams of prisoners lolled on the outer wall, ostensibly watching the game below.

The raiders propped a ladder against the wall of the old Turkish bath house, then scrambled up to the roof to attach two large charges of explosive to the fortress walls. At the sound of the detonation, the game in the courtyard came to an abrupt finish and the prisoners ran to their cells. Those marked for escape were already in place near the two gaping holes in the thick outer wall. Hand grenades and burning mattresses added to the general confusion, though it seemed that the explosion had amply disoriented the prison guards. The prison governor stood on the terrace of the administrative wing, yelling: "Stop it!" but nobody took any notice of him.

The first escapee emerged from the breach in the wall in less than two minutes. Seeing British soldiers outside, he backed away thinking that the raid had failed. Then, identifying the face of a friend from the Tel Aviv IZL, he blurted out the agreed password.

When most of the escaping prisoners were in the narrow alleyway next to the Arab market, they began to attract the attention of people in the nearby cafés. Some wandered over to investigate, but backed away at the sight of IZL guns aimed at them. The escapees ran to the truck that waited by the city gate. None of them noticed that the three-man team stationed by the wall were not on the truck—Avshalom Haviv, Meir Necker, and Yaakov Weiss had not heard the trumpet sounding retreat. They were caught and sentenced to death.

At the sound of the explosion, Dov Cohen, commanding the force left outside the city walls, had ignited the gasoline poured on the road, jumped aboard his jeep, and raced to the east gate. He could see that the escaping truck was already moving into the narrow road alongside the railway depot—and a group of genuine British soldiers, who had heard the explosion while on the beach, were coming in the opposite direction. He tried to catch the truck and yell instructions to the driver, but it was too late. The driver attempted to pull out to the left but hit a cactus fence. The engine died and they were stranded exactly opposite the British soldiers, now in firing positions.

The occupants of the truck ran for cover. Meanwhile a van had driven up behind the truck. Dov Cohen stopped it and ordered the Arab driver out of his cab. The man refused and Dov shot him. The IZL truck driver ran to the cab and started to pull the dead Arab clear—but was hit by a bullet and died immediately. Nobody else among the group knew how to drive, so Dov had no alternative but to yell to his men to scatter while he grabbed a Bren machine gun and, firing from the hip, gave them covering fire. His covering action lasted a few moments until a machine-gun burst caught him in the face. Within minutes British reinforcements had arrived, and were gathering up the IZL and *Lehi* dead and wounded. Among the six dead escapees and three rescuers was Michael Ashbel, who had been saved from hanging by the abduction of the British officers some months earlier. Counting the three who were caught and hung, the Acre rescue cost twelve lives. The twenty-eight successful escapees found their separate ways to the agreed rendezvous, and were hustled off to hiding places.

The raid caught the imagination of the international press, some papers even comparing it with the storming of the Bastille. But in Tel Aviv and Jerusalem, there were those who questioned whether the effort had been worth it. The official leadership of the Jewish community, who were waging an intensive and promising diplomatic campaign, expressed their acute displeasure; the raid could return them to square one, and strengthen the British argument that their presence in Palestine was essential to the maintenance of law and order and prevention of bloodshed between Jews and Arabs. The *Haganah* made public statements about the cost of lives of the raid.

Begin has never forgiven the *Haganah* for its attitude: "We never contemplated criticizing *Haganah* operations where they lost men. Quite the contrary, we related to them as brothers in arms fallen in battle. They repaid us in disgraceful fashion."

The cracks in the walls of Acre Prison proved to be cracks in the British Mandate in Palestine. The breaching of a thick-walled fortress was a strike at British morale. There was more to come.

On August 16 a military court sentenced the three men captured in Acre to death by hanging. Days earlier the IZL had kidnapped two policemen and was holding them in a deserted apartment. The Jewish leadership asked the populace to cooperate with the Palestine police in the hunt, and *Haganah* men were ordered to help also. The abduction was viewed as an act of provocation likely to put an end to all the diplomatic hopes. The search succeeded when, sensing the approach of police units, the IZL guards fled. The two men were free, but Begin did not give up hope of saving his three men from the hangman's rope. Two days after confirmation of sentence by British military headquarters, Marvin Paice and Clifford Martin, both sergeants in the British Army Intelligence Corps, were on their way out, in civilian clothes and accompanied by a Jewish friend, from a café in Natania. At one o'clock in the morning, as they were passing the town hall, a car pulled into the club beside them and three masked men armed with submachine guns jumped out.

"Hands up! Whoever moves gets shot!"

"We're unarmed," Paice replied calmly.

The three men were ordered into the car and the two sergeants were chloroformed. The car headed for an orange grove outside the town, where their Jewish friend was bundled out, tied hand and foot, and admonished not try to move until dawn.

He got free of his ropes and walked to an army camp, where he reported the incident. Meanwhile the kidnappers and their captives were safely in an abandoned factory building near Natania. The sergeants were hustled into a concealed bunker beneath the building and told that they were being held hostage for the safety of three condemned men. The bunker was equipped with food, beer, cigarettes, oxygen bottles to supplement the air supply, and a field toilet.

Here they were held while British patrols walked overhead, oblivious to the existence of the underground chamber.

The IZL attempted to convince the British that the two men were somewhere in Tel Aviv, abandoning a truck carrying stretchers, field dressings, and ropes nearby. They did this primarily for the benefit of the inhabitants of Natania, who were convinced that the kidnapping would result in continuing curfew and retaliation against them. Their enemy, however, doubted that the kidnappers could have got through the cordon thrown around Natania.

The British brought pressure to bear on the Jewish Agency, which in turn approached the IZL. But the Agency's contacts with Begin no longer existed, so the *Haganah* intensified its own search.

Despite the community leaders' opposition to the kidnapping, they tried to persuade the authorities to commute the death sentences outstanding on the three IZL men. The Chief Rabbi approached the High Commissioner. The Hebrew press published pleas for clemency, while warning the British that if the executions went ahead as planned, the communal leaders would be powerless to help the two sergeants. But the British were adamant.

For Begin it was a serious dilemma. He was far from certain that he would find the resolve to order the execution of the sergeants. On the other hand he was certain that if the IZL captives had been officers, the authorities would have given in to the demand for commutation of sentence. However it was too late for that; the British were now on their guard against further abductions.

The moment of truth arrived. To the vociferous

disgust and anger of the entire community, including opponents of IZL—and there were plenty of those— the three men in Acre Prison were taken to the gallows. Begin summoned his operations officer, Paglin.

"There is no doubt that we must carry out our execution. Our credibility depends on it. On the other hand I'm not sure that it's possible."

"Why not?"

"Because Natania is surrounded by troops."

"We can get around that."

"Maybe. But I don't want any of our men caught in the act of taking them to their execution."

"I can promise you that, but whether our men get caught after the execution is another matter . . ."

Begin knew that risk existed in every IZL operation, but his credibility was at stake. If he ordered the release of the two sergeants, the British would be free to execute any IZL man that they took in the future —and any further threat would be meaningless.

"All right," Begin said. "What do you propose?"

"I'll go to Natania to see for myself," Paglin decided. "If it can be done without getting caught, we'll do it."

So Paglin went to Natania and met his men in the town. In the late afternoon he went with some of them to the bunker.

"What are you going to do with us?" the sergeants asked.

"Your men executed ours, and in so doing they passed sentence on you."

"You are going to hang us?"

The IZL man nodded.

"When?"

"Immediately."

They climbed to the factory above. Paice went to his death without a word.

"We're guilty of nothing," said Martin, as they tied a handkerchief over his eyes.

"I realize that you're the victims of British policy," answered an IZL man, "but as a soldier you know who is responsible for that policy."

Martin's lips twisted as he mumbled a silent prayer.

The two bodies were wrapped in blankets and returned to the bunker. Before dawn they were brought up again, taken to the nearby grove, and hung from a tree. The IZL men then planted a few mines around the tree. The CID would certainly come to investigate the scene of the crime, and it was an opportunity to get a few more of them. A phone call was made to the Natania town hall, notifying them of the place. When the IZL heard that a crowd of Jews was heading there, they added a warning that the area was mined—which was promptly relayed to the British military authorities.

The British arrived to find the two sergeants hanging by their own neckties. The IZL had kept its promise. For fear of booby traps the bodies were towed clear by a jeep, which hit a mine. No one was hurt, but Paice's body was blown up, adding to the horror. The British had mistakenly assumed that the warning referred to the bodies, and not to the area around them.

The Jewish authorities expressed their shock and disgust. Golda Meir made a sharp and bitter statement. Again the community was split in two—those who considered the execution degrading and inhuman, and those few supporters of IZL who claimed that there had been no alternative.

In an attempt to lessen the criticism, the IZL published a "charge sheet" against the two sergeants, listing: illegal entry to the land of Israel, suppression of the Jewish aspiration for liberty, the carrying of illegal weapons for use against Jewish freedom fighters, and so on. The list of crimes, circulated in a handbill, boomeranged. In fact it was one of Begin's few real mistakes in the propaganda war. Nobody could take seriously such charges brought against men who were only carrying out orders. If there had been Jews prepared to defend the act of execution itself, as a retaliation against the British hangings and a way to prevent additional hangings, nobody was prepared to justify the retroactive and fabricated sentence.

A letter from Sergeant Paice's father addressed to the head of IZL had arrived in Palestine—but too late. Its publication proved embarrassing. Begin decided to make use of it, however, in a broadside entitled: "An Answer to a Bereaved British Father."

We, the soldiers of Israel, understand the feelings of a father anxious about the fate of his son. We are also sons of fathers and fathers of sons. And God is our witness that we did not want the growing bloodshed in our vandalized and conquered land, by tyrants thirsty for blood and oil. This small country is our only land. We wanted to bring to it our brothers, we wanted to build it as a land of freedom and peace. But we were not allowed to, and the Jewish blood spilled like water, the fault of that same cruel overlord, is now augmented by the burning drops of blood of Hebrew heroes who vowed to liberate

287

their land and free their people—or die. Therefore, Mr. Paice, it was not to us that you should
have addressed your plea for mercy, but to those
who murdered the sons of aged Necker and aging
Haviv, and who ignored their pleas. To those
who murdered the only brother of Idit Weiss,
and ignored her pleading. To those who murdered, directly and indirectly, tens of thousands
of innocent men, women, and children, who
stole countries that were not theirs, who condemn
to extermination entire nations—it is to them
that you should have turned to spare fathers
and sons, including British fathers and sons who
are killed for the crime of denying others a right
to live. And now, go to them, in Downing Street,
and tell them—as all British fathers should whose
sons were conscripted for the most disgraceful
task in the history of the world—You are the
murderers! You murdered my son!

Those who met Begin during this period will still
testify that, much as he knew the executions of the
sergeants to be necessary, he was sickened by that
necessity. The specter of it was to haunt him through
his years as leader of the opposition in Israel's
Parliament. To his opponents of the left wing and
center parties, Begin and his *Herut* Party represented
extremism and political adventurism. To large sec-
tions of the Israel public, he was the continuation
of the IZL, and as such no better than the leader
of a bunch of terrorists. The obvious sadness with
which Begin sought to repudiate this public image
only served to strengthen it. And if anything could
upset his outward urbanity, it was mention of the

hanging of the two sergeants. The fact is that the British, after this incident, no longer took Jews to the gallows.

In 1972 Begin paid his first visit to England. The memory of that decision was once more jolted back to life. Members of the families of the two sergeants staged demonstrations against him. The communications media asked uncomfortable questions, and got the by now well-known response: "I understand only too well the feelings of the two families, but what choice did we have? We were in the midst of a war for our liberation. The British régime threw its full military might against us. They treated our fighters as if they were common criminals instead of prisoners of war. When they sentenced men to death, we warned them that we would answer in kind."

It was obvious that of all the actions by the underground that Begin headed, the two most alive in the memories of the Englishmen who demonstrated against him in London, and who demanded that he be brought to trial, were the blowing up of the King David Hotel and the execution of the two sergeants. On the other hand his old adversaries respected him. When they met him they were surprised to find that he was unprepossessing in build, immaculately dressed, and a thorough gentleman. Yet, though they shook hands, the old scars remained in their hearts.

An Israeli journalist visiting London happened to run into Colonel Grey, the last commandant of the Palestine police, who told him that of all the acts of the underground, only three had shaken the administration sufficiently to influence their thinking about leaving the country.

"In 1947 Britain was still an empire," he said, "and

an empire can permit itself to be unjust, even tyrannical and terrifying. It can permit itself defeats on the battlefield or in the diplomatic arena; but it cannot allow itself one thing: to lose prestige and become a laughingstock."

The three things that had shaken Britain's hold were the flogging of officers, the break into Acre Prison, and the hanging of the sergeants.

"When the underground killed our men, we could treat it as murder; but when they erected gallows and executed our men, it was as if they were saying 'We rule here as much as you do,' and that no administration can bear. Our choice was obvious. Either total suppression or get out, and we chose the second."

CHAPTER 16

TB in Rosenbaum Street

Alongside a photo of the fictional Yisrael Sassover, Menachem Begin keeps in his living room a picture of a frail man with elongated features. The late Yisrael Epstein was a good friend, perhaps the best. A senior member of the IZL command, he was one of the few men that Begin consulted on decisions. Begin himself would later admit that, in moments when the cause seemed to be claiming too many sacrifices, it was Epstein who revived his spirit and perhaps even talked him out of resigning as head of IZL.

Begin knew Epstein back in his days as *Betar* commissioner in Poland. He had run across him in his visits to Vilna, and he and Aliza had been Epstein's house guests while looking for a home of their own. It was Epstein who took Aliza Begin home from the maternity hospital after she had given birth to a daughter, Hasia, on May 2, 1946, and it was he who lent his own name to Begin's daughter. To the boy Benny he was a favorite uncle.

Late in 1946 Epstein was sent to Europe to raise funds for the IZL, in order to finance illegal immigration. He arrived in Italy at precisely the moment when an IZL team was planting explosives in the British Embassy in Rome. Epstein was picked up by the police together with some of the others. Based on his Palestinian citizenship, the English asked for extradition in the hope of finding out what he was doing in Italy. Epstein was afraid that they would deport him to the Eritrean detention camps, where his days of usefulness would be over. He believed that the mission that brought him to Europe was of paramount importance, and so he decided to escape from the Italian prison. But he was discovered by a guard, shot, and fatally wounded.

Begin was not a scout troop leader. He had learned to live with death. But Epstein was too close a friend —perhaps even his mirror image, with the same fervent belief in God, the same deep historic sense, and the same respect for the spoken and written word.

The photo of Yisrael Epstein went with Begin when he moved, in 1947, to a new apartment in Tel Aviv, where he would stay until his elevation to the premiership thirty years later. The move from Yehoshua Bin Nun Street was not a sudden decision. IZL security officers were concerned that too many British policemen seemed to be spending time near their leader's home. Even though it appeared at first to be sheer coincidence, they were taking no chances. Begin himself worried about something else: since the combined revolt, the heads of *Haganah* and the Jewish Agency had become accustomed to the sight of him with a beard, and there could be no guarantee that they would not pass on a description to the British.

Though they did not know where he was living, one word in British ears—and every bearded man in Tel Aviv would be suspect.

There was another reason to discard his disguise and cover address. An Egyptian Jew was building a hotel nearby, and the activity surrounding its construction was hardly conducive to the complacency of a man seeking anonymity. So Yisrael Sassover vanished one night from Yehoshua Bin Nun Street and, next morning, Dr. Yona Koenigshoffer appeared in residence at 1 Rosenbaum Street, Tel Aviv. The choice of name was dictated by the fact that the original Dr. Koenigshoffer had mislaid his passport. All IZL Intelligence had to do was switch photographs and Begin had a new identity.

The only person who had difficulty in adjusting to the switch was Benny, who could not understand where his father's beard had gone, or why the family name had suddenly changed. The new name was not designed to help him in his contacts with the children of the new neighborhood.

One of the neighbors was struck by the pallid appearance of this Dr. Koenigshoffer. Not knowing, of course, that it was the result of having shaved off his beard, she decided that he must be suffering from tuberculosis—a fact that disturbed her. Fearing that Koenigshoffer had come from Petach Tikva, she asked a relative there whether the name meant anything to him. Back came the confirmation that there had indeed been a Koenigshoffer in Petach Tikva, and he did have tuberculosis. Next morning she rapped on the Begins' door and suggested that Dr. Koenigshoffer should get a medical examination. Begin declined politely, hoping the anxious woman would spread the news through the neighborhood. Tuberculosis would be a good cover, and it would certainly keep the neighbors away and forestall any questions about why he did not go out to work each morning.

The man from whom Begin rented the apartment also had no idea who his new tenant really was. The lease was signed by Dr. Kahan, who explained that his relative, Dr. Koenigshoffer, was too ill to appear in person.

Benny was reaching the age at which children ask questions. Curious about his father's job, he pestered both Aliza and Menachem and only got evasive answers. Then, one day, Begin discovered that his son was not a supporter of the organization that he headed. The neighborhood kids were playing war on the British, and Benny chose to be a member of *Haganah*. But this was no time to entrust his secret to a child, not even his own son.

The period after Begin's change of address was one of extensive activity in IZL, the main event being a raid on the Jerusalem Officers' Club that took place on March 1, 1947. Dressed as British soldiers, a squad drove up to the building, staged a frontal attack, overcame the sentries, and placed explosive charges. The building collapsed on the heads of the occupants, killing seventeen officers and men and wounding twenty more. That same day other IZL units staged attacks on two army camps in central Palestine, killing and wounding ten more British soldiers. Military vehicles were destroyed in Haifa, and landmines made driving treacherous throughout the country.

The next day martial law was proclaimed in the main cities of Palestine. Public institutions were closed, special military courts for fast judgments convened, and roadblocks set up where there were large concentrations of the population to check the identity of all passers-by. Barbed-wire fences were installed around government buildings, prompting wags to christen the new enclaves "Bevingrads," after the British Foreign Secretary.

Winston Churchill asked in the House of Commons: "Is this house aware that the British Army in Palestine is four times greater than that in India? Is it not too great a burden to maintain 100,000 troops and to spend on them £40 million a year?"

The action against the Officers' Club was a turning point for IZL. It was the first operation carried out on the Sabbath, something which Begin had never allowed even though most of his men were not orthodox Jews. Moreover the club was located close to the Yeshurun Great Synagogue—as if to flaunt desecration of the sanctity of the day. At first there had been reservations. Paglin spelled out the risks involved, but recommended approval nevertheless. When he went to Jerusalem to reconnoiter the target, he discovered that a Jewish bus passed by the building every few minutes—and the passengers were likely to be hurt. In his opinion the only time that the job could be done was on a Saturday, when public transport was at a standstill. He returned to Tel Aviv sure that Begin would not agree.

There had been circumstances in which Begin was forced to make decisions that went against the grain. One of these concerned the problem of raising money for the IZL. His men were ordered never to use their weapons against Jews, and to avoid any internecine violence. But threats were certainly involved. They were also used to force restaurant and movie house owners to close down and refuse to serve the British. One contention held that terror knew no limits; what was used today against the British could be used tomorrow against the community's representatives. The official Jewish attitude toward *Lehi* was different. Although the Jewish Agency wanted no part of it, it did at least recognize that *Lehi* was prepared to subject itself to *Haganah* supremacy, for all that it might disagree with the official policies. In other words Natan Friedman-Yellin and his colleagues did not see themselves as an alternative to the duly elected democratic Jewish institutions, as Begin and his comrades did.

Begin countered the argument that the community's leadership represented the public with his own belief that, in times of emergency when the national fate hung in the balance, one does not dabble in formalities. For him, the degree of intensity of the struggle against the British was the only yardstick of authority.

From mid-1946 to mid-1947 IZL activity was at its height. Not a day went by without some action somewhere in Palestine, whether demolition of telephone poles or strikes at police posts—anything to make the British uncomfortable and their lives untenable. Not only were they living and working behind barbed wire, but they were forced to travel in convoy. The IZL kept up the pressure until it seemed like a steady barrage of harassment, of mines, bullets, and explosives.

At the same time the IZL also waged a propaganda war. Posters appeared on every street, sometimes even while the British watched, powerless to intervene because they knew that armed IZL men would be somewhere in the background offering cover. The IZL radio was no less active, and thousands listened to its broadcasts, which always began with the song "To Conquer the Mountain" and the station signal: "The Voice of Zion from Underground, the Voice of Liberated Zion, the Voice of the *Irgun Zvai Leumi*." At first they only broadcast for five minutes a day from a transmitter concealed in the apartment of Esther Naor, sister of David Raziel—one-time commander of IZL. The British tracked down the transmitter and arrested Esther and her husband. The children were taken in by their grandmother, and to pay a brief visit with them was one of the few reasons that brought Begin out of hiding.

The IZL voice was not silenced for long. This time the British were warned that they would pay with their lives for any attempt to silence the transmitter. Whether the warning did the trick or not, the British stuck to attempts at jamming broadcasts thereafter; but the IZL operators simply switched to other channels, followed by their thousands of listeners.

Both the posters and the broadcasts carried the clear imprint of Begin's style. They were dramatic and emotional, often leaving the impression that history itself was speaking. Gradually the length of broadcasts stretched to twenty-five minutes a day. To Begin, with his eternal faith in the magic property of words, the broadcasts were no less important than the armed warfare.

Begin himself spent long hours listening to the radio, waiting to see how the outside world reported on the performance of his organization. He was so engrossed in this reaction that his colleagues began to believe that his timing of operations was based on the impression they might make on world opinion. The British press was raising the specter of IZL operations within the United Kingdom itself, and the thought pleased Begin. It was a propaganda coup. Although the IZL did not have the kind of capability for operations that far away, he did his best to encourage the idea, and enjoyed watching the British embarrassment.

At first the broadsheets, posters, and handbills were printed at the press of an IZL sympathizer who slipped them in between his own work; but the need gradually arose for an independent press. The IZL set one up in south Tel Aviv, but it fell into British hands during Operation Season. Begin would not give up. For him the printed word was no less important than dynamite. So they bought another, and installed it underground, beneath a carpenter's shop, which gave ample cover for the noise and also allowed the truckers who brought wood to bring in paper and take away the final product hidden in their furniture deliveries.

Anyone who now talks to Begin about this period, which he still views as the crowning point of his life, is likely to come away with the impression that, from the moment of the IZL's declaration of revolt, the *Haganah* and the Jewish Agency sat with their arms crossed. But this is far from the truth. Though the IZL undertook very daring operations, and despite the fact that its share in achieving Jewish independence in Palestine is almost undebatable, the *Haganah* was by no means inactive. Spearheaded by the *Palmach*, it was a highly organized and disciplined force whose function was, in Clausewitzian terminology, to continue diplomacy by other means. And it was the

Haganah that provided the firm base on which David Ben-Gurion later built the army of Israel.

While Begin was escalating the campaign against the British, the *Haganah* was acquiring more weapons and training its crack echelons. Ben-Gurion was convinced that the Arabs would oppose the creation of a Jewish State by force, very probably with the help of the neighboring countries, and for this Israel would need a regular military arm. In addition, while IZL was busy harassing the British, the *Haganah* was methodically supplying cover to illegal immigration on the assumption that, apart from the humanitarian need of sanctuary for the refugees, the community was going to need every available pair of hands for the impending conflict. *Haganah* agents in Europe organized groups of people, chartered ships, loaded them with human cargoes, and guided them into the shores of the Holy Land. On the beaches the immigrants were met by a cordon of armed *Haganah* and *Palmach* men, who often had to fight their way into the hinterland where the refugees found shelter in Jewish settlements. Some of the ships were caught and turned back. Some of the immigrants were thrown into detention camps on the nearby island of Cyprus; but thousands got through under cover of night and the willing protection of the *Palmach*. And the protection was not only passive. When the *Palmach* struck at coastal radar stations, it did so to prevent the British from spotting the incoming cargoes.

The efforts to settle desolate tracts of land also continued, on the assumption by the community's leaders that the people and the plow were what determined frontiers. The last furrow would be the border. Moreover the new settlements that sprang up literally overnight, despite all the British attempts to prevent them, were self-sufficient military outposts, complete with well-hidden underground arsenals and *Haganah*- and *Palmach*-trained farmers, who would prove capable of defending themselves against the regular armies of the Arab states.

In early 1947 voices were again heard in the Zionist left in favor of restraining the dissidents. Now there was a new danger. What would happen if, in the middle of the battle for independence, the dissidents decided to use their weapons in order to gain control over the community? Who would stop them then? These questions were to hover uneasily over the relationships between IZL and the community. Obviously his adversaries did not know Begin very well, and therefore credited him with altogether too far-reaching aims. The man who argued for restraint during Operation Season never planned to turn his weapons on fellow Jews now. He had already proved that on numerous occasions; however, to his opponents he did appear to be an uncompromising extremist, not above taking the law into his own hands. Further, given the traditional enmity between the left and the Revisionists, Begin indeed must have seemed to present a very real danger.

Operation Season might have been renewed, but in 1947 the *Haganah* and *Palmach* had more urgent things to do. In any case, Season had left a bitter taste in the ranks of the *Haganah*. They disagreed with the IZL, detested its leadership, scorned the emotionalism of its propaganda—but they still admired the courage, however misguided, of the IZL's men.

In early 1947, with between 600 and 1,000 operational men, plus backup echelons numbering some

5,000, the IZL was far different from what Begin had originally found when he took over. His close associates were still of the East European Revisionist stamp, brought up in the traditions of *Betar,* who revered the memory of Zeev Jabotinsky whom they called "teacher of the generation." Their behavior remained that of old world Polish courtesy. But the men in the ranks were a different matter. Many of them were from the poor districts around the big cities—a fact of considerable significance in understanding Begin's subsequent political policies as leader of the *Herut* Party.

The parties of the Zionist left controlled all the key positions in the community, in education and culture as in politics, and they were the ones who set the style and tone of life in Jewish Palestine. The Israel Labor Party of 1977 is vastly different from that of the late 1940s, probably far closer to the British variety than to the more radical European socialist parties. Yet it still pays lip service to the conventions of those days: the dignity of manual labor, the return of the Jew to the soil, and labor as a value in itself. They preached to the youth to set up kibbutzim, to tame and reclaim the deserts, to share in building the infrastructure of the State that must certainly come. And the youth themselves, brought up in the various movements of the left wing, were an exclusive club, within which the *Palmach* was the most exclusive of all—one that drew for its values and for its very active and intimate social life on the heritage of the labor movement.

The so-called marginal youth of African and Asian origin tended not to identify with the *Palmach* and its leadership of mostly Russian and East European antecedents. Thus, for those who wanted active involvement in the struggle against the British, the road to the IZL was an obvious and natural one. And the influx of Oriental youth, from an underprivileged environment, gradually tilted the organization away from the closed society of Polish and East European *Betar* graduates into an army for whom *Betar* meant very little.

The trend is still evident in the party on which Begin relies for his support, and which eventually brought him to power. Indeed the pockets of poverty were the citadels of Begin's electoral strength. Paradoxically, the socialist parties never established a foothold in these communities, while the right wing under Begin knew how to exploit their pent-up anger. Given the security and foreign problems with which Israel has to contend, and the concomitant inability to devote sufficient attention and resources to the elimination of poverty, the paradox is perhaps inevitable. Equally as inevitable are the changes that the social reality has wrought in the mentality of the organization that inherited the mantle of the IZL.

But some things do not change, and one of these is Begin's personal style. Unlike those of previous governments, his cabinet meetings are usually short. Consensus is almost absolute on every issue, and in that it is reminiscent of IZL staff meetings. There have been remarkably few moments throughout his career when Menachem Begin has been in the minority among his own party, and only rarely has he had to force his opinions on others. On the occasions when it has happened, the result has been crisis. Generally his associates agree with him so readily that their viewpoints seem to be adjusted to his in advance.

Begin's opinions, even on subjects in which he cannot be expected to be well versed, are fixed and dogmatic. He directed the pace of IZL activities from within his own four walls, often deciding on strikes against targets that he knew only from the map. His opponents used this fact to criticize him, while his supporters claimed that it proved his extraordinary intuition and ability to assess situations from the reports of others.

In mid-1947, while Begin was still far from the corridors of power, just such a situation arose in Tel Aviv when the IZL was planning a major operation. Opposite one of the "Bevingrad" enclaves they had purchased a small warehouse, ostensibly to store potatoes, from which they intended to dig a tunnel under the compound, line it with explosives, and undermine the British-occupied buildings. The plan called for a warning to be delivered to the British to vacate all their barbed-wire enclaves, so there would be little chance of them discovering the actual target in time. But the *Haganah* discovered the plan. The United Nations Select Commission on Palestine (UNSCOP) was already in the country, and the military arm of the official Jewish establishment accused the IZL members of an attempt to impress the UN delegation with the power of their tiny organization to dictate the pace of events. Whether the accusation was well founded or not, a number of UN delegates had agreed to meet Begin—and a meeting was set up through the good offices of the AP correspondent in Tel Aviv.

The meeting took place without the other members of the Commission being aware that it had been planned, in the home of the poet and IZL sympathizer Dr. Yaakov Cohen. Those who came were driven around Tel Aviv, switched from car to car, while the

IZL checked that they were not being followed. Finally they were brought into the presence of a man who differed vastly from their preconceived notions. Begin himself was pleased when they told him so. It was his first diplomatic encounter at international level. Justice Emil Sandström and Dr. Ralph Bunche were well-known world figures, and Begin acknowledged the fact in his own gentlemanly manner by rising to his feet, and offering Sandström—chairman of the Commission—his own place at the head of the table. The Swede hastened to note that a precondition for the discussion was that it would not be made public while the Commission was still in Palestine.

Begin readily agreed, then answered Sandström's questions about IZL and the history of the battle against the British. With Begin were Haim Landau and Shmuel Katz—the latter destined eventually to be the prime minister's Advisor on Information Services. In describing the Holocaust of Nazi Europe, and parallel events in Palestine, Begin began to talk so loudly that Sandström was compelled to stop him.

"Please lower your voice. They must certainly be able to hear us outside."

Begin apologized. The Justice then asked a further question:

"I would like to know, sir, on what you base your rights to this land?"

"The Land of Israel has always been Jewish territory," Begin replied. "There was a Jewish State here 3,000 years ago. It was destroyed by the Romans, and the Jews went into exile. In all their years in the countries of the Diaspora, they did not forget this land, nor did they abandon the dream of returning someday. It is, therefore, our natural right."

"And what, in your opinion, will be the fate of the Arabs resident in this country?" Sandström asked.

"The land that they hold will continue to be theirs; they will be citizens with equal rights in the Jewish State. As for the soil, I must add that the Jewish government will have to carry out agrarian reform. Jews and Arabs will benefit from it, for you must know that too much land is presently held by too few people."

"Will your organization accept the views of the Jewish majority, even if they differ from yours?"

"The majority of this generation of the Jewish people is not entitled to forego the historic right of the Jewish people to its homeland. It belongs to all the coming generations as much as to this one. I am convinced that the Jewish people, as such, will not accept any solution contradictory to Jewish tradition. If it does so, then, sir, it is still early to determine what will be the viewpoint of the *Irgun Zvai Leumi*. We are educating the youth to loyalty to principles, and you do not forsake principles because of opportunistic needs."

Next, Sandström asked a leading question:

"Would it be true to say that you do not enjoy extensive support among the Jewish community?"

"If we don't have that kind of support, sir," responded Begin swiftly, "perhaps you would tell me how we can nonetheless fight against a British enemy superior to us in manpower and equipment? Maybe our war does bring suffering to many Jews, but it is a war of liberation. In the final analysis we are fighting for them."

The Commission members could conclude, as have many statesmen who have come into contact with

Menachem Begin, that most of his arguments were bedded in law. He relies on international or natural law. This, for example, was his anchor in claiming the nonjurisdiction of British courts, as representing an illegal administration. Conversely they could conclude that his views were also rooted in fresh historical memories—and particularly the Holocaust; he suggested that the Commission should visit Europe to talk to the survivors of the concentration camps.

Begin himself came out of the meeting very satisfied. Though he could not publicize it, his organization appeared to have achieved international recognition as a body whose opinion must be heard. Furthermore he sensed from the tone that the British Mandate was nearing its end; after all, most of the questions had related to a future free of the British presence. Of course he had no doubt that independence of the Jewish community in the land of Israel was not going to be given by any committee, or even by any Great Power. There would be a fight, but the light at the end of the tunnel was finally in sight.

CHAPTER 17

Dir Yassin

Two members of the UN Select Commission on Palestine, Dr. Jorge Garcia Granados and Professor Enrico Fabregat, had an even better chance to get to know Begin when a further meeting was held. Both were decidedly pro-Zionist, and Begin spoke to them as friends. He repeated the war aims of IZL, stressing that his organization was opposed to any proposal to partition Palestine. His visitors did not disagree with IZL's political platform in principle but noted that their colleagues on the Commission were unlikely to agree—particularly since the Jewish Agency had already expressed willingness to accept one of two suggestions: either the partition of Palestine into Jewish and Arab states; or a federal union under a central UN-sponsored government, with no limitation on immigration to the Jewish area. Begin replied that neither solution was acceptable to IZL, and he gave reasons that are still echoed in his policies today: "It is impossible to isolate the Jewish people from the

Land of Israel. A nation cannot agree to the carving up of its homeland."

Begin's demand of the UN was already formulated: dismemberment of the British Mandate, and the conversion of the Land of Israel—on both sides of the Jordan—into a democratic Jewish State, founded on the principle of equality to all its citizens. The idea was the Revisionist ultimate hope that found expression in the IZL emblem: a hand clutching a rifle, superimposed on a map of Palestine that included both sides of the Jordan River.

The actual boundaries of Palestine have long been in dispute. Some religious circles contend that they were determined by Divine Providence and confirmed by God's covenant with His chosen people. Obviously, following that line of thought, any withdrawal from the territories occupied by Israel in 1967 must be opposed as sacrilegious. However, even in these terms, the frontiers of the Promised Land as mentioned in the Bible are not altogether clear. For example the southern border is given as the Egypt River, but whether that is the El-Arish Wadi or the Nile, no one knows. In fact there was only a short period, during the reigns of David and Solomon, when the actual frontiers coincided closely with the "map" of the Promised Land.

Not even the maximalists in Begin's party today seriously consider the possibility of restoring the so-called Land of Israel on both banks of the Jordan (even though a Revisionist song speaks of exactly that). The Land of Israel Movement, which operates under the party's patronage and has as its aim Jewish settlement on the West Bank, views the Jordan River as the eastern frontier of its "entire land." But in

1947 Begin thought he was capable of acquiring the absolute maximum.

"What will you do if partition is accepted by the Jewish Agency?" Granados and Fabregat asked.

"I assume that the Agency will arrest us. Probably, for the first time in history, the Jews will open concentration camps for other Jews."

Begin parted from the two with a heavy heart. He was convinced of the justice of his demand, yet realized that it was unacceptable to the friendly members of UNSCOP—although this, of course, did not make him moderate his position. Obviously, even if the British Mandate was nearing its end, the IZL's battle still had to go on.

At the end of August 1947 UNSCOP submitted its recommendations: the majority for partition, and the minority for federation. The decision was now up to the General Assembly. But on September 28 Arthur Creech-Jones, the British Secretary of State for the Colonies, told a UN committee that, though His Majesty's Government would not enforce a settlement against the will of the Jews and the Arabs, "in the absence of a settlement [the British government] had to plan for an early withdrawal of British forces and amendment of the British administration from Palestine."

This change of attitude did not include the opening of the gates of Palestine to refugees. A few weeks after Creech-Jones's statement, 4,000 immigrants were deported to detention camps in Cyprus. The underground war of IZL and *Lehi* went on. Meanwhile Begin was coming around to the view that the fight ahead would be over the size of the Jewish State.

On November 29, 1947, the UN General Assembly

adopted the UNSCOP majority recommendation to partition Palestine. Tens of thousands of people back in Palestine listened to the dramatic roll-call vote, broadcast direct from New York, then emerged into the streets of the cities and towns to hug friends and strangers, to sing and dance. Restaurant owners invited their patrons to eat and drink on the house. The whole of Jewish Palestine celebrated. True, the partition left the community with very little territory and indefensible borders. It tore chunks out of the heart of the country and gave Jerusalem, the historic capital of the Jewish people, to the United Nations as an international city. But even that could not detract from the spontaneity of rejoicing. For the first time since the Romans had come to the Holy Land, the Jews were to have an independent land of their own—and the only land that really meant anything to them.

Begin's reaction at best was hostile. He was more concerned with what the UN decision was not giving. On November 30, he published a brief communiqué in the name of IZL:

> In the United Nations Organization a decision was taken for partition. The state to which we aspired from early youth, a state that will give the nation its freedom and promise our sons their future—that state still remains the objective of our generation. It will not be easy to reach it. A great deal more blood will be spilled for it.

The Arab response to the partition decision was not long in coming and proved the truth of Begin's grim prophecy. An attack on a Jerusalem-bound bus, at midday on November 30, signaled the beginning of

Arab attacks on Jews throughout the country. For the Arabs this course of action would prove counter-productive; instead of peaceably inheriting well over half of Palestine west of the Jordan, their conviction that they could prevent the creation of a Jewish State by force was eventually to result in their becoming homeless refugees.

Realizing that the Arab community was being incited by a nationalist and uncompromising leadership, Begin concluded that they were probably counting on British help to reverse the UN decision. In the meantime he was developing his own independent foreign policy, which was in part expressed in IZL posters condemning partition:

> In the name of our indisputable historic right, we hereby announce and declare to the world: the partition of our homeland is illegal. We will never recognize it. The signatures of institutions and individuals on the partition contract are invalid. They do not bind the Jewish people. The Jewish people will continue to fight in the full awareness of the righteousness of its cause of the liberation of our land, and the ingathering of millions of its members on its soil on both banks of the Jordan. The stratagems of the treacherous British oppressor, the calculations of alien powers, and the acts of betrayal by misled leaders—all will be shunted aside. Historic justice will be done. The entire Land of Israel will be returned to the Jewish people—for all eternity.

At the same time Begin made efforts—again by way of handbills—to make the Palestinian Arabs understand what they would be getting into if they tried to prevent the establishment of a Jewish State:

The British régime still hopes to remain in the Land of Israel as guardian of order and as the tool for peace. The oppressor wants to achieve his purpose by way of a bloody war between Jew and Arab. He knows that his régime is bankrupt and faces total elimination. His only salvation is in bloody clashes between you and us—clashes that will throw the country into anarchy. Therefore, he incites you to raise your hand against us. Agents pass among you and call on you to go to war, from which only one element can draw any benefit: the cursed oppressor régime.

Arab neighbors, we call on you not to be drawn in by incitement and provocation. We call on you to maintain good neighborly relations with our people. And not for them alone but also, primarily, for yourselves. Your men have already claimed victims from our brothers. Women have been murdered. We have not yet responded to these treacherous attacks, for we still want to believe that you will abandon that tragic road of provoking your Jewish neighbors. All of us, without exception, want peace with you. But we are all ready for war, if you force it on us. If you compel us to go over to counterattack, you know what will be the fate of the murderers. You know that we have stood for years in the face of 100,000 British soldiers—and they could not overcome us. You will understand, therefore, that if we are forced to put an end to the attacks by your people in direct service to the British, we will reach to every place the murderers come from and strike them with all our might.

Arab neighbors, we turn to you in a last warning. Leave the citizens of the land of the Jews alone. Do not violate the peace between the two peoples. Do not create an abyss of blood between them. In this land we will live together and progress together to a life of freedom and happiness. Do not reject the hand that is extended in peace. We will shake the hand of a good neighbor in friendship, but we will cut off without mercy the hand of the murderer.

As might have been expected, the IZL appeal fell on deaf ears. The Arabs of Palestine were too incited by now, and a massive conflagration could no longer be prevented. Begin's men prepared for war; but like *Lehi* their experience only extended to small-scale guerrilla warfare. The *Haganah* and *Palmach*, on the other hand, had spent years preparing for the battlefield proper, learning fieldcraft and organizing in military-type units. Thus while they deployed to defend Jewish population centers and mount well-planned offensives, the two smaller groups (IZL and *Lehi*) answered terror with terror: bombs in the Arab market in Jerusalem, explosives in Arab cafés, hit-and-run attacks on population centers—always as retaliation. Although Begin's war was that of a small guerrilla force compared with Ben-Gurion's program to train a unified national military machine, it did not prevent him from declaring that IZL would take on itself the task of carrying the war beyond the partition frontiers.

Recruiting stations were opening up in all the

towns and cities of Jewish Palestine, but IZL members preferred to maintain their organization's small, independent frame. Then, on the morning of April 10, 1948, began an operation which to this day is marked by hard feelings and controversy.

Shortly before dawn, a combined IZL-*Lehi* detachment launched an attack on Dir Yassin—an Arab village to the west of Jerusalem. *Haganah* headquarters in Jerusalem, preoccupied with keeping the Tel Aviv-Jerusalem road open, learned of the IZL plan in advance. David Shaltiel, the senior *Haganah* officer in Jerusalem, sent a note to his IZL and *Lehi* counterparts stressing that a hit-and-run raid, or the driving out of the inhabitants of the village, was not in the general interest since it could only leave the way open for Arab irregulars to occupy the village. However the IZL men claim that Shaltiel did approve the operation. The Arab irregular armies were firing continuously at traffic on the Jerusalem road, and Dir Yassin could be a potential trouble spot. Conversely the village elders had already declared that they intended to remain peaceful and, according to some accounts, had denied entry to the Arab belligerents. In an article published in *The Times* (London) in April 1971, Begin answered accusations against him and his organization by saying that the village had participated in attacks on traffic and on the western suburbs of Jerusalem.

To this day it is not altogether clear why the two organizations chose to attack this particular village. Maybe they viewed it as a threat to Jerusalem's suburbs. The IZL and *Lehi* claim that Arab reinforcements reached the main Arab force in Dir Yassin. Be that as it may, the IZL and *Lehi* men came upon a sleepy village. Not until they had opened fire and it was returned by the some half dozen watchmen were the other villagers aroused to protect themselves.

According to the plan, an IZL armored car equipped with a loudspeaker was to enter the village from the other side, broadcasting an announcement that the route of retreat to Ein Karim was left open to the villagers, and they were advised to use it, after surrendering without a fight. But the armored car fell into an improvised tank trap—and its message was not heard by the villagers. The people of Dir Yassin were able to halt the initial onslaught. None of the attackers had expected resistance, and now they had difficulty in coping with it. They sustained their first casualties, and found themselves short of ammunition. The situation was growing more difficult by the moment.

In danger of being pinned down by the Arabs, the operation commanders asked the *Haganah* for help, and Shaltiel responded by sending ammunition and a *Palmach* squad to cover evacuation of the wounded. The battle raged from house to house. It was early afternoon before all resistance was finally overcome. Arab sources say that according to Arab eyewitnesses unarmed men, women, and children were killed during the attack. A few survivors were loaded into trucks, driven through Jerusalem, and returned to Dir Yassin, where they were shot in cold blood. A part of this story was told the next day to a Red Cross representative by three survivors found in the wreckage of the village.

The IZL and *Lehi* consistently told a wholly different version, insisting that it had been a straightforward attack which had run into very stiff opposition. There were claims that white flags were put up by the local defenders and the Iraqi soldiers in the village, who had then opened fire on the approaching IZL men. A bitter battle had ensued, and the Iraqis had tried to escape disguised as women.

Whichever version is correct—and that will probably remain shrouded in the mists of history—the fact is that a great many women and children were killed. Begin would say, many years later, quoting from a Foreign Ministry brochure: "The men were shocked to find that, alongside the bodies of Palestinian and Iraqi soldiers were those of women and children." He added: "The responsibility for their deaths lies directly with the Arab soldiers, who according to the rules of war should have evacuated them from the village when they turned it into a fortress, well ahead of waging battle for it."

The IZL men also disproved the charges of parading the survivors and then shooting them, claiming that they were released at the entrance to the Old City of Jerusalem.

Nobody knows what prompted the massacre which, according to *Haganah* burial teams moved in the next day, claimed the lives of approximately 200 men, women, and children. It seems that the combination of inexperience and a tight situation simply made the IZL and *Lehi* soldiers lose their heads.

When the British heard of the massacre, they contemplated sending in RAF planes to bomb the new occupants of Dir Yassin, but dropped the idea when *Haganah* members moved in. The sight that met their eyes was horrible. Yeshurun Schiff, the unit commander, radioed a report to Shaltiel, who promptly ordered him to disarm the raiders. Schiff protested that they would refuse, and convinced Shaltiel to back down from a demand to open fire, saying that it would signal civil war in the Jewish community at a time when other problems were far more urgent.

The *Haganah* remained at one end of the village, and the IZL and *Lehi* men at the other—with a barrier of hatred between them. No attempt at communication was made.

The Jewish community as a whole condemned the Dir Yassin massacre. David Ben-Gurion sent a cable to King Abdullah of Jordan, disassociating the Jews of Palestine in the sharpest possible terms. The Chief Rabbi of Jersualem imposed boycott—the Jewish equivalent of excommunication—on all who took part in the attack. The Jewish Agency Executive and the *Haganah* issued statements protesting and condemning the dishonoring of the Jews' legitimate battle for independence.

Dir Yassin was a turning point in relations between Jew and Arab. True, there had been a century of bloodshed. For decades marauders had attacked outlying settlements, Arab town dwellers had sometimes turned on the Jews with whom they lived ostensibly at peace. From time to time the Arabs had been making pogroms on their Jewish neighbors. In 1929 and again in 1936 the extreme Arab nationalists massacred hundreds of innocent Jews, including women and children. And the British were always doing their best to worsen the relationship between the Jews and Arabs. One should not assume that history would have developed differently had the events at Dir Yassin not taken place.

But Dir Yassin was the catalyst that accelerated certain processes. First of all, it deepened the gulf of hostility. The Jews had retaliated in the past, but always measure for measure. This was the first occasion on which Jews took the initiative and struck at a peaceful Arab village.

Secondly, Dir Yassin provoked the Arabs into making one of their biggest mistakes. In the jockeying for position that went on during April 1948, in the final days before the British withdrawal, attempts by Arab irregulars and armed gangs to isolate settlements and even suburbs, and to interrupt Jewish traffic on the roads, were failing miserably. The battle for the Jerusalem road cost the life of Abdul Kader el-Husseini, the foremost Palestinian Arab military leader—a loss that left his forces around the city in a state of shock. Arab propagandists and the Arab media, in the double hope of drawing the neighboring Arab countries into the conflict and of restoring the Palestinian resolve to fight, began to retell the details of Dir Yassin and added details of their own Oriental imagination. This proved counter productive. The Arabs of Palestine panicked and began to run. Entire communities emptied almost overnight. When the *Haganah* attempted to straighten lines and strengthen communications, in preparation for the now inevitable Arab invasion of Palestine, they found that the Arab populations of mixed towns—so recently ready to torment their Jewish neighbors—now opted to cross the borders into Jordan and Lebanon. And when war followed, Jordan and Egypt imposed their sovereignty on Arab Palestine. The Palestinians had miscalculated. The move begun with their resistance to partition was sealed in part by their reaction to Dir Yassin.

In the Jewish community dissidents of IZL and *Lehi* were once more hounded, in even more vigorous terms, by all the epithets used to describe them in the past.

But now to "Fascists" and "terrorists" was added "murderers." The truth is that some of the *Lehi* leaders, including Natan Friedman-Yellin, were also ready to condemn the Dir Yassin incident, although Friedman-Yellin said that it was understandable if it had happened in the heat of the battle.

Ever since 1948 the Arabs have used Dir Yassin to substantiate the justice of their position in the conflict over Palestine. Their constant argument has been that the Jews came to the country to drive out its Arab inhabitants, notwithstanding any claims they make to the contrary. And the mass condemnation of the incident made no difference.

The British were already leaving, though some of them still believed that the clashes between Jews and Arabs could still change the decision. And the Jewish Agency was preparing for the role of interim government in the new State. But for the moment its main effort was in readying the community for independence. David Ben-Gurion, the chairman of the Agency Executive, was now almost certain that the regular Arab armies of Egypt, Jordan, Syria, and Lebanon, perhaps with other groups, would invade the new State.

At four o'clock in the afternoon of May 4, 1948, in Tel Aviv Museum, David Ben-Gurion declared the establishment of the State of Israel. That same day the regular armies of the Arab states invaded Palestine and the newborn State was fighting for its life. There was no time to celebrate independence—or even to ponder the greatness of the hour. Although after 2,000 years of exile and persecution the Jews again had a sovereign homeland, now every able-bodied man and boy, and many women too, were on the front lines in cities and settlements, holding off superior and better armed columns of Arab soldiers.

The inhabitants of Rosenbaum Street in Tel Aviv realized that the man on the front pages of the daily papers bore a startling resemblance to their neighbor, Dr. Koenigshoffer, although he did seem a little pale and frail for the leader of an underground army. Then, suddenly, the nameplate on the door was switched to "Aliza and Menachem Begin."

Begin did not really know Tel Aviv. His excursions from the apartment had been limited to hurried walks through back streets, always escorted, to attend some meeting of the combined revolt or to visit Paglin in his own southern Tel Aviv home. His first real stroll alone was a few days before the British finally departed. A crowd had collected in Mograbi Square to listen to an IZL broadcast, relayed by loudspeakers. The British were no longer interested, but the official Jewish organizations were not happy about the news being spread by IZL from the rooftops throughout the city, and so they tried to break up the crowd.

Begin went to see for himself. He walked briskly past the Habimah National Theater toward Allenby Street. If anyone recognized him, there was certainly no hint of it. At Mograbi there were a few familiar faces, and some people did glance at him with a flash of recognition in their eyes, but no one said a word, although one acquaintance later admitted that he was astonished to see Begin in public after so many years in hiding.

He had left home at seven in the evening, and didn't return until three in the morning. Occasionally he encountered British police, but they did not even give him a second glance.

Begin agreed to place his men under *Haganah* operative orders, though they maintained their own command structure, weapons, and strongholds. The British were still in the country, so Begin and his men were still classified as wanted by the law-enforcement agencies. But no one was really interested in him any longer. Thus the IZL was free to consolidate in the areas where it felt at home—the poorer suburbs of the main cities—and which were mostly close to Arab areas from which snipers were constantly operating.

On April 25 the IZL opened an offensive against Jaffa, which bordered on southern Tel Aviv. Though they still lacked the experience, this was clearly a large-scale military mission, aided by the results of IZL raids on an ammunition train and a British arsenal a few days previously. The day before their offensive began, Begin appeared in person before the men who were to take part, most of whom were seeing him for the first time. It was still risky, but this after all was their first overt operation—and to hell with the British.

With the experience at Dir Yassin still in their minds, IZL mortars bombarded Jaffa for five solid days. Despite the softening up, Arab resistance was stiff and the IZL had a tough time breaking through to the shoreline to complete the first stage. Meanwhile the British, harassed by Arab accusations of pro-Jewish bias, moved tanks and infantry into the city and threatened a bombardment of the attacking forces.

Begin was observing the campaign from advanced headquarters in an abandoned schoolhouse. His sober mood was lightened by the addition of newborn Leah to his family. The baby, born on February 22, three months before, was named after his wife's sister, killed by the Nazis. Begin saw IZL dead and wounded being brought back, and had ample opportunity to realize that overt war was totally different from what they had been doing before. On the first day the IZL assaults were thrown back by Arab defenders, and his men began to doubt their ability to take the city. However, for Begin, success was essential. Not only had the IZL decided to free Tel Aviv from constant harassment by Arab snipers in the neighboring city, but Jaffa also represented anathema to Begin's philosophy. The Arab city had been allotted to the Arabs under the partition plan. To him that fact posed a constant threat to the heartland of the Jewish State. Although the *Haganah* was also mopping up nests of snipers and Arab armed gangs around the outskirts of Tel Aviv, the official attitude was still one of not violating the UN-drawn borders; unpalatable as they might be, the Jewish Agency was still prepared to accept them as a necessary evil. The IZL, on the other hand, was eager for conquests beyond the frontiers they did not accept.

The IZL failure was making triumphant headlines in the Jewish press, and *Haganah* was hinting that it might need to restrain the dissidents. For Begin, this was rubbing salt into gaping wounds. But he was not yet ready to give up the attempt. He knew that the *Haganah* operations around Tel Aviv would hamper the movement of Arab reinforcements to Jaffa, forcing the inhabitants to fall back on their own resources and whatever help they might get from the British garrison. The second day was also not particularly successful. Begin resolved to hold the lines as they were, without any further futile assaults. Paglin, however, had other ideas and managed to convince his commander to extend the battle for one more day. They were able to fight through to the beach, cutting off the Manshiah Quarter that separated the two cities.

At this stage the British did intervene. The result was a standoff, with the upper hand, if any, being held by the IZL. Under the terms of a compromise agreement the *Haganah* took over the IZL forward positions and kept the peace together with the men of a Scottish regiment. But within three weeks it became evident that the Arabs of Jaffa, having heard who the assailant was, had opted to abandon the town. The IZL had lost 42 men and 400 were wounded; the Arab population had dwindled from 70,000 to 3,000. The IZL's three days opened an argument over refugee property and refugee rights to return home that has persisted for three decades—so far.

On May 14, 1948, the British departed from Palestine, leaving behind the graves of 338 civilians, policemen, and soldiers, who had been killed since the end of World War II.

On May 15, as the Arab regular armies crossed the frontiers, the *Haganah* and *Palmach* moved to meet them. Clearly the IZL would be involved sooner or later, although the prevailing atmosphere between IZL and the Provisional Government of Israel was one of mutual suspicion. As far as Begin was concerned, there was a common enemy. That was more important than any internecine rivalry. Therefore it was without any hesitation that he placed IZL under the command of the newborn Israel Defense Forces.

Unlike other underground and guerrilla leaders around the world, Begin emerged into a society in which he had no place in the new government. To most he was still the leader of an extremist renegade faction—the representative of the Revisionist movement, with all its unpleasant connotations. Many even had the impression that his role in events was over, that he would emerge from underground anonymity into the public anonymity of a man whose share in history belonged to the past. Begin himself, on the night of May 17, 1977, was to say that the underground and the rise of the State of Israel were the greatest hours of his life. Perhaps he felt that more strongly than anyone else, but certainly the thirty years in between would not destine him to a vacuum of anonymity.

CHAPTER 18

The "Sacred Howitzer"

The ship was bought by the IZL in the spring of 1948 for $131,000, and promptly renamed *Altalena,* Zeev Jabotinsky's pen name. The IZL originally intended to use it to transport Jewish immigrants from America and Europe—men who would take part in the war to defend the homeland. That plan changed as a result of some unexpected events.

IZL agents had been active in Europe since the beginning of the campaign against the British, seeking weapons wherever they could be purchased. Their sources ranged from semi-official to anarchist and Communist groups. But, that spring of 1948, they suddenly found that large quantities of weapons at a reasonable price were available from an unexpected source: the government of France. Nobody quite knows to this day why Georges Bidault, the Foreign Minister of France, was so willing to supply the IZL with arms—which, ironically, were taken from British army surpluses stored in French warehouses. Perhaps he thought to restore French influence in the Middle East through the back door; or maybe as a Christian Democrat he was impressed by IZL assurances that no harm would come to the French religious institutions in Palestine. Bidault, a friend of England, had never particularly liked Jews or Zionism; yet he instructed the French General Staff to hand over equipment valued at $5 million.

With the Arab armies knocking on the doors of Jerusalem and Tel Aviv, the thousands of rifles, machine guns, mortars, and ammunition crates could well be a decisive factor. Indeed, as the IZL completed its negotiations and began to load the *Altalena,* with French help, the Egyptian army was deployed a mere 25 miles from Tel Aviv and the future of the fledgling State already in doubt. Under the auspices of the United Nations a truce was declared. The terms of the truce allowed no importation of armaments— even had there been sources willing to supply the young State. Nevertheless Ben-Gurion understood that without weapons and ammunition Israel could not withstand the onslaught for any extended period of time. The best and most experienced men were scouring the world for weapons, in the knowledge that the survival of Israel was dependent on their success. Some guns were getting through, under the noses of the UN truce supervisors, but it was still only a trickle.

The *Altalena,* with her virtually priceless cargo, sailed for Israel at 20:30 hours on June 11, 1948. There were two problems still ahead: how to run the gauntlet of watchful eyes on the Mediterranean; and to whom to deliver the cargo should the *Altalena* succeed in getting through. The shipment included 5,000 rifles, 3 million bullets, 250 Bern submachine guns, 250 Sten guns, 50 artillery pieces, 5,000 shell artillery, 150 Spandau machine guns, and additional explosives.

Eliahu Lankin, a veteran IZL member, was responsible not only for the 1,820-ton landing craft and its military cargo but also for 940 *Betar* members and IZL sympathizers on their way to fight in the war. The captain, passengers, and cargo were all IZL "property." Yet the IZL no longer existed formally.

Although Menachem Begin had responded to Ben-Gurion's call to disband the IZL immediately upon the Arab invasion, on the grounds that a sovereign State could not tolerate private armies or afford to divide its military resources, he did not renounce his right to fight against the partition boundaries, which he believed a victorious Israeli army would in any case cross. As the *Altalena* approached Israeli shores, Begin was in the paradoxical situation of being the head of an organization that did not exist. According to the agreement for dissolution of the IZL, its headquarters staff were temporarily supervising the orderly enlistment of IZL personnel into the Israel Defense Forces, along with their weapons and equipment. The job was to be completed within one month. But the IZL and *Lehi* did have a separate and independent existence in Jerusalem which, according to the partition decision, was not a part of Israel but an international city and therefore did not fall within the jurisdiction of Begin's agreement.

Begin's parting from his senior officers—some he knew personally, and others he had heard of but never met, but all were members of his "fighting family"—was alike sad and happy. Sad, because they were breaking up, and most of the members of the organization would be joining an army composed of the old enemies from Operation Season and countless other clashes. But happy because after all the objective of ridding Palestine of the British and securing Jewish independence had been achieved— and because he had been assured that his men would remain together in special units; their officers would be drawn from *Haganah* and *Palmach,* but they would be among friends.

As part of the agreement the IZL was to discontinue its separate procurement efforts, and to place its contacts at the disposal of the official emissaries of the State—who were aware of the *Altalena* and her cargo. Begin himself did not know that the *Altalena* was sailing until she was already at sea, and then he began to worry that the IZL would be accused of violating the truce. His assistants tried a number of times to make contact with the vessel in an attempt to delay the voyage. Meanwhile during the night of June 15 Begin sent an urgent invitation to Ben-Gurion's two assistants, Levi Eshkol and Yisrael Galili, to come to his temporary headquarters, where he told them about the ship. The two men demanded that a message be sent to delay the *Altalena* until a decision could be taken on whether to risk a truce violation by unloading the cargo. Eshkol and Galili then reported the conversation to Ben-Gurion. Next morning Galili contacted Begin again to tell him that the ship could come and should do so as quickly as possible.

While IZL radio operators still tried to contact the ship, Begin talked to Galili about the weapons, demanding that 20 percent be turned over to his men in Jerusalem. Galili did not object. But Begin was not finished yet: he also wanted first priority on the remainder for those battalions of the army where his men were now serving. This Galili immediately rejected, saying that the load would be turned over to the Defense Ministry and General Staff, and it was up to them to decide on the allocation.

"The Ministry of Defense will pay you for it," he assured Begin.

"We don't want a penny. The weapons are dedicated to this war, but I do have the right to see that our men serving in the army will get them. Look at it this way, Galili, if the ship had come in a few weeks ago, all the weapons would have been given to our people—and you wouldn't have objected to them arriving in the army properly equipped, so why object now?"

"In that event," said Galili, "we will not be able to help you unload the ship."

That conversation is still subject to conflicting interpretations, with one side arguing that Menachem Begin wanted to create a private army within the Israel Defense Forces (IDF), and the other insisting that the accusation was the result of traditional enmity rather than of established fact. It has further been suggested that Ben-Gurion was never given the full details by his two assistants; since he always refused point blank to meet Begin, this could well be at the root of the misunderstanding. However there can be no question about the fact that members of Begin's staff urged him not to give in easily, and that they were suspicious of the national leadership under Ben-Gurion, which could be expected to compromise with the Arabs as to the basis of the partition borders.

In any case on the night of Friday, June 18, there

was a degree of uncertainty about the army's willingness to help unload the *Altalena*. On the one hand Galili had categorically refused, while on the other hand an army liaison officer attached to Begin's headquarters said that the IZL could expect assistance. To be on the safe side, they set about recruiting every available IZL supporter to give a helping hand.

On Saturday the ship was offshore, but things were still uncertain. Begin's most recent offer was to store the weapons in an IZL warehouse under a joint IDF-IZL guard—but that too had been rejected by the Ministry of Defense. Amihai Paglin demanded that the entire cargo be unloaded by members of the IZL, for their own use, and without assistance from the army.

The *Altalena* groped through total darkness to drop anchor at 03:00 hours 40 yards away from a jetty at Kfar Vitkin, north of Tel Aviv. Meanwhile Galili had reported to the General Staff on the latest developments. Yigael Yadin, Director of Operations and acting Chief of Staff (Dori, the Chief of Staff, was seriously ill) sent a staff officer to the beach to ascertain Begin's intentions. On the way there he passed through IZL roadblocks, manned by men whom his companions identified as IDF soldiers, who had apparently taken "leave" to help their old organization unload the boat. At Kfar Vitkin beach the officer met Paglin and told him that he had come to invite Begin to a meeting with Galili in a nearby army camp. Paglin's reply was that if Galili wanted to see Begin, he could come to the beach. The officer could see IZL men obviously armed with weapons straight off the ship. They seemed tense and Paglin himself appeared to be wary of a trap. When Paglin again refused to call Begin to a meeting, the officer left to report to Galili. A directive was promptly issued to Major General Dan Even, the area commander, to deliver an ultimatum to IZL:

By special order of the Chief of Staff of the IDF, I order the confiscation of all weapons and war materials that have arrived on the shores of Israel in the area of my jurisdiction, and their immediate placing at the disposal of the State of Israel. I have been instructed to demand of you all the weapons that have come ashore, to place them in my safekeeping, and to inform you that you must contact the High Command. You are required to carry out this order immediately. If you do not agree to do so, I will immediately use all the means at my disposal to implement the order. I hereby inform you that the entire area is surrounded by army units and the roads are blocked. The complete responsibility for the results, in the event of a refusal to comply with this order, is yours. You have ten minutes in which to reply.

Begin did not take the ultimatum seriously. According to one version, he demanded that General Even come to him on the beach under a white flag. Begin's refusal to comply with the ultimatum only served to strengthen the suspicions as to the IZL motives. He later argued that he had been taken in by a government trick, since no one had told him in advance not to bring the ship to shore. He had, in fact, been led to understand that she must arrive as soon as was humanly possible. Moreover, he repeatedly insisted, he had never intended to bring the weapons ashore against a government directive and army orders. Opponents of Begin reply that when given army orders, he disobeyed them.

Galili was in no hurry to carry out the orders. Instead he sent Mayor Oved Ben Ami of Natania, an IZL sympathizer, to persuade Begin not to risk confrontation with the government and army. But Ben Ami was no luckier than his predecessor. Ben-Gurion, who was being kept up to date on events, then ruled that there could be no compromise: either the IZL must obey orders or all available force was to be used. The days of negotiating agreements with Menachem Begin were over, he said.

On the beach at Kfar Vitkin the atmosphere was one of approaching civil war. Some of the IZL army recruits had deserted their units so as to reach the boat. Those who had not deserted were placed in detention and disarmed. Major General Yitzhak Sedeh, commander of the *Palmach*, order Lieutenant Colonel Moshe Dayan to take his battalion to Kfar Vitkin. Dayan broke through an IZL roadblock, then handed over command to his deputy, using the excuse that he had to attend a funeral. On the seaward side Israeli naval craft were closing in on the *Altalena*.

Most of the passengers were already ashore. Still on board were the crew and a number of passengers who had volunteered to help with the unloading of cargo. Begin came aboard, and was delighted to find his old friend Eliahu Lankin, who had been sent to a detention camp in Africa during Operation Season. On shore, Paglin concluded that there was no hope of getting the weapons and transferring them to an IZL storehouse, so he ordered a boat that had just come in with a fresh load of ammunition to return to the *Altalena*. Minutes later Begin radioed from the ship.

"What's going on there?"

"We have very serious problems. I'm returning the weapons to the ship."

"Hold on. I'm coming back."

On shore once more Begin listened to Paglin's reasoning and rejected it. He was not afraid of the army of Israel, but only that the UN would be alerted to a ship unloading weapons. He could not believe that the Israeli army would present a real danger.

"Do you really think that Jews will open fire on us?"

"I suggest that you let me go on board with the men and weapons, and that we sail out of here. Then we'll see. When the truce is over, we can decide where to land. Maybe I'll decide on Gaza. If I do, I'll let you know."

"Leave it as it is," Begin said. "I'm afraid you're just tired. No one is going to fire at us."

"If you don't agree, then you must relieve me of the job"

This was their first serious disagreement after years of close cooperation and trust, but Paglin was convinced that Begin's judgment was wrong this time. Begin promptly summoned Yaakov Meridor from the *Altalena* to take command on the beach, and sent Paglin off with a suggestion that he catch up on lost sleep. But Meridor's assessment was similar to that of Paglin, and he ended up by virtually ordering Begin off the beach and onto the *Altalena*—with the understanding that the ship would sail to Tel Aviv, where the presence of IZL members and sympathizers would make the army think twice about firing on the beach crew.

Begin was about to thank his men for their efforts when Paglin's prediction came true: IDF machine guns opened fire. Begin was unceremoniously shoved into a launch, protesting about the interruption of his speech. According to one version he was actually carried bodily onto the boat. As the launch headed for the *Altalena,* the two Israel navy corvettes offshore opened fire. Captain Fein, an American Jewish naval officer, upped anchor, maneuvered to protect the launch, took the occupants aboard, then sped southward. The corvettes signaled the *Altalena* to change course westward and out of Israeli territorial waters; but, as Fein ignored them, they dropped astern, unable to match the speed of the newer craft.

The fledgling Israel air force also flew sorties over the *Altalena,* but the pilots, including IZL sympathizer Ezer Weizman, were reluctant to attack. Meanwhile on Kfar Vitkin beach the two sides were counting their casualties. The IZL had suffered six dead, and the army of Israel lost two men.

The *Altalena* cruised past the Tel Aviv harbor, and ran aground facing the main swimming beach—a few hundred yards from the Kaete Dan Hotel, which housed UN headquarters. Here Begin could assume that the government of Israel would not dare take action against them, in full view of the largest Jewish city in the country. And he presumed the United Nations already knew about the *Altalena* and her cargo. As dawn rose over Tel Aviv, the rumor spread like wildfire and crowds poured down to the beach to see for themselves. Meanwhile IZL members serving in the army were deserting their posts in droves, on the assumption that they might be needed if an attempt was made to stop the unloading by force. Some of them swam or rowed out to the ship, and others lined the beach. The message was clear: Tel Aviv beach was in IZL hands.

Early in the morning the operations officer of the Israel navy was summoned to Ben-Gurion, who wanted to hear the officer's suggestions on how to get the *Altalena* under control at once. But none of them was acceptable, because none met Ben-Gurion's prime criterion of "immediately." He was afraid that any delay could mean civil war. With their external enemies, they didn't need any new problems. Ben-Gurion then ordered General Yadin, the acting Chief of Staff, to bring enough military strength into the city to force an unconditional surrender of the *Altalena*. Next he summoned an urgent cabinet meeting, and told his colleagues: "It's an attempt to run over the army and murder the State." The religious members of his coalition were shocked that Jew had fired on Jew at Kfar Vitkin, and that both sides had sustained losses; now they wanted him to avoid bloodshed at any cost, even at the price of compromise with the IZL. Ben-Gurion was adamant. If the IZL surrendered unconditionally, he would be prepared to forget the whole business and waive any criminal proceedings. If not, then the army would be ordered to act fast. Ben-Gurion's stand was voted on and approved by the majority of the Provisional Government, with the religious ministers voting against. Ben-Gurion immediately ordered the army to carry out the government's decision.

The only unit on the spot consisted of *Palmach* headquarters staff, who were located in the Ritz Hotel facing the *Altalena*. While the handful of staff officers and clerks drew weapons and hand grenades, reinforcements from the *Palmach* Yiftach and Negev brigades, and a company from Carmeli Brigade, were rushing into the city. The *Palmach* units attempted to block IZL supporters who were moving through the streets toward the beach, where the two sides were clashing. At this point, however, the government forces were too few. Obviously in the long run the army would win, but most of its units were deployed along the truce lines and engaged in training a considerable distance from Tel Aviv. The *Altalena*, meanwhile, lowered a launch full of men and weapons. Then the balance began to change as army units from nearby camps, and soldiers in Tel Aviv on furlough, moved onto the beach.

The street clashes were turning into a shooting war although no one really knows who fired the first shot. The IZL was not aware of it, but the *Palmach* unit at the Ritz Hotel, commanded personally by Yigal Allon, the senior officer of the *Palmach*, was cut off, and the entire city could have fallen into IZL hands. Even though small arms fire was hampering the unloading of the *Altalena*, the sight of heavy machine guns being mounted on deck, pointing at the Ritz, prompted Allon to ask for artillery support. His own weapons could rake the decks of the ship, but were powerless against the IZL men on the blind side of the hotel. As the first boat from the ship was making its way to the beach, a young *Palmach* officer threw a hand grenade in the direction of the IZL men. His name was Yitzhak Rabin.

While Begin and Fein were sweating out the action on Tel Aviv beach, Amihai Paglin was planning to capture the seat of government in Ramat Gan, just outside Tel Aviv. With another IZL officer he started out from Natania to Tel Aviv in a taxi. But just outside the town an armored car pulled alongside the taxi and ordered it to halt. Paglin was detained by the IDF. Although he made a number of attempts to escape, when he finally succeeded, it was too late to be of any help to the *Altalena*—or to be any threat to the legally constituted government of Israel.

Allon had to wait for the covering gunfire. The few howitzers that the IDF possessed were all located close to the front line, for use against the Arab armies. Finally one was turned round and brought into range. Allon had meanwhile agreed to a forty-five-minute cease-fire to evacuate the wounded—and a delegation headed by Tel Aviv Mayor Rokach was trying to convince Ben-Gurion to declare a truce. But at 16:00 hours, shortly after the cease-fire was to have taken effect, shellfire began to rake the *Altalena*. The second shell, intended as a warning, instead of harmlessly falling into the water plowed through the deck of the ship, exploding among ammunition cases in the hold. IZL claimed that the *Palmach* forces were trying to kill Begin, who was aboard the ship. Fein and his first mate raced to activate sprinkler systems, then returned to the bridge. As captain Fein was ready to raise a white flag, for he knew that otherwise they would lose everything—ship, cargo, and crew. Begin was opposed to this, but Fein ordered his radio operator to stop him from interfering. The white flag fluttered overhead. Although Begin continued to demand that it be taken down. Fein's first concern now was for the wounded, and he was not interested in the IZL leader's orders. Begin was pinned down to the deck, the radio operator's knee firmly in the small of his back. The captain ordered the crew to abandon ship. When only seven men were left, Fein and Lankin turned to Begin and ordered him overboard. Begin refused, insisting that he would be the last man off. Without any further ceremony Fein told two seamen to lower Begin into a raft.

On shore the main effort was directed to helping the wounded. The exchange of fire, and the direct hit on the *Altalena*, now covered in black smoke and reeling from a chain of explosions, had cost the IZL fourteen dead and sixty-nine wounded.

Throughout the rest of that day and night the security forces rounded up all the IZL men they could catch in the Tel Aviv area. That evening Begin himself in a choked voice, almost sobbing, broadcast over the IZL radio. His speech was a long account of the *Altalena* affair, starting with the need for the weapons, and ending with a chain of accusations of bad faith against the government and its representatives. Finally, in broken tones, Begin issued a plea to stop the war of brother on brother. Claiming that he was not certain of his ability to restrain his own men, he begged the public to support the effort. As he finished, still facing the open microphone, he burst into tears. What he said sounded like the obituary of the IZL, but the tone of his speech would prompt his opponents in the years to come to refer to Begin as a "hysterical demagogue." Menachem Begin would write years later: "Let them ridicule me. I know that there are tears that no man, even a hard fighter, should feel ashamed about. A tear comes not only from the eye. Sometimes—like blood—it comes from out of the heart . . ."

338

One week later the Provisional State Council—forerunner of the elected Knesset—convened in Tel Aviv. Representatives of the moderate right wing condemned the handling of the *Altalena* affair, claiming that compromise had been possible. Ben-Gurion responded in a fury that if the *Altalena* had not been destroyed, she would have destroyed Israel. There was no place for private armies and armories in a sovereign State, he said.

The question as to whether Begin really intended the weapons for the IZL has never been resolved. More and more Israelis tend to believe that he did not plan to take them because, much as he disliked the existing leadership, he recognized its legality. If, on the other hand, he did insist at Kfar Vitkin, and in his earlier talks with Galili, on transferring part of the weapons to IZL warehouses, it was not just in response to pressure from extremists in his own circle but more importantly because both he and they were still imbued with the underground mentality.

Ben-Gurion's attitude and his instructions to open fire if necessary must certainly have been prompted by the traditional hatreds between the camps—hatreds which, ever since the Arlosorov murder, had led members of the Zionist left to believe that the Revisionists were only biding their time before attempting to seize power by nondemocratic means. And the *Altalena* certainly seemed to be the harbinger of the moment for which they had waited. Afterwards Begin's parliamentary opponents always knew that the mere mention of the *Altalena* could divert Begin's attention from the business of the day while he again heatedly defended his version. Years after the tragedy Begin related that one of Ben-Gurion's close friends had told him: "My conclusion is that Ben-Gurion was intentionally misled in the *Altalena* affair . . ." He would not disclose the man's name. But Ben-Gurion never showed any signs of regret about the affair that caused the death of sixteen IZL men. He even said that the old howitzer which was used to fire on the *Altalena* "should be placed in the Temple." It is still referred to as the "Sacred Howitzer."

The sinking of the *Altalena* marked the end of the IZL. But Menachem Begin, whose eyes had for some months been on politics, moved on to take charge of the *Herut* (Freedom) Party, the founding members of which were his old comrades of IZL.

CHAPTER 19

Day of Fury

Shortly after emerging from underground, Menachem Begin told an Italian newspaper that he wanted to cease public activity and deal with his own affairs, perhaps even as an attorney. He may have honestly meant it, but in retrospect the years in IZL were unquestionably long strides down the path that led to politics. The transition was only natural. After all, few underground leaders have turned their backs on politics after independence was achieved—and the IZL's anti-British activity was in effect a forerunner of active Revisionist policies by other means after the British left Palestine.

However the Revisionist movement after the declaration of revolt, in 1944, was not what it had been before. At the beginning it seemed that it was merely a legitimate facade for the activities of IZL. Under Menachem Begin, the IZL had drifted farther away from the movement that was its political parent and spokesman. Begin applied his own political judgment

341

to IZL strategy, mostly in consultation with his own staff, all of whom were more concerned with operative aspects. The IZL attitude was that the degree of adherence to Jabotinsky's teaching could be measured only by the degree of willingness to fight against the British. Paradoxically the IZL leaders could with ample justification answer the Revisionist politicians' contention that political activity was the only legitimate course, with the argument that they were still living in Jabotinsky's era and believing—as he did —that Jewish independence was dependent on British goodwill.

When the State of Israel came into being, Begin was the recognized leader of the Jabotinsky camp, in addition to which he could—unlike the Revisionist legalists—bask in the glory of a freedom fighter. The Revisionist Party was small, very introverted, and mostly composed of old-timers who were still adhering to the past as if nothing had changed.

In a broadcast given over IZL radio on the day the State was founded, May 15, 1948, Begin praised his own organization for its stubborn stand against the British régime just ended, while implying that the struggle would now move into political channels. He also spoke on foreign affairs:

We must foster relationships of friendship and understanding with the great American nation. We must foster relationships of friendship and understanding with the peoples of the Soviet Union. Let us not conceal the truth. In the past there were hostile relations between the country of revolution and the liberation movement of the Jewish people. Those relations cost our people blood and tears. But, following the heroic war of the Hebrew underground, a revolutionary change has taken place in these relations. The Soviet Union recognized our right to sovereignty and independence in our homeland. And we will never forget that the victorious Russian army saved hundreds of thousands of Jews from the claws of the Nazi predators.

Begin then cited the need to protect democracy and to concentrate efforts on increasing immigration without consideration for the country's capacity to absorb large waves of immigrants. He said nothing about any move to politicize the organization that had emerged one day earlier from the underground, yet it was self-evident. In fact discussions had begun within the IZL staff immediately after the UN decision of November 29, 1947. Having fought the British, the IZL would go on to fight partition—it being obvious that the leadership of the Jewish community was ready to accept a divided homeland without protest.

Haim Landau—Begin's close associate in IZL and later a minister in his government—said many years afterward that had it not been for the partition decision, Begin would quite probably not have rushed into politics, and IZL would have disbanded on the day the State of Israel came into being. Some of its leaders, including Begin, would probably have settled down to relatively passive roles among the rank and file of the Revisionist Party.

The *Altalena* incident might have added impetus to the process. Begin and his comrades were learning once again that their socialist opponents were in control of all the institutions of the new State, and that the trades union had become of decisive influence in public and social affairs. Begin's close associates are also convinced that he was afraid the IZL's part in winning Jewish independence would be forgotten. Not that this was a conclusive factor, yet it was a consideration in pushing Begin into politics. Indeed it seems that he clung to the underground era as something valuable, to hang onto forever. He said as much in his 1977 election night speech, when he noted that it was the highlight of his life.

Others believe that he was motivated by a genuine concern for his men, who were emerging into a world controlled by their enemies. The men at the top of the army had commanded Operation Season, and the heads of the Jewish Agency were now ministers of the government of Israel. Particularly after the *Altalena* incident, Begin felt a compulsion to create for his comrades a seat of power on the political map.

All these factors were instrumental in his creation of the *Herut* Party, which offered itself at the elections to the first Knesset in 1949. True to its IZL ethic, *Herut* adopted as its own the insignia of a complete land of Israel on both sides of the Jordan, and placed that concept in top place on its election platform. This was the issue on which the party fought its first election. But as time went by, moderation set in to the point where they talked only of conquering the West Bank and Gaza, and of stationing the army of Israel on the Jordan River.

From its very inception *Herut,* in keeping with its Revisionist background, favored a somewhat conservative liberalism in social and economic policy. The platform included principles accepted in the modern welfare state: national health insurance, guaranteed right to work, guaranteed minimal education —and equal rights for the country's minorities, including the right to an independent educational system, as well as complete freedom of religion and culture. Contrary to the secularism of Jabotinsky and veteran Revisionists, Begin has always favored a religious viewpoint to the point of constantly opposing the separation of "religion and state."

Experienced adversaries could find in Begin's political program plentiful evidence of political semantics: the use of fine words to support concepts that would hardly invite opposition, yet were unattainable in practice; for example, preservation of friendly relations with every country in the world. Nobody would disagree with that, but no one knows how to achieve it in the modern polarized world. In other words his opponents were at liberty to accuse Begin and his program of promoting high-sounding concepts without the practical means of achieving these principles.

The most controversial demand in the program was for continued war until the entire "Land of Israel" was liberated. The vast majority in Israel were more concerned about survival than about expansion beyond the frontiers as they were in 1949. During the course of the War of Independence, however, the partition picture had changed drastically. After the initial Arab invasion, the Israel Defense Forces began to repel the invaders and almost inevitably crossed the frontiers to do it. Thereby the authorities were in part following Begin's policy, though out of necessity rather than conviction.

The political map of Israel showed a heavy preponderance of power on the left, both in the ruling Mapai Party and in the more extreme Mapam, which would later merge into the Labor alignment. And the power was not solely electoral. The General Federation of Labor, or *Histadrut,* possessed a sphere of influence that included centers of economic strength, both in agriculture and industry, and of social importance, such as pension and insurance funds—and, as a result of circumstances, the General Sick Fund. Historically these, together with an extensive cooperative consumer movement in production and services, had originated in the needs of settling a desolate land with no other organized bodies that could take responsibility for pioneering both economically and socially. Given this highly developed infrastructure, it was not surprising that the new immigrants arriving after the War of Independence should gravitate toward the labor camp, which could provide both productive work and social security. In fact, without the *Histadrut* and what it represented, the new government of Israel would have been faced with a totally insurmountable task.

This then was the political constellation against which Begin intended to do electoral battle. In addition his *Herut* Party was but one faction of revisionism, the original party being far from ready to recognize the leadership of the IZL "fighting family," as Begin persisted in calling them. Nevertheless he expected to receive 30 to 40 percent of the votes cast at Israel's first election, on January 25, 1949, and this primarily as a result of his own oratorical talents.

He did indeed know how to captivate an audience. It has been said of Begin's speeches that he needs the contact with his listeners, for his delivery depends both on accompanying gestures and inflections of tone. His newspaper articles, for example, are deemed by many to be boring diatribes, even though the words and phrases differ in no way from his speeches.

Begin's first public rally—held in Zion Square, Jerusalem, in August 1948—drew crowds, some of whom came out of curiosity to see the ex-underground leader. In that speech he promised that the IZL, which still existed in Jerusalem, would continue to fight against the UN decision to internationalize the city, and for its unification as the capital of Israel.

His next appearance, in an open-air movie house in Tel Aviv, gave rise to comparisons with Jabotinsky. Those who had heard the Revisionist leader in person claimed that Begin was an imitator, though more emotional than his teacher. It often seemed that he was excited by the sound of his own words, and that he believed in their power to change reality.

Tens of thousands heard him, but nothing he said could change the political realities, which predated independence. The traditional hatred for the Jabotinsky camp was now transferred to Begin. Veteran settlers in the country still remembered the split in the Zionist movement when Jabotinsky had declared the independence of his faction; and many people still recalled with pain the killing of Arlosorov, which had given the Revisionist Party the status of an outcast. The younger members of the community were very much aware of the IZL's refusal to accept the authority of democratically elected institutions. And over all of them lingered the memory of various operations such as the King David Hotel, the hanging of the sergeants, Dir Yassin, *Altalena,* and others. Most believed without any question Ben-Gurion's version that the IZL had brought a cargo of arms on the *Altalena* with the express objective of rebellion against the government. None of this fitted into the image of political leadership that the majority of Israeli electors had in mind as they embarked on their first steps as a sovereign democracy.

Herut came out of the election with 11.5 percent of the popular vote, and 14 members in the 120-seat Knesset. The bulk of these votes came from the families of IZL members and from Oriental communities in the suburbs of the big cities. The results were disappointing to Begin. Nevertheless the party's newspaper published a brief statement on the day after the election: "The will of the majority, even if they be mistaken, is decisive. This is democracy, and we shall honor the will of the majority and of the régime. However, we demand that the majority also respect the will of the minority and the opposition."

Begin could, and did, find consolation in the fact that the vote in army polling stations showed a higher pro-*Herut* percentage than did the overall national figures—a proof, as he frequently remarked with pride, that the youth could understand his policy and respect his past performance.

The traditional Revisionist Party, which contested the election on a separate ticket, did not win a single seat. Its members accepted the verdict and merged with *Herut*. However the new party was showing signs that election defeat was influencing its internal affairs. Though IZL traditions still prevailed on some members to refer to Begin as "the commander," he was subject to the political pressures of others. Nobody disputed his leadership, yet the first signs of splits were evident. The parliamentary party was not entirely composed of IZL members. Alongside Begin and Haim Landau were men such as Hillel Kook, who had been for years on IZL missions in the United States; Uri Zvi Grinberg, poet and nationalist mystic, who supported the organization but never fought; and Ari Jabotinsky, son of the late leader, who had ceased to be active in IZL when Begin took command. Perhaps understandably, there was a distinct correlation between past distance from the IZL high command and present lack of common language with its commander. Some of *Herut*'s parliamentary representatives were pressing for union with the middle-of-the-road General Zionist Party. Others insisted that the future lay in *Herut* pentration of the *Histadrut*. Ari Jabotinsky consistently opposed Begin's religious orientations; as his father's son, he could not support the unification of organized religion and state. Grinberg was running his own maverick course as ardent crusader for immediate war to conquer the entire Land of Israel on both banks of the Jordan, and to drive the Arabs out of Jerusalem.

But for Begin's vigorous leadership, the *Herut* Party might have been doomed to immediate factionalization. Some of its members did desert the ranks, but the desertions only strengthened Begin's control to the point where—with the dissenting voices no longer on the inside—Menachem Begin and *Herut* became synonomous. Within the parliamentary party, and the institutions of *Herut*, many were willing to accept Begin's opinions as rulings of "the commander." He consulted only with his close associates from the IZL, whom he still addressed by their underground code names. Indeed with some of them, such as Haim Landau and Amihai Paglin, he still does.

Paglin, who had always been more extreme than Begin and never ready to accept the latter's restraint in circumstances such as Operation Season, was one of the few IZL officers who did not find a place in *Herut*. Begin sent him abroad on various missions and gradually shunted him aside into insignificant jobs. Paglin, who understood little of politics, finally terminated his formal membership in the party.

Though Begin's political opponents in the Knesset were primarily pragmatic politicians with long records of deeds, and though they disagreed with almost everything that the "Fascist demagogue"—as he was sometimes called by his opponents in the heat of debate—had to say, they listened to his speeches out of sheer fascination with his rhetorical talents and power. In the Knesset he convinced nobody who was not ready to be convinced. Outside those walls his performance was a different matter.

The question of whether or not to accept reparations from the German government for damage done to Jewish lives and property during the Hitler period became a major national debate. The German Reparations Agreement was to be a turning point in the history of Israel, both economically and socially. It was also indisputably a factor in pushing Menachem Begin even further out into political isolation, where he was less well placed to seize power and where his opponents could use the issue against him.

On January 7, 1952, few people were out in the Jerusalem streets, and, apart from the eternally curious, all steered well clear of the temporary home of the Knesset, a building that belonged to a bank. The surrounding area was ringed with barbed wire and cordoned off by a human wall of hundreds of policemen armed with nightsticks and tear gas grenades. The only people allowed through the barriers were

Knesset members and employees and a few hardy newspapermen.

The trouble had begun a few months earlier. Waves of mass immigration, shortages in natural resources, and an underdeveloped industry had brought Israel to an intolerable economic situation. In fact, after four years of independence, the young State was on the verge of financial bankruptcy and collapse—and the $65 million aid from the United States was too little to buy time for urgently needed development.

All kinds of proposals had been brought to the government of Israel, but none contained feasible or attainable solutions to the problem. Then Treasury Director General David Horowitz suggested that Israel should demand from the Federal Republic of Germany reparation for Jewish lives and property lost during the Nazi period. It seemed a useless proposal.

Israel's boycott of Germany was so total that Israeli passports were stamped: "Good for all countries except GERMANY." But Foreign Minister Moshe Sharett was finally persuaded to go along with the idea. Working in absolute secrecy, Horowitz's economists in the Ministry of Finance prepared the groundwork for discussion. Early in 1951 a demand for financial reparations was submitted to the Four Power Commission that virtually controlled Germany, but they rejected it as not being their business. With no alternative, and with distinct misgivings, the Israeli government redirected the request to Chancellor Konrad Adenauer.

Adenauer pounced on the Israeli application as if it were manna from heaven. Germany was still far from reinstatement in the family of man, quite apart from her needs for the kind of outlets that would foster her own economic rebirth. A gesture to Israel could help the rehabilitation of Germany in both contexts. David Ben-Gurion was also well aware that in accepting reparations, he would be helping to reinstate the "enemies of humankind." Although he insisted to Begin and his supporters that he hated the Germans no less than they did, there was a strong streak of pragmatism in the first prime minister of Israel. His primary task was to consolidate the State of Israel and, without Germany, it now appeared to Ben-Gurion to be an impossible one.

The news—when it broke—caused deep shock waves and consternation in a country where many citizens were survivors of the Holocaust and has lost kin in the Nazi gas ovens. The protests against Ben-Gurion's move went far beyond the bounds of parliamentary opposition led by Begin. There were strong, almost overpowering, emotional overtones. Apart from Communists, orthodox religious circles, and Begin, Ben-Gurion had to contend with opposition from within his own party. Against a storm of fury he proclaimed: "We must take care of our people, and what is more just than that we should be able to rehabilitate them and erect for them a home with the monies of those who bear moral responsibility for the loss of their property in Europe?"

Begin and the *Herut* Party set to work with a will to defeat the move to approve reparations from Germany. For the first time since his emergence from underground, Begin succeeded in rallying to his flag people who had no association with his camp or politics. Others were organizing demonstrations, but this occasion seemed almost tailormade for Begin's emotional oratory. He appealed to the Israelis' honor and pride, reaching deep inside troubled souls that needed little persuasion.

"If negotiation with Germany can happen, then anything is permissible in the State of Israel," Begin cried, speaking at a meeting held in a central square in Tel Aviv two days before the Knesset was to convene to ratify the reparations agreement. From the quietness of the crowd there was no indication of what would happen two days later in Jerusalem.

The Knesset convened in the knowledge that West Germany had already allocated $1 billion to Israel, apart from personal compensation to be paid directly to the survivors of the Holocaust. Feelings were running high enough to cause the recall of members from trips abroad for the controversial vote. On Begin's orders one member of *Herut* who had suffered a heart attack was brought into the parliament building on a stretcher.

Thousands of *Herut* members and various opponents to any agreement with Germany poured into Jerusalem to attend a public rally near the Knesset building. As David Ben-Gurion rose to tell the Knesset, "We will not allow the murderers of our nation also to be its heirs," Begin was talking to the crowd outside. In a voice breaking with emotion he told them: "There is no sacrifice we will not make. We will be killed rather than let this come about. This will be a war for life or death. A Jewish government that negotiates with Germany can no longer be a Jewish government."

His audience was in an ugly mood. Many of them had seen the inside of Hitler's extermination camps and still bore the tattooed numbers on their arms. Begin was now ranting: "When you fired a cannon at us, I gave an order—no! Today I give an order—yes! . . . There is no German who did not kill our fathers. Every German is a Nazi. Every German is a murderer. Adenauer is a murderer. . . .

"This will not be a short or cold war. Maybe we will go hungry for want of bread. Maybe we will again part from our families. Maybe we will go to the gallows. No matter."

He was close to tears as he stepped down and walked toward the Knesset to take part in the debate inside.

The crowd followed. As they approached the building, the police tried to stop them but gave way to the angry stream of people. While police barricades crashed to the ground, the mob pelted the Knesset building with stones. Years after, Amihai Paglin would claim that the stones were brought the day before, by provocateurs. The open space in front of the main doorway was now a battleground. The groans of the wounded and the shouts and curses of policemen mingled with the din of police and ambulance sirens. The debate continued in an atmosphere made even more tense by the racket outside. Suddenly Knesset member Yochanan Bader of Begin's party ran in and screamed: "Gas against Jews! That's how you welcome reparations!" There was no need for explanations. Wisps of tear gas used by the guards at the door to try to keep the crowds out of the building were seeping into the debating chamber. As the cries of protest rose within the room, a hail of stones broke a number of the windows high up in the walls of the chamber. Glass splinters flew in all directions. Dust, smoke, and gas combined to bring tears to the eyes of Knesset members.

Toward evening the storm died down. The police were holding hundreds of rioters, and scores of police and demonstrators were hospitalized. At this point Begin ascended the Knesset podium to make his speech:

> I appeal to you at the last moment as a Jew to Jews, as the son of an orphaned nation, of a mourning nation. Stop! Don't do this thing—it's obscene! There has been nothing like this ever since we became a nation, and I'm trying to give you a way out . . . As an adversary I wouldn't give it to you. As a Jew I will resist! Go to the nation. Hold a referendum!

When Begin began to speak of the police behavior, Ben-Gurion had heard enough. "Your hooligans," he bellowed.

"You are a hooligan," Begin responded.

An uproar followed. Clearly Begin would not be allowed to continue without an apology to the prime minister—but he demanded a similar apology from Ben-Gurion. It looked as if a fight might break out at any moment in the Knesset chamber.

"If I don't speak here, then no one will," Begin shouted.

The Speaker of the Knesset declared the session closed, to be reconvened in the evening, but Begin again took the stand to resume his interrupted speech. "There are some things dearer than life—and this is a matter for which people are prepared to leave their families and go to war. There will be no negotiation with Germany! Nations have gone to the barricades on lesser issues. We are ready to do anything to prevent this!"

It was a speech unprecedented in its forcefulness.

"You have prisons, concentration camps, an army, police, detectives, cannons, and machine guns. No matter! Over this issue all that power will splinter like glass on rock. You have already arrested hundreds; perhaps you will arrest thousands. We shall sit with them. If necessary we shall be killed with them. But there will be no reparations from Germany!"

Even as Ben-Gurion rose to respond to the debate, Begin's opponents were trying to brand his speech a blatant attempt to rule by the law of demagoguery. The prime minister began by warning against being taken in by the words of a demagogue, as he called Begin.

"A democracy knows how to defend itself against that; and if there is a need for defense, then it will be undertaken by the army and the police."

By a majority vote the Knesset decided to enter into negotiations to receive restitution payments from Germany. The actual negotiations began at the end of March 1952. At the last moment Begin and other members of his party tried to prevent the start of the negotiations by asking for a mass meeting to take place in Tel Aviv.

The demonstration was the largest Israel had ever known. About 70,000 people gathered in one of the central squares of Tel Aviv. Many of the people were not even members of Begin's party. The anger of the crowd was frightening. As the time for the demonstration drew near, the tension grew and there was fear of physical violence. Ben-Gurion, advised of rumors that damage might be done to union buildings, decided not to call on the police and army but instead had thousands of members of professional unions and kibbutzim bused into Tel Aviv.

The two opposing sides met face to face. It was an angry but disciplined crowd. Begin turned to the audience: "I call on you, Mr. Ben-Gurion, even though there are great differences between us. For the sake of the memory of the millions of our brothers and sisters who were destroyed and for the honor of Israel. Stop! Recall our representatives from Germany and stop all contacts with Germany regarding restitutions. We don't want any contact with the Germans, nor their money. There is no countervalue nor restitution for spilled Jewish blood. Mr. Ben-Gurion, the God of Israel will decide who is right."

The crowd was already heating up, but Begin had no desire to have a repetition of the unfortunate incident in Jerusalem. Begin's opponents claim that even before he began his speech a note was passed to him that thousands of kibbutz members would step in if the demonstrators became violent, and that thousands more were guarding public buildings. Begin implored the crowd not to allow itself to be incited to violence. He asked those gathered to raise their hands and take an oath not to allow the government to accept restitution payments from Germany unless a referendum was called. At the end of the meeting Begin himself led the marching demonstrators, many of whom carried black flags.

In the Knesset, Begin's speech was broadly criticized by Knesset members. He was suspended from taking part in Knesset activities for two weeks. Begin retorted that the suspension was an act of "moral and political cowardice."

From time to time Begin's opponents still remind the public of the contents of this memorable speech. They recall his statement, which included a call to return to the underground and the threat of violence against government decisions. Although since those days Menachem Begin has created the image of a liberal, moderate, and democratic leader, at every election the events in the Knesset of January 7, 1952, have been reiterated, even in 1977. But by then they had lost their impact.

Begin never harbored hatred for the British, against whom he had fought; but he never forgave the Germans. Later on he and his party members would continue to urge the public not to buy German goods. But as the years passed, he moderated his views on the importation of German-financed capital goods. His general opposition to contact with Germany surfaced once more in 1965 when the Israeli government wished to establish diplomatic relations with West Germany. "Can anyone deny that the Nazis of yesterday constitute the Germany of today?" he demanded in the Knesset. "Have they died, been killed, or have they disappeared? I cannot accept the Prime Minister's assertions that we are in a conflict between emotion and intellect. In this instance the two are inseparable. There is no division between pure and sacred logic and cold intellect and reason. They are integral and indivisible. It is up to us not to normalize relations, before the eyes of the world, between the exterminated and the exterminators."

The morning after Begin was elected prime minister,

in May 1977, the Bonn government expressed fears about a possible deterioration of relations between Germany and Israel. Begin's views on the subject were well known. But on assuming leadership of the country he revealed the pragmatic side of his personality. When in October 18, 1977, West German commandos succeeded in liberating hostages aboard a hijacked Lufthansa airliner at Mogadishu, in Somalia, one of the cables that arrived in the office of the German Chancellor was signed by Menachem Begin. The Chancellor could interpret Begin's congratulations as a gesture that the prime minister of Israel was reconciled to normalization of relations between their two countries.

Later Begin went further than that, and in his capacity as prime minister has met the German ambassador to Israel. This too could be interpreted as a change in Begin's dogmatic attitude toward the Germans.

CHAPTER 20

". . . *Excepting* Herut . . ."

The German reparations crisis left bitter memories. It enabled Menachem Begin's adversaries to present him as anti-democratic, someone who did not recognize democratic rules and was dominated entirely by emotion.

Moreover Ben-Gurion believed, and he made no secret of it, that if he had not ordered the army to fire on the *Altalena*, the IZL would have tried to take over by force. With the passage of the years, and as he grew to know Begin better, Ben-Gurion's suspicions of the former IZL chief began to mellow. But at the time of the German reparations parliamentary debate, and for some time afterwards, Ben-Gurion was convinced that Begin was a dangerous man.

Whenever Ben-Gurion was asked to form a new government, or was seeking parliamentary support for one of his measures, he adopted the political formula: "All parties are eligible excepting *Herut* and the Communists"; and indeed that became his political credo when seeking likely partners for one of his coalition governments.

Often one had the impression that Ben-Gurion's enmity for Begin went beyond politics and arose from a deep personal antipathy. He even refused to mention Begin's name in parliamentary debates. Taking the rostrum to respond to opposition arguments, the late prime minister would term his political rival "the man sitting next to Dr. Bader" (the *Herut* economic expert), and he adopted unparliamentary terms to attack him.

However sharp-tongued and aggressive Begin might be in political debate, he observed the rules of parliamentary decorum. He was devastingly sharp with Ben-Gurion, but after the reparations incident, he endeavored to remain within the bounds of politeness. Their verbal confrontations generally took place over historical arguments. Ben-Gurion did his best to exploit this aspect. Sometimes he would ostentatiously stalk out of the Knesset hall whenever Begin took the rostrum. When he did remain in his place, he would invariably try to divert a current political argument back to an ancient quarrel. Whenever the government was in trouble on some current issue, Ben-Gurion would introduce some insulting remark aimed at Begin and connected with the recent past. He was aware that he need only shout *"Altalena"* to bring Begin to his feet from the opposition benches. This kind of conditional reflex on Begin's part served Ben-Gurion's purpose time and again, and saved his government from some embarrassing questions, forgotten in the shouting match over the IZL's fights with the *Haganah*.

Ben-Gurion's hostility seemed quite irrational to

Begin. It seemed to him that it would have been fairer if the hatred came from his side of the house. After all, his men had been victims of "the Season," and the fatal casualties of the shooting at the *Altalena* were his followers, not those of Ben-Gurion. "He is simply a bad man," Begin once explained to a confidant who was trying to get to the roots of such deep hostility.

Actually it is difficult to fathom a personality as complex as David Ben-Gurion's. He was famous for his capacity to hate his political opponents; at the same time it did seem that his hatred for Begin was irrational. There are those who hold that part of his feelings about Begin derived from the period immediately after the *Altalena* incident, when Ben-Gurion did not go so far as to order Begin's arrest although dozens of the IZL's key men were detained. Perhaps Ben-Gurion was apprehensive lest the arrest of the IZL commander might cause a serious rift with Begin's supporters at a time when the Arab onslaught was still going on. Perhaps in their parliamentary slogging matches, Ben-Gurion wished to settle that account.

Although Begin was aware of Ben-Gurion's tactic of diverting attention from embarrassing situations for the government by attacking him, he was never able to control his reactions, and fell time and again into Ben-Gurion's trap.

During these years former IZL men suffered from alienation and isolation. Although the underground has disappeared, the hatred for the IZL remained a very palpable emotion. Indeed in many places of employment a former IZL man could not get a job.

It was at that time that Begin wrote *The Revolt,*

his memoirs of the underground. There are few such books among the memoirs of statesmen and former resistance leaders. It is more like a long and emotional speech. Although Begin is a brilliant speaker, and one of Israel's best parliamentarians, his style does not lend itself to easy reading. Alongside facts from the days of the fight against the British, mostly lacking in any personal angle, the book contains a long series of emotion-ridden phrases. The impression is that the author was reliving the most romantic period in his life while recapitulating the events of those times. He argued with his opponents on paper with the same enthusiasm as he did in real life.

While Begin indulged in his memories, the government fought a losing battle on the economic front. The new State found it difficult to feed the masses of bewildered Jewish refugees who were drawn to their ancient homeland from the four corners of the earth, converting the land into one huge immigrant reception camp. Ben-Gurion introduced an emergency economic program, with rationing of food and other basic commodities. As happens everywhere, the black market began to flourish, and many Israelis started to blame the socialist government for the austerity. In the first Knesset elections in 1949, at the height of the War of Independence, Mapai, the Labor Party, controlled 46 seats of the Knesset compared to 14 for *Herut;* another 7 went to the General Zionists, a bourgeois party. The elections for the second Knesset in 1951 saw *Herut*'s number decline to eight seats, while Labor lost only one and the General Zionists, in a landslide, went up from seven to twenty seats.

It was apparent that the General Zionists gained most of their new votes from *Herut* from people who were afraid of Begin and his fiery rhetoric, and who believed the worst his opponents said about him. Moreover Begin's focusing on nationalist issues, on the need for liberating all parts of the ancient homeland, put them off, as did his harping on who had played the bigger role in expelling the British. Voters disliked the socialist austerity régime and wanted jobs and homes, and the General Zionists promised them these things. The 1951 elections changed the political map. Ben-Gurion dropped his old left-wing coalition party, Mapam, and replaced it by the General Zionists. This party eventually renamed itself the Liberal Party, and in time formed its alliance (named the *Likud*) with *Herut*.

Menachem Begin as head of a tiny party with eight seats had little to do. He had sustained a bitter disappointment. A man of weaker fiber might have despaired and abandoned politics, but it was at such a nadir in his political career that Begin believed even more deeply in his political path and in the mission thrust on him by Jewish history. Ever since his youth as an activist in Polish *Betar*, Begin had been accustomed to being in the minority. His mentor, Zeev Jabotinsky, provided his disciples with a prime personal example, imbuing them with the belief that all the benefits of power were worth less than faith in the righteousness of one's way. In effect, the Revisionist movement remained in the wilderness from the day it was formed until May 17, 1977, when Begin's party emerged victorious in the Israeli elections.

It is worth noting that at the time the State of Israel was founded, it was not at all clear whether it would remain a democratic society and be run according to parliamentary rules. When the Interim

Council of State, a kind of embryonic Parliament, was formed after the declaration of independence, its leaders were not all persuaded that an opposition would serve the national interest. Even Ben-Gurion was quoted as saying that a free press could better serve the purpose than a parliamentary opposition. Only when Begin ran in the first elections at the head of the *Herut* Party did he demonstrate that there could be no evading the accepted Western democratic system. It has been said that if Begin, by his restraint after the *Altalena* incident, stopped the situation from deteriorating into civil war, then his party taught the majority to learn to live with parliamentary democracy.

Begin wrote down the aims of the opposition in Parliament. The man who fought Great Britain so bitterly now began to look admiringly at the British as the prime example of a democratic society. "We will serve our people in the Opposition," Begin wrote in his party newspaper, "and it will be a national service no less important than being in government. The task of the Opposition is to provide an ideological alternative to the incumbent government, to criticize what needs criticizing, and to support the government, when it so deserves."

Mapai became *the* party of government. Before the State was born, it had laid the foundations of its power; now it reaped the harvest. The large number of immigrants quickly learned the ways of Israeli politics. They learned that in order to get work, they had to look to the ruling party, which also gave them homes, medical services, and schools for their children. Already those foundations were beginning to crumble and the seeds of the fall of 1977 were being sewn.

The first steps away from its ideological sources put Labor on the road that eventually would lead to its defeat, largely because it had run out of impetus but also because there seemed little to distinguish it from Begin's party.

Paradoxically the Arabs helped more than a little to bring about Begin's victory at the polls. Israel's state of siege obliged the Labor leadership to serve as a permanent war cabinet. They had to set aside their social and economic targets. Ben-Gurion was guided by one basic motivation—to foil the Arabs' plans to annihilate Israel. He set out to make Israel into the most powerful country in the Middle East, and to use any possible means to this end. The labor movement, which based itself on the aspirations of European social democracy, found itself educating its youth to military values.

Obviously this was the direct outcome of Israel's struggle for survival in a sea of Arab enmity. Hardly two years had elapsed since the bloody War of Independence, during which five invading Arab armies had been driven back, when the Arabs opened their war of attrition against the Jewish State. From the early 1950s hardly a day passed without armed Arabs infiltrating into the country. The killed Jewish farmers in border villages, set fields on fire, planted mines, blew up homes, killed women and children, assaulted lines of communication, and obliged the Israeli army to launch reprisal raids into Arab territory to get at their bases.

These were the years that molded Israel's image as a society under siege. Its citizens were aware that at any hour they might have to defend their lives. Begin never ceased demanding far-reaching punitive operations against the killers from across the borders, but the official policy of the government took the wind out of his sails. Almost all of Begin's highly vocal demands were carried out by the administration, quietly and without prior announcement. Israeli command units hammered time and again at terrorist bases over the border. The average Israeli saw that Begin made demands and Ben-Gurion got things done. Indeed during his years in office the "Old Man," as he was known, enjoyed the glory of being the man who brought the Jewish State into being and who built up Israel's military power. Even Ben-Gurion's most persistent critics could not take this away from him.

Begin once commented of him: "He is said to be my harshest adversary. But I can say to his credit that Jewish history will never forget him for having proclaimed the birth of the Jewish State after two thousand years of exile."

In the 1955 elections *Herut* retrieved some of its lost strength when its representation rose to fifteen seats, mainly as a result of public uneasiness over Israel's security difficulties as a mini-war was waged by her enemies across the borders. In these elections the winners in 1951—the General Zionists—saw a decline to thirteen seats (from twenty), which made *Herut* the biggest opposition faction. Most significantly, although the dominant Mapai Party retained its power, its representation declined by five seats.

The election results made Begin a very happy man. He saw in the doubling of his party's strength further confirmation of the reward for perservering in the face of adversity. But over everything hung the threat of approaching war as the armed infiltration from across the borders relentlessly increased. And way beyond this local element, the Soviet Union's penetration into the Middle East contributed to the sense of the inevitability of military confrontation.

The Israeli Intelligence Service had been aware of the growing political alliance between the Soviet Union and Egypt. Ever since the British lost their dominant position in Egypt, the Israelis had argued that this could only lead to the rise of a pro-Russian régime there. They were to be proven right with a vengeance. The Soviets gained their foothold in the Middle East following the signing of an arms deal with Czechoslovakia by the charismatic president of Egypt, Gamal Abdul Nasser, in 1955. From that time huge quantities of Soviet arms made in Czechoslovakia began to pour into the arsenals of Egypt. Nasser never concealed that the purpose of these weapons was to destroy Israel.

The arms deal along with the belligerent declarations that accompanied it caused deep anxiety in Israel. Suddenly it seemed likely that the mini-war along Israel's borders might be converted gradually, or even in one move, into a large-scale war. It was against this deteriorating background that Menachem Begin urged a huge rally attended by 25,000 supporters in one of Tel Aviv's public squares: "War is preferable now rather than waiting for the day when the Arabs attack us." To roars of approval the *Herut* leader declared: "From a moral viewpoint, such a war is in order, because it is not a war of evil intent but for justice. It is not a war to conquer foreign lands, but to liberate our homeland. Not a war to shed blood, but one for peace, for the Arabs and us."

In the interviews he gave at the time to Israeli newsmen, Begin continued to argue that time was working in the Arabs' favor and that if Israel hesitated to launch a preemptive attack, she might find herself in a position that would preclude such deterrent action ever again. It was Begin's view that this was not only a question of liberating the ancient Jewish homeland from foreign rule but of a defensive war for the very survival of Israel.

While the government looked with growing anxiety to the south, beyond the border with Egypt, Begin focused his attention on the eastern border and beyond, to the West Bank of the Jordan, land annexed to the Kingdom of Jordan in 1949. For him ancient Judea and Samaria were an integral part of the ancestral homeland. Irrespective of the security and political situation, Begin was convinced that Israel should use the first available opportunity to move against Jordan and retrieve her ancient territory. He was less interested in Egypt, which held only a small area, the Gaza Strip.

The war clouds looming over the Middle East enabled Begin to retrieve the losses his party had sustained in the 1951 elections. As the 1955 election campaign got under way, it was apparent to all that the *Herut* leader was riding on this wave. Large crowds were drawn to *Herut* rallies in cinemas and in the open air to hear Begin's bitter attacks on the "corrupt rule of the ruling party." Mapai provided him with a lot of ammunition. He protested that the main government party only took care of its supporters and terrorized the others. He complained that the health services and welfare facilities of the huge trade union federation were being denied to supporters of *Herut,* as well as jobs in the larger companies. These were well-known facts at the time, but few protested about them in public.

Begin was much more cautious in his speeches about German reparations. "I do not promise you palaces, for they have been stolen by the corrupt rule of Mapai. But I do promise you a life of human and national honor," he cried.

Then, as on a few other occasions in his political career, Menachem Begin fell into a trap he had laid for himself, perhaps unconsciously. And his Labor opponents knew just how to use his actions against him. On the eve of the 1955 elections Begin toured the southern districts of Tel Aviv, one of his party strongholds. He drove from one rally to another—thirteen in all on one evening—in an open Cadillac limousine put at his disposal by an American Jewish admirer. In order to make a path for the car, one of Begin's aides organized an entourage of young party supporters riding motorcycles. The sight of the huge Cadillac with Begin waving to his adoring supporters, accompanied by motorcyclist outriders making a tremendous noise, aroused considerable disquiet and even fears throughout Tel Aviv. On Election Day the newspapers carried lengthy reports of the noisy procession of *Herut* through the city, evoking a bad reaction from many voters. Even those who agreed with Begin's criticism of Mapai's corrupt rule found themselves panic-striken at the idea that the alternative might be Menachem Begin of the Cadillac and the motorcyclists. The negative image was a fine gift to Begin's adversaries and they exploited it to the hilt. The polling booths opened without Begin having time to rectify the damage and explain that what had happened was not planned by him. It is clear that were it not for that procession, *Herut* would have done very well at the polls.

Begin was to say later: "In politics, it is easy for a party to decline after having been in the ascendancy. It's even easier to fall after a decline, and more difficult to recover after a loss. We have learned that as long as we keep our faith, we can convert defeat into victory."

As October 1956 approached and the skies darkened over the Middle East, the internal political temperature began to subside. War was on the doorstep; obviously the threat rendered internal arguments less acute.

David Ben-Gurion, together with the leaders of Great Britain and France, planned the campaign against the Nasser régime. Their plan, formulated under the noses of the Americans, was based on the premise that Israel would use the pretext of the mini-war being waged against her across the Egyptian border in order to cross the frontier and attack Egyptian forces in the Sinai Desert. When the Israeli forces reached the Suez Canal area, the British and the French would intervene to stop the fighting and separate the warring armies, and thereby once again take over control of the Canal, which had just been nationalized by Nasser.

The operation was kept a closely guarded secret; only a few ministers in Ben-Gurion's cabinet knew anything about it. Although the premier trusted his armed forces and had confidence in the protective air cover promised by the French, he was ridden by anxiety shortly before the deadline. As a statesman with profound historical insight, Ben-Gurion was deeply concerned about the Jewish people's survival in Israel. The constant attacks into Israel over the past year or two had had a negative effect on civilian morale. The infiltrators, with Egyptian sanction, had sought to undermine internal security in Israel, getting as close as 15 miles from Tel Aviv and ambushing buses on main arteries. The worst incident was the attack on a school building when a dozen youngsters were murdered in cold blood.

But Ben-Gurion's will was firm, despite the anxiety that racked him just before the troops were due to move. The final touches to the campaign were made in consultation with his top aides at his bedside in his home, today the Ben-Gurion Museum in Tel Aviv.

Although Ben-Gurion kept the operation plans a close secret, he did involve the opposition leaders in his preparations, for he wished to secure full parliamentary support. Thus, a few days before Israeli troops and armor began to move into Sinai, Begin found himself a guest at the Ben-Gurion home, wondering about the meaning of this unusual invitation. The premier was ill in bed. Ben-Gurion told him: "I called you here to include you in the secret of a fateful decision. I do beg of you to keep it a secret and not tell anyone, even your closest comrades."

Ben-Gurion proceeded to unveil details of the military planning. When he had finished, Begin rose to his feet, walked over to the beside, and clasped his hand. "I applaud your courageous decision. You can be sure of our support," he said.

This support materialized when the Knesset met in special session a few days later, even as battles were still raging in the desert. For once Begin praised Ben-Gurion, giving his warmest possible blessing to the government and to the Israeli army for their brilliant move.

This harmonious relationship continued even outside Parliament. Early in 1957, shortly after the completion of the Sinai campaign, Begin was invited to make a lecture tour in the United States. He hurriedly contacted the premier, realizing to what extent Israel was now under political attack and that the United States led those who demanded an Israeli withdrawal from Sinai. He also knew that the American Jewish establishment opposed his proposed lecture tour because they thought of him as an extremist.

"Perhaps my views might damage Israel's information campaign at this moment. So I wanted to consult you before I leave," Begin told the premier. Ben-Gurion replied: "There are some things that one should think over but never talk about."

This was more than a slight inkling that Ben-Gurion was not all that far from Begin's ideological concept, despite their verbal confrontations inside and outside Parliament. At any rate, during the Sinai campaign period both of them favored a pro-French orientation, and this commonly held concept helped to improve their personal relations.

But their verbal cease-fire did not last long. In 1957 Ben-Gurion decided to order an Israeli pullback from Sinai. He did this with a heavy heart. More than once he had declared that parts of Sinai were integral areas of Israel and he had even revived ancient memories of the Kingdom of Israel, evoking applause from Begin and his party. As a realistic and pragmatic statesman, however, Ben-Gurion appreciated that he could not oppose the combined resolve of the United States and the Soviet Union. But when he ordered the Israeli withdrawal, Begin accused him of handing over the fruits of victory to the enemy.

The heightened tension between the two leaders may be seen against the background of the approaching general elections of 1959. Ben-Gurion began to defend his withdrawal decision. Begin and his supporters launched a nationwide drive protesting the pullout. "Don't withdraw," they begged Chief of Staff General Moshe Dayan; but to no avail. The IDF moved out of the Sinai Peninsula and the Gaza Strip. This move was largely based on the solemn promise of President Eisenhower to ensure Israel's right of a sea passage through the Tiran Straits into the Red Sea. But when Nasser blockaded the Straits ten years later in 1967, no one in the White House or State Department knew about it.

Ben-Gurion and Begin began again to exchange sharp epithets during Knesset debates. "A real statesman is not permitted to feed the lowest instincts—nor is he capable of it. He must take action, not declaim. A demagogue can do anything one fears," said Ben-Gurion, in one of his harshest speeches.

Then once again the shadow of Israeli-German relations loomed over internal affairs when the government decided to sell arms to the German armed forces. Begin spoke with wrath from the Knesset rostrum, denouncing any move toward a rapprochement with Germany. In comparison to his speech against the German Reparations Agreement, this one was in a minor key; but Ben-Gurion was not going to let him off. When it came to his turn to respond to the opposition, the premier simply quoted passages from Begin's earlier speech, declaring: "We have to remember that this man promised to leave the House and not be silent or rest until the reparations agreement was voided. Look at him—is that the man who has kept his word? Did he do as he promised?"

Early in 1959, as the elections again drew near, the personal rivalry between the two men reached new tension. In every election speech Ben-Gurion attacked Begin with the most cutting epithets. Begin tried hard to maintain a low profile during the campaign, well aware of the harm that had been done to his image by the campaign procession of the previous elections. He focused on the long-drawn-out rule of Mapai:

"If a party is in power for too long a time, that invites considerable dangers to civil liberties and the national future. We deeply believe in the great truth of liberalism. Man was not created for the state; on the contrary, the state was formed to serve man."

He strove to project an image of political liberalism, and his main election slogan was: "We will bring down Mapai and set up a National-Liberal Government."

For the first time, Begin endeavored to bring the bourgeoisie closer to him, especially those segments who had never supported the left, and in the past had been inclined to the IZL but disliked *Herut*'s style. He did his best to convince them that he was a truly liberal politician devoted to the democratic system. While never abandoning the principles that had guided him since his early days in *Betar*, he began increasingly to emphasize his devotion to liberal ideas.

This helped him at the polls. In 1959 *Herut* ended up with seventeen seats, making it the second largest party after Mapai, which had forty-seven seats. Now ensconced as leader of the opposition, Begin began to free himself to some extent from his old negative image as an extremist. He became a respectable element in the Israeli political establishment. But the path to power still remained a distant and difficult one.

CHAPTER 21

The Wilderness of Opposition

Begin had not led *Herut* to victory at the polls in any of the elections so far, yet few questioned his authority as leader of the party. There were defections over the years, some perhaps as a result of the absoluteness of political opposition, others because they believed that Begin's constant electoral failure should have made him step aside and make room at the top for others. The remnants of the old Revisionist Party were also discontented at being shoved aside. Meanwhile Begin himself was concerned with moderating the extremist image of the party under his leadership.

In the early 1960s the border situation was relatively stable and tranquil—a fact attributed by most to the outcome of the 1956 war. In these circumstances Begin found it difficult to return to his old slogans about liberation of the homeland from the Jordanian occupiers. While all was peaceful, nobody wanted to hear the kind of talk that could only lead to another war.

The reparations speech that had caused Begin's suspension was long in the past, and *Herut* had almost lived down the memories of stones thrown at the Knesset building. Begin's own rhetoric and legal knowledge was acquiring him a reputation as a skilled parliamentarian—a reputation enhanced by the fact that he was one of the few members who never missed a Knesset session, and who threw himself into his legislative work as if it was all that mattered in life. On the days when the Knesset met in full session, he was early to arrive and quick to greet even his political opponents with a handshake and some pleasant words. He was now recognized as an affable and polite gentleman, whose company was eagerly sought in the Knesset cafeteria by friend and foe alike. His colleagues were impressed by the fact that Begin did not let leadership of a party go to his head.

While other politicians made use of their status to enjoy a good life, Begin was not tempted. His home was still the same modest Tel Aviv apartment. He had time for all comers, and diligently answered all his mail. When the Knesset was in session, he stayed in one of the more modest Jerusalem hotels and took his meals in the Knesset cafeteria. Although *Herut* provided him with a small car and driver, he used it only when traveling in his official capacity. Otherwise he was often seen on Jerusalem city transport, or waiting in line for a ticket to a local movie house. An ardent moviegoer, Begin never missed a good western or historical movie until television finally replaced the urge for outside entertainment.

From the mid-1960s, after his faithful secretary Dov Alpert died of cancer, Begin was served diligently by Yehiel Kadishai, who gave up his private business in a ticket agency to return to the service of the man who had been his commander both in *Betar* and the IZL. Kadishai, who is now head of the prime minister's bureau, was one of the few people who could read Begin's handwriting—and one of his first tasks was to dictate to a typist the manuscripts of Begin's weekly newspaper column.

Then, on April 1, 1959, came a minor incident that was to remind his opponents of their old antipathies. In the middle of a parliamentary debate on the state budget for the year, news reached the floor that Israel Radio had just broadcast the call-up codes of three reserve echelons of the army. Amid the uproar, a representative of the National Religious opposition who was attacking the budget announced that now was obviously not the time for criticism of the government. Begin promptly asked for the floor, and waded into a speech with the heavy overtones for which he was famous.

"The General Staff of our army has declared a general mobilization," he began, then went on completely oblivious to voices attempting to remind him that only three units had been called. ". . . If our army, mobilized as a result of what has happened, is called into action, we shall all stand behind it."

Within hours it was learned that the radio announcement was a mistake. Instead of a carefully worded statement that the mobilization was part of an exercise, the radio station had been allowed to make an overly dramatic "real" call to the reserve. Ben-Gurion took the floor to accept responsibility, and noted that the general involved had been removed from his post. Now Begin was free to revert to type: the opposition leader attacking the government for a blunder. But the damage was done. He had rushed to support a possible war without even knowing the reason for the mobilization, or what its objectives were.

Ben-Gurion was meanwhile becoming embroiled in an affair that was radically to alter the entire left wing of Israeli politics. In 1954 he had retired temporarily from politics, and settled in a Negev kibbutz in an attempt to encourage Israeli youngsters to follow his example and bring life and productivity to the wasteland that constituted one-half of Israel's total territory. While he spent his days as a shepherd in the desert, Egyptian Intelligence apprehended an Israeli-directed sabotage ring, composed mostly of local Jews, which had been assigned a number of strikes against American institutions in Egypt in the hope of further provoking deteriorating relations between the United States and the cadre of young officers who had deposed King Farouk. The plan was ill advised, both because of its moral implications and because the members of the ring were neither trained nor prepared for their assignment. Two of them were hanged, the rest were sentenced to various terms of imprisonment—and one of their mentors, an Israeli Intelligence officer, committed suicide in his prison cell.

Though the public was not made aware of the full details, a storm broke out in leadership circles. Military men were quick to blame the political echelon both for the decision to go ahead with the plan and for the fiasco of its failure. The politicians were just as quick to blame Army Intelligence. The soldiers claimed that Ben-Gurion's successor as Defense Minister, Pinhas Lavon, had issued the orders, while he protested that he had known nothing about it. The debate now revolved around one question: Who gave the order?

Ben-Gurion was on the sidelines at the time, with no desire to become involved. Lavon was maneuvered into resigning by the current prime minister, Moshe Sharett, and Ben-Gurion returned to the Defense Ministry and, eventually, the premiership. Ben-Gurion himself was always inclined to believe Lavon's guilt in the affair.

However, the Lavon affair was not yet over. In the early 1960s Lavon, now secretary-general of the *Histadrut* (the General Federation of Labor) as the result of a gesture made toward his political rehabilitation by Ben-Gurion, produced evidence that seemed to indicate the forging of documents by those same Intelligence officers who had tried to lay the blame for the Egyptian fiasco on him. In a widely, and perhaps deliberately misunderstood move, Ben-Gurion insisted that the evidence be presented to a legally constituted committee of enquiry headed by a Supreme Court judge. His opponents in his own party, perhaps motivated by a wish to cramp Ben-Gurion's style, argued forcefully in favor of a Knesset enquiry—a concept that offended the Old Man's sense of justice. No matter whether Lavon's name was cleared or he was found guilty of giving the original orders, Ben-Gurion could not and would not accept that any parliamentary body could take precedence over the judicial system in a matter of justice and legal guilt or innocence. The traditional leadership of the Labor Party split into two camps, the bigger of which was against Ben-Gurion. As tempers rose the actual issues of principle were lost, and Ben-Gurion's insistence that a parliamentary committee meeting behind closed doors would be sheltering the guilty parties began to be interpreted as a personal vendetta against Lavon.

Given the split in Mapai ranks, the 1961 elections could have been Begin's big chance; but he did not have a strong enough grip on public opinion, nor had he managed to shake free of the extremist label. And, in any case, for all that the public watched scandal gnaw away at Ben-Gurion's stature, they were convinced that the government and Mapai were synonymous. Clearly whoever came out on top of the internal war in Mapai would be the man who would lead Israel into the future. Paradoxically, therefore, the problems of the left wing made *Herut* and the opposition a completely secondary and minor issue in Israeli politics. *Herut* held its own in the election, and Begin was content to see that as a victory; but in fact the party was simply standing still. For some of its supporters this very fact was adequate evidence that *Herut* could never achieve power.

On the eve of the election the General Zionists united with the Progressive Party to form the Israel Liberal Party, which now offered itself as an alternative to a Labor-dominated government. The new union represented more of a threat to *Herut*'s status as the main factor of opposition than it did to Mapai, yet its poor showing in the election allowed Begin to mock its grandiose ambitions, and this he did in terms of "a party of small merchants and landlords," lacking any clearcut policy and entirely devoted to second-level internal problems. But he was beginning to realize that *Herut* alone would never dislodge the left wing. While Mapai was casting around trying to repair the rifts that had split Israeli Labor into factions, Begin started the same exercise at his end by quiet overtures to the Liberals on the possibilities of an alignment of the two parties.

By 1963 David Ben-Gurion's political career was waning. The Lavon affair, apart from weakening the régime, had exhausted the Old Man both politically and personally. At this point Isser Harel, the head of Central Espionage—the *Mossad*—brought Ben-Gurion evidence that German scientists and engineers were working in Egypt on the design of unconventional weapons for eventual use against Israel. Harel was indiscreet enough to release this information to the editors of the daily newspapers. In retrospect it appears that he was seeking the necessary backing to allow Israeli Intelligence to go to work against the German scientists; but in fact the revelation only served to further weaken Ben-Gurion. When the Knesset convened to discuss the news, the debate turned into a frontal attack on Ben-Gurion's pro-German policy. Israel had received reparations. Israel had supplied Uzzi submachine guns to the West German army. The prime minister himself had offered legitimacy to the Federal Republic by proclaiming the country to be "a different Germany." Now the voices of all parties were raised in protest against that same Germany, contending that the scientists were continuing with Hitler's "final solution."

The members of Army Intelligence were quick to discover that the whole thing was nowhere near as serious as it had been made to appear in the media and in the Knesset debate. The opposition however were not aware of this. Harel's version was good enough for them and, as usual, Begin was in the forefront of the attack on the government.

Ben-Gurion was not present to hear Begin's almost traditional assault on Germany. He was on vacation in a hotel in northern Israel, fuming over Harel, who had resigned because of differences of opinion on how to deal with the German scientist threat. Golda Meir, then Foreign Minister, filled in for him in the Knesset while he listened to the proceedings over the radio. He knew that Golda was not enamored of his German policy, yet he expected her to put up a good defense. Now not only did she seem to be soft-pedaling the whole thing, but Begin was putting up an unusually strong performance. Ben-Gurion was alert to potential dangers of this kind. He had already written in a letter to a friend that Menachem Begin was a disciple of Abba Ahimeir, the Revisionist extremist who had been arrested in connection with the Arlosorov assassination. Now he would seek the opportunity to level the charge directly at Begin in a Knesset speech, immediately after his return from vacation.

Ben-Gurion came to the Knesset armed with quotations from the writings of Ahimeir. He launched his attack with a sentence that caused an uproar: "I was no partner of theirs when they glorified the name of Hitler." He was not allowed to finish. The *Herut* members were on their feet screaming insults at the prime minister. The Speaker of the Knesset, himself a member of the left-wing coalition, closed the session, aware that this time the Old Man had gone far beyond the bounds of good taste. Ben-Gurion retracted his statement, but when he read in the next day's paper a bitter criticism of the comparison he had tried to make, he was provoked into writing a letter to one of the journalists who had attacked him.

> Begin is clearly a Hitlerist type. He is a racist willing to destroy all the Arabs for the sake of the completeness of the country, sanctifying all means for the sake of the sacred end—absolute rule. I see in him a severe danger to the internal and external situation of Israel. I cannot forget the little I know of his activity, and it has one clear significance: the murder of scores of Jews, Arabs, and Englishmen in the demolition of the King David Hotel; the pogrom in Dir Yassim and the murder of Arab women and children; the *Altalena*, which was designed for the seizure of power by force; the stoning of the Knesset by an incited rabble on the instructions of Begin—and had I not used the army to prevent the rabble from breaking into the Knesset, there would have been a massacre of Knesset members. These are not isolated acts, but a revelation of method, character, and aspiration.

Ben-Gurion predicted that if Begin took over, he would replace the high command of army and police by his hooligans, and would rule the way Hitler did in Germany, suppressing the workers' movement with force and cruelty and indulging in a political adventurism that would destroy the State. "I do not doubt that Begin hates Hitler, but that hatred does not prove that he is any different. When I first heard him make a speech over the radio, I could hear the voice and screeching of Hitler. And when I saw in the Knesset the fervor on the faces of Begin and Ben

Eliezer, I was familiar with that murderous expression."

If the German scientists in Egypt contributed to the end of Ben-Gurion's régime, it was not due to Begin's opposition. Begin was too small to do that. Already weakened in his leadership by the Lavon affair, Ben-Gurion could see that some of his party colleagues were hesitating to back him up in his treatment of the German scientists' affair as the relatively minor incident that it was. He drew the obvious conclusion. Resigning the premiership, he did his best to see that Finance Minister Levi Eshkol, his own choice, replaced him, and he retired to his Negev kibbutz.

When the fuss died down, Begin went back to the now traditional task of rebuilding his image. Clearly he was satisfied being a member of the Knesset, head of the opposition, and a member of two of its major committees: Foreign Affairs and Security, and Constitution and Law. Then came the day in 1964, when Begin could inform Kadishai—who still remembers the gleam in his boss's eye—of the ultimate in legitimization of *Herut:* "Yehiel, the government is about to decide to transfer the bones of the head of *Betar* back to Israel."

Kadishai knew that Begin had been trying to have this done for years, yet while Ben-Gurion was in power it had been out of the question. The Old Man had detested Jabotinsky, and would hardly have been inclined to that kind of gesture.

When Jabotinsky had died twenty-three years earlier in New York, his will was found to contain a request that he be buried where he died, or cremated; but added to that request was a sentence that became a commandment to his followers: "I request that when a Jewish government arises in the Land of Israel, it will order my bones reinterred in the Land of Israel."

Begin and his colleagues had long looked forward to the day when that dream would come true. Had they wanted to, they could have carried out Jabotinsky's last wish themselves. But they respected the concept that the government must take the step—and Ben-Gurion obviously would not. Eshkol, when approached by Begin, shook the *Herut* leader with a provision of his own: he would agree to it only if Zeev Jabotinsky was reinterred on Mount Herzl, in the plot reserved for Zionist leaders. This was beyond Begin's wildest dreams.

Ben-Gurion's reaction was not long in coming. He did not attack the government's decision, but he did use the occasion to publish a series of articles attacking the opinions and beliefs of the dead *Betar* leader, whom he considered the sworn enemy of the Jewish workers' movement. This time Begin restrained himself. In the *Herut* journal he praised Jabotinsky's achievements, and ignored Ben-Gurion's broadside. When the coffins of Jabotinsky and his wife arrived in Israel, it was as if *Herut*, the IZL, and *Betar* had all finally attained legitimacy. Even the fact that the government refused to bear the cost could not detract from the occasion. *Herut* members willingly paid, and even painted their rented command cars in military colors to compensate for the army's refusal to supply transport from the airport to the cemetery.

So Jabotinsky took his place among the other Zionist leaders. Even those who had disagreed with him and what he represented had respected his achievement. Begin indirectly benefited from that recognition; once the burial at Mount Herzl was over, no one could any longer refer to him as the politician "outside the camp." In practical political terms, of course, the act was meaningless. Mapai had achieved the union of the left-wing parties, while the Liberals presented a challenge on the right wing. Faced with isolation as a small political force, Begin now decided to move out from his tiny circle in the hope of making power attainable.

The General Zionist element of the Liberal Party was a potential ally. In the distant past they had opposed Jabotinsky, but never with the ferocity of the left wing. Toward the end of the British Mandate, while not supporting the IZL, they had at least objected to its outlawing by the community. Since independence, they had attempted alliance with Mapai in order to enjoy some of the crumbs of power, but had found it a generally disappointing experience. Ideologically their opinions were closer to those of Begin, though they were not at all interested in the nationalistic component of his credo. The main thing they had in common was their detestation of Mapai socialist rule.

The Progressive elements were a different matter. They had always been closer to Labor than to the right wing; their leaders were moderates who detested Begin's personal style no less than his opinions. They did not like socialism, but were even further from *Herut* ideology. Their union with the General Zionists was somewhat unnatural. As Begin began his overtures, the first cracks materialized in the Liberal Party. The Progressives opposed any negotiation with him, while the General Zionists were willing. From the first moment it was clear that the talk was of a united appearance before the electorate, but not of a full merger between the two parties, which were so totally different in their political mentality. It was to be little more than an answer to the Labor alignment.

The Progressives tried to torpedo the move, but the negotiation went into high gear as the elections approached. Begin's new friends were discovering that he was a gentleman, generous and willing to forget the past. With the rift in the Liberal Party inevitable, the Progressives, now named the Independent Liberal Party, struck out on their own—while the main party concluded its pact with Begin and formed *Gahal*, the "*Herut*-Liberal Bloc." At the celebration of the signing of the agreement, a smiling Begin assured his partners that they would not be serving the nation in opposition for much longer.

The two parties maintained their independent frameworks and institutions, but set up a joint management to direct parliamentary maneuvers. Begin was to all intents and purposes now the leader of a much bigger party by virtue of the fact that *Herut* was larger than the Liberal Party. But that was merely the formal reason. In practice his position derived both from his dominant personality and from the fact that *Herut*'s interests lay with Israel's main problems of security and foreign affairs, while the Liberals were more involved with economic matters.

The *Gahal* partnership had an immediate and meaningful by-product: Begin's new partners were influential in moderating his views, even to the point where the new party actually joined the *Histadrut* in an attempt to undermine something of Labor's position within its own fortress. The Liberals convinced Begin that the move was necessary. To break the power of organized labor, it had to be done from the inside. Convincing his *Herut* colleagues was not so easy, and there was also a main obstacle: the *Histadrut* had to accept them. The doors were locked, quite naturally, against anyone who did not subscribe to the socialist ideals represented by the organization of labor. *Gahal* was willing to swallow the somewhat unpalatable condition that joining the union meant accepting the rules by which it operated. Nevertheless the doors remained locked. The *Histadrut* was perfectly capable of appreciating the danger of the Trojan horse. And here the law courts came to the aid of *Gahal*, in establishing that any party had the constitutional right to organize workers within a labor union. The day *Gahal* penetrated the labor union is a meaningful date in the political career of Menachem Begin.

One year after the election that established *Gahal* as the main opposition in the Knesset, Begin's own position was threatened within *Herut*. The scene was the party's eighth convention. The ceremonial opening was graced by the presence of Prime Minister Eshkol, a confirmation of the fact that the party had indeed achieved legitimacy in Israeli politics. Once the ceremonies were over, it became clear that there was internal opposition in *Herut*—perhaps as a result of its own constant opposition within national politics. Not an election passed without the party leadership believing that victory was theirs, followed by the disillusion of defeat when the votes were counted. Now there were voices calling for fresh blood at the top to replace the men who led them time and again to defeat. Of course no one dared question Begin's authority, yet he could sense the ground shifting beneath his feet.

"The plot is clear," he fumed to his close associates. "They want to turn me into a led leader, and I have no intention of agreeing to that."

But Begin took the initiative by announcing that he would not seek reelection as chairman of the party. His old colleagues were reminded of an occasion when Begin had actually declared that he was leaving the party, and had started to do his articles as a lawyer. He retracted then, and many now believed that this announcement was another tactic to get his own way in the face of the internal opposition. One man did take the abdication seriously: Shmuel Tamir.*

Tamir, in his youth, had been a member of the Jerusalem Intelligence office of IZL. Early on in *Herut* he caught Begin's eye, though he enjoyed no particular status in IZL or the party. Tamir in fact was an exception—Palistinian born, of a good family, with a father who had links to the left-wing aristocracy. Tamir was one of three IZL veterans who accompanied Begin on his first trip to the United States, and he remained there a few months after Begin's return to Israel. When he got back he drifted away from politics, completed his legal training, and set himself up as a successful lawyer, becoming involved in most of the prominent political cases that hit the headlines in the early days of statehood. Fame and fortune came easily to Tamir. When he finally returned to politics, it was not at first as a member of *Herut*. Together with Jabotinsky's son, he set up a new party called "the New Régime"; but it did not last long. Eventually he drifted into *Herut*, where Begin welcomed him and suggested that bygones be bygones.

*Who would become Minister of Justice on behalf of Professor Yigael Yadin's Democratic Movement for Change.

391

He included Tamir in the party administration and the team that negotiated the establishment of *Gahal*, then allocated him a certain place on the party's list of candidates for the upcoming election. But Tamir, an ambitious man, was ungrateful. On the eve of the party convention he denied belonging to the internal opposition. When Begin announced that he was withdrawing his candidacy for the chairmanship, however, Tamir was quick to jump into the breach.

Tamir's candidacy was an undoubted impertinence; the *Herut* membership list was full of men with more experience and proven loyalty to Begin. The veteran leadership responded with an anger only matched by Begin's own reaction. Nobody had ever seen their leader so angry before. He was convinced that Tamir had maneuvered him into a trap and was now ready to plunge the knife into his back. Begin took his place on the platform of the convention and launched into a three-hour analysis of Tamir's path of treachery. It was one of his best speeches. After he had finished, the hall was completely silent. But Tamir remained unimpressed. He had prepared a surprise of his own. Amihai Paglin, one-time operations officer of the IZL and a favorite of Menachem Begin's. Paglin had drifted away from politics and was never active in *Herut*, but Tamir invited him to the convention because he was still a leading figure in the "fighting family." As Paglin ascended the platform to make his speech, someone observed that he was not formally a member of the party; but he was silenced by a call from the hall: "He joined this morning." Tamir had thought of everything.

"You have surrounded Begin with a wall of iron," Paglin announced. Though heckled from the floor, he continued to attack the *Herut* leadership and argue for fresh blood—and, clearly, he was also referring to Begin himself.

"Down from there!" Begin's supporters yelled.

"Anyone who wants to take me down had better come up and do it!"

For a few moments it seemed as if there would be a fight and that the "fighting family" was on the verge of a civil war of its own. Begin was having difficulty in digesting what was happening. He was used to being in a minority, but had never faced insurrection within his own ranks and from some of his best friends. People who knew him insisted that that week of the convention was the hardest of his political and public career. Certainly it was a display of ingratitude toward him of a kind that he could hardly stomach.

But, apart from Tamir and a few hotheads, no one for a moment believed that Begin would cease to be the leader of the party—even if it meant a split. It was finally demonstrated that Begin and *Herut* were indivisible. Tamir and his people were thrown out of *Herut* and established their own "Free Center" Party. Begin remained alone at the top. This time there was a new experience to add to all his earlier bitter memories.

CHAPTER 22

Minister Without Portfolio

To many young Israelis in the 1960s the parliamentary battles between Menachem Begin and his adversaries seemed an anachronism. The question of who actually drove the British out of Palestine was no longer of any interest to anyone apart from the aging members of *Herut* and a handful of veteran *Haganah* officers. And on current events party discipline was so thorough, and the people concerned so rigid, that debates on the floor of the Knesset were predictable down to almost the last word.

Israel's situation as a garrison State was ironically forcing Ben-Gurion's government into policies reminiscent of the theories of Jabotinsky. Circumstances necessitated the creation of "an iron wall against the Arab world," as the Revisionist leader had described it, and the preponderance of security problems had inevitably led the new State to virtually become a fortress. The security situation to a great extent determined the social forms of Israel. A good part of the budget would always be allocated for defense expenses. Since the establishment of Israel, all the resources had been applied to the main goal: survival.

On defense and security there was little disagreement between *Herut* and Labor. Consequently it was even harder for the population at large—many of whom had not lived through the enmities of the 1930s and 1940s—to understand the uncompromising attitudes of those to whom the recent past was so important. Eshkol's decision to allow the reinterment of Jabotinsky's bones in Jerusalem had blunted emotions, and even granted *Herut* a certain legitimacy—the comfortable acceptability of middle age that catches up with all youthful revolutionaries and hotheads.

By the nineteenth anniversary of Israel's independence, it all seemed to belong to prehistory. As in every democratic Parliament, seemingly bitter adversaries in the Knesset chamber happily drank coffee together in the Members' Snack Bar.

In May 1967, on the eve of Independence Day, as the Israel Defense Forces were making final preparations for their symbolic "mini-parade" through the streets of Israeli West Jerusalem, Army Intelligence received its first indications of something dramatic happening in Egypt. The following morning those spectators in the stands who were near enough could have noticed Chief of Staff Yitzhak Rabin bending over to whisper urgently in Prime Minister Eshkol's ear. The public would later find out that Rabin was reporting that Nasser's tanks were rolling across the Suez Canal bridges into Sinai, clearly an offensive buildup.

Developments followed with great speed. Pronouncements from across the border, and photos of the mob scenes in Arab countries, left little doubt that the Arabs were hell bent on achieving the final destruction of Israel. They could not have picked a worse time as far as Israel was concerned. Where Ben-Gurion had been a resolute wartime leader with the physical presence and inspired speech of a biblical prophet, Levi Eshkol was a mild-mannered expert on economic affairs with little understanding of military matters—and during this period Israel's problems did indeed seem to be economic, for the country was in the throes of recession, with mounting unemployment. Ben-Gurion, the man who had forged Israel's army and who had no understanding whatsoever of economics, was now a self-made political exile far from the center of power.

After the Lavon affair (the full details of which have still not been verified) Ben-Gurion's leadership had no longer been undisputed, and some of his opponents wanted to exploit the opportunity to inherit his position. At the head of a small band of loyalists, most of whom were not members of the old, established, and aging leadership, Ben-Gurion had departed to set up his own party—the Israeli Workers' List (RAFI)—fuming publicly about corruption in the ranks of Labor politics.

As has often been the case in Israeli history, the wisdom of hindsight has justified Ben-Gurion's controversial viewpoint. However, at that point he was leader of a party smaller even than Begin's *Herut*. Ironically, after Ben-Gurion's departure for the tranquility of final retirement, the party split into two—with one faction returning to the labor fold and the other gravitating toward Begin.

By May 1967 all this was in the past. While the

international situation deteriorated by the hour and it seemed that Israel faced certain destruction, the Israeli public found itself decidedly uneasy about the quality of leadership if the country was headed for total war.

The loud voices from across the border were fuel to the fears of the Holocaust generation. Cairo Radio described in detail exactly what would happen to the Israelis when the victorious Egyptian army occupied Tel Aviv. Many Israelis were furtively homesick for the days of Ben-Gurion's inspiring, if controversial and stormy, leadership. But the authoritarian leader, now in his eighties, sat in his Negev kibbutz writing his memoirs. His warning to Chief of Staff Rabin not to risk war was not yet common knowledge. Eshkol, unable to grasp the military implications yet willing to listen to his military advisors, was forced by a majority cabinet vote into opting for strenuous diplomatic moves to gain international support rather than exercising the military option of preemptive war.

On the international scene, the nations of the world—apart from a few brave and traditional friends—were silent. The 1956 Sinai campaign had resulted in the stationing of UN troops along the border between Egypt and Israel. Needled by mockery from the other Arabs to the effect that he was hiding behind UN skirts, Nasser demanded the withdrawal of the UN contingent. General-Secretary U Thant acceded, and the world did not protest. To Israeli minds the picture was clear: the world would stand in silence on the sidelines as the Arabs closed in for the kill.

The suggestion that Ben-Gurion, the aging lion, should be recalled to replace Levi Eshkol at the head of an emergency government came, strange as it may

seem, from his most vehement political enemy—
Menachem Begin. Exactly how it came about is now
lost to history, but the fact remains that the suggestion
was being discussed in the corridors of the Knesset,
and had certainly been raised with Begin on two
separate occasions—once with Moshe Haim Shapira
of the National Religious Party, who served as Minister of the Interior in Eshkol's coalition cabinet, and
again with Shimon Peres of Ben-Gurion's own Rafi
Party. It was obvious that under different conditions,
no one would even think of the idea. But at the end
of May 1967 Israel was standing with her back to the
wall. It became clear that Syria and Jordan might
join Egypt in the now inevitable war. And the uneasiness of the Israelis with their government had turned
into an absolute lack of confidence.

Eshkol, who was aware of the talk behind his back,
adopted the habit of inviting opposition party leaders
to take part in cabinet meetings that discussed the
security situation, since this was no longer a matter
for party politics. On the occasion of one such meeting Begin had the opportunity to take Peres aside.

"The situation seems too serious for the present
government to handle," he said quietly.

"I'm convinced of that," Peres responded.

"In my opinion we must do everything to put matters in the hands of Mr. Ben-Gurion."

Though Shimon Peres, as a long-time associate and
confidant of Ben-Gurion, knew perfectly well of the
traditional rivalry and even hatred between the two
men, he was not at all surprised by Begin's overture.
Assured of Peres's support, Begin promised to feel the
pulse in other political parties. All seemed to be in
agreement, even among the Labor Party. But they

were reckoning without the party's secretary-general, Golda Meir, who, prompted by hostility for Ben-Gurion and loyalty to her friend Eshkol, was determined to torpedo any such idea.

Meanwhile Begin was faithful to his promise. Having received assurances from all concerned, but having been told by the National Relgious Party that as members of the coalition they could not bring the suggestion to Eshkol, he declared that he would do it. Begin was greeted with quiet courtesy by Prime Minister Eshkol, who used the opportunity to bring him up to date on the security and diplomatic situation. The formalities over, Begin launched into the subject that had brought him to the prime minister's office.

"I have come to propose a very tough suggestion, and I don't doubt that a man would need all his spiritual resources to accept it. However, if you don't accept it, I would ask of you just one thing: forget I ever suggested it."

Eshkol, a wily and experienced politician, had a shrewd idea of what was coming.

"You must add Ben-Gurion to your government," Begin continued.

Eshkol said nothing and Begin felt uneasy. But he went on: "I don't need to tell you about the gulf between him and me, or about the insults he has heaped on me in the Knesset throughout the years. If I nevertheless say that he should head the government now, it is a sign that the situation is truly critical. I suggest that you hand him the premiership and continue to serve as his deputy."

It was a long time before Eshkol responded.

"Look," he said finally, "two such horses can never pull the same wagon." In his heart Begin knew that

Eshkol was right. Nobody could force him to give way to his bitterest enemy—particularly when his own party was against it. However the *Herut* leader kept his options open with the other parties in case there was a change of mind on Eshkol's part.

On Saturday, May 27, Ben-Gurion's wife, Paula, called on an old friend.

"Please," she said, "we're having guests tonight, and I don't have anything to give them to eat and drink. Could you help me?"

"How many guests will there be?"

"I don't know the exact number, but one thing I can tell you: Menachem Begin will be among them."

"Begin?" The friend could hardly believe her ears.

"Yes, Begin. In fact, I consider him a very nice man. I'd like him to feel friendly toward us."

Moments later the friend was at the Ben-Gurion home, with baskets full of cakes and fruits. Mrs. Ben-Gurion was busy fixing up the guestroom.

"I see you're excited," said her friend.

"I think Begin's a nice man, and I'll tell you another thing. In all his years of opposing my husband, there never was a time when if he saw me, he was not quick to greet me and shake my hand warmly. In my opinion, he's not as bad as people try to make him out."

That evening Begin and some of his colleagues went to Ben-Gurion's Tel Aviv home on Keren Kayemet (now Ben-Gurion) Boulevard. This was only the second time in his life that Begin had set foot in the house. The first occasion was in 1956, when Ben-Gurion invited him to hear about the impending Sinai campaign. Now he sat quietly listening to the Old Man describe preemptive war by Israel as a dangerous adventure. Israel must seek Great Power assistance, he said, then ensure that Egypt was clearly seen to be the aggressor. Begin realized that Ben-Gurion's hostility toward Eshkol was too deep. There was no chance of bringing those erstwhile friends and partners, now bitter opponents, together.

On May 23, 1967, Nasser closed the Straits of Tiran —Israel's sea lane to Africa and Asia. If an Israeli government accepted that lying down, then it was the beginning of the end. All sides were now convinced that Ben-Gurion was not the answer. The consensus was that Eshkol should be made to resign his Defense Ministry responsibilities in favor of Moshe Dayan. In return, Begin was prepared to promise the support of his party to the government. Again Golda Meir objected, and Eshkol was not prepared to step down unless his party thought it necessary.

By this time public pressure was mounting. The entire reserve army was mobilized and the economy at a standstill. Things could not go on this way without a collapse internally. Begin openly declared that he was willing to join a national coalition and share in the heavy responsibilities. But he had one condition: Moshe Dayan must be Defense Minister.

"We ourselves have some good candidates for this post," Begin told the leaders of the other parties, "but we prefer a man from another party, as we want a national coalition, one that can lead the nation to war. And apart from that, Dayan is the right man in the right place."

Were it not for public backing, Begin's proposal might not have been accepted, but the public was in no mood for party politics at this stage. Indeed Israelis have never before had such a clear premonition of impending doom. The ripples at home and the clamor in the Arab world began to penetrate the thinking of the ruling Labor Party, which finally decided to overrule Golda Meir and Levi Eshkol. The road to a national emergency government was now open.

The one man who still opposed his own party joining a coalition was David Ben-Gurion. Dislike and distrust of Eshkol was so deeply engrained that the Old Man told a meeting of his *Rafi* secretariat, convened to decide on whether to join the coalition: "That man must not be allowed to head the government. We must do everything to get rid of him." Though his colleagues were inclined to agree with his assessment of Eshkol, they could not accept the timing. Peres was well aware of the gravity of Israel's situation, and wanted to see his comrade, Moshe Dayan, in the Defense Ministry running the inevitable war. Ben-Gurion was in a minority of one.

That same evening Menachem Begin formally informed the prime minister that his party was willing to join the emergency government. A few hours later the prime minister's secretary called back to invite Begin to a cabinet meeting at which fateful decisions would be made.

While the incoming Defense Minister, Moshe Dayan, was racing in his private car to reach the meeting on time, Begin was calling up three old friends: Yaakov Meridor, Arye Ben Eliezer, and Yohanan Bader. He wanted them to accompany him in his car as far as the prime minister's office on this, his first trip as minister in the government of Israel. At the entrance to the office, the car stopped and the four men got out. Begin embraced each and then shook hands. They stood and watched as he walked into the building. For them it was a historic and almost unbelievable moment. There were tears in Meridor's eyes.

The cabinet meeting of June 1, 1967, did indeed make fateful decisions. Four days later Israel embarked on what history would record as the Six-Day War—the war that changed the map of the Middle East and the results of which are still a major issue in the agenda of world affairs.

On the morning of June 2, on his way to the Knesset to take a seat at the cabinet table, Menachem Begin ordered his driver to turn aside to Mount Herzl so that he could visit the area set aside for the graves of the leaders of Israel and Zionism. He stood for a moment at the foot of Zeev Jabotinsky's grave.

"Sir, head of *Betar*, we have come to inform you that one of your followers is now serving as a minister in the government of Israel."

The gesture was typical of Begin, but the beginning of June 1967 was not an appropriate time for Israelis to reflect on the political miracle. Menachem Begin had been rehabilitated. The most maligned man in Israeli politics was in fact taking the first step that would lead him ten years later to the prime ministership of Israel.

CHAPTER 23

The Thousand Days

For nineteen years Menachem Begin had dreamed continually of the day when, in his own lifetime, Jerusalem would be reunited and the West Bank of the Jordan restored to the Jewish homeland. To that end he never referred to the Jordanian administration as anything other than "the occupying régime." Yet as the years went by, he moderated his public demands for a war of liberation to the point where they seemed no more than an empty slogan. Such are the ironies of history that Begin today can publicly take credit for never having forsaken the dream of reuniting Jerusalem, and establishing the border of Israel on the Jordan River.

But early in June 1967 few Israelis had either the time or inclination to indulge in such fantasies. The noose was tightening, and national morale at its lowest point. The reserve army was stationed along frontiers that were long and awkward to defend. As the waiting period stretched from days into weeks, the economy—already in recession—slowed to a standstill. Every able-bodied man from eighteen to fifty was in uniform.

The appointment of Moshe Dayan to the Defense Ministry raised morale, and the coalition government gave people the feeling that the country was fielding its best team, even if that team was not entirely united in its view of what needed to be done. Foreign Minister Abba Eban, believing up to the very last moment that war could be avoided, was clutching at any comforting statement from Washington. Prime Minister Eshkol, on the other hand, wanted the waiting period in order to obtain certain American assurances that the Russians would not intervene—and if the Egyptian president happened to withdraw his troops from Sinai and lift the blockade of the Straits of Tiran in the meantime, so much the better.

Begin knew that war was inevitable even before he joined the government. He was convinced of the Arab determination to destroy Israel, as he had been from the very first day of independence. He was one man who was prepared to take the Arab propaganda statements at face value.

Less than twenty-four hours after he took his place at the cabinet table, the decision was taken: Israel would try to break the military might of the Egyptian army. But the question was whether the Egyptians would be fighting alone. After all, the whole buildup in the Sinai Peninsula had been the result of a Syrian claim that Israeli troops were massing along the northern border—a story fabricated with active Russian assistance. And to the north, Syrian guns and emplacements were located high above Israeli settlements. Nights spent in deep shelters—and even school classes in shelters—had become a fact of everyday life along the frontier with Syria. The Syrian-held (Golan) Heights were synonymous with terror and it was hardly likely that the occupants would be content to sit with their arms crossed. Far more likely was a Syrian drive to cut Israel in two while her army was engaged against Egypt to the south.

The eastern frontier with Jordan was no less troublesome. Arab Legion guns were within range of most of Israel's coastal plain, including the city of Tel Aviv. Jerusalem was cut in two by the frontier, and its horseshoe shape meant that Jordanian snipers could harass almost every section of the Jewish city. Nevertheless anxious Israeli eyes were on the southern frontier with Egypt—the strongest and most dangerous of enemies. The assumption was that the Jordanians would not intervene. But nothing was left to chance. On the morning of June 5, 1967, as three Israeli armored spearheads probed into the Sinai Peninsula, a message was transmitted to King Hussein from Levi Eshkol: If you leave us alone, no harm will befall Jordan.

The assumption was wrong, and the warning disregarded. At close to 11:00 A.M. Jordanian artillery began a bombardment of Jewish Jerusalem—and of every other community within range.

Back in 1949, shortly after Israel had signed the armistice truce with her neighbors, the IDF General Staff started making plans for liberating the Old City of Jerusalem. For the Israelis, Jerusalem represents much more than just a city, or even a capital; since the dawn of the Hebrew nation countless generations of Jews have dreamed about Jerusalem. And countless prayers have been written, in which the biblical phrase of the Babylon exiles was repeated: "If I forget thee,

O Jerusalem, let my right hand forget her cunning."

Today only one remnant of the Jewish glorious past survives in Jerusalem—the Western Wall of the Temple. From military posts in western Jerusalem the Israelis could not see the old stones, and they longed for the day when they could pray again to their Lord by the wall.

But there was another, more prosaic, aspect to the Israeli feeling about Jerusalem. In 1948 it had been feasible for Israel to take over at least the Jewish Quarter of the Old City, if not the whole city. But Israel's troops had failed. The Jordanian Legion had conquered the Jewish Quarter, and this was traumatic for many soldiers who by 1967 were senior officers in the IDF. For nineteen years they had dreamed that, one day, they would rectify that failure.

When Jordanian Legion posts started bombarding western Jerusalem that June morning in 1967, it was the signal for the realization of that old dream.

A different Israeli government might have ignored the Jordanian provocation; with Menachem Begin as a minister, it was impossible. True, there were some ministers who feared fighting on two fronts. But those with military records, such as Moshe Dayan and Yigal Allon, had a different assessment of the military situation. No less sure were the chief commanders of the IDF.

Their confidence was confirmed by the first three hours of the war, which actually made its outcome simply a matter of time. In those hours the Israeli air force in a planned attack destroyed the airpower of the Arabs. The sky was now the uncontested domain of the IAF, and Israeli airplanes could start giving massive support to the ground forces in Sinai. Almost anything would be feasible.

As the news of the bombardment of Jerusalem reached Tel Aviv shortly before noon, Begin had a premontion of history being made. He said as much to the Education Minister and one-time commander of the *Palmach,* Yigal Allon. That afternoon, amid growing excitement about the reports from the battlefield in the south, Allon cornered the prime minister.

"Begin and I want Jerusalem."

Later that afternoon, Begin, accompanied by his secretary Yehiel Kadishai, drove up to Jerusalem on a side road to avoid the Jordanian shells falling on the main highway. His destination was the Knesset, where the new members of the National Unity government were to be sworn in. At the entrance to the building Begin asked Kadishai to wait for Eshkol, and to tell him the moment he arrived that he, Begin, was asking for a cabinet meeting before the full session of the Knesset began.

The meeting convened in the Cabinet Room, but not for long; the sergeant-at-arms drove the ministers out with a warning that the room was too exposed to Jordanian shellfire. The leaders of Israel trooped down to the basement of the building, where they accepted Begin's proposal to liberate East Jerusalem and the Old City. Then, and only then, were Begin and Yosef Sapir sworn in as the two ministers representing *Gahal*—Begin's union with the Liberal Party.

That same night Israeli paratroopers were locked in bloody battle in northern Jerusalem, attempting to break through to the isolated garrison on Mount Scopus. For nineteen years Israelis had protected the Hebrew University campus to the east of the city through the armistice agreement with Jordan that allowed a relief convoy once a month. By the morning of the third day, the paratroopers were through to Scopus and the Mount of Olives behind the Old City, which was now virtually encircled. At this stage their orders were: "Isolate the city from reinforcement, then wait for it to fall like a ripe fruit."

On the second night of the war Menachem Begin was listening, as usual, to the BBC News from London, and heard the newscaster mention that efforts were being made to achieve a cease-fire between Israel, Jordan, and Egypt. He was alarmed. The IDF did not yet have the Old City and the Western Wall, and he had visions of yet another battle stopped at the wrong moment, yet another historic opportunity lost. At five o'clock in the morning he phoned Levi Eshkol. The prime minister listened to Begin's fears, then suggested that he call Moshe Dayan immediately and ask him to be at his Tel Aviv office at 7:00 A.M.

The result of the seven o'clock meeting was an order to the General Central Command: "Don't only encircle—conquer!" A little while later ten husky paratroopers, tears of emotion rolling down their cheeks, stood at the foot of the Western Wall of the Second Temple—the holiest site in Judaism.

As a religious man, Begin believed that historic justice must eventually triumph, and therefore that the Israeli army could not fail in its mission. Despite his momentary anxieties, his spirits were soaring at the thought that he would be an eyewitness to the event he had helped to shape.

On the sixth day of war the armies of Israel stood on new borders, far beyond any imaginable one week earlier. To the south Israeli soldiers could look far into Egypt across the waters of the Suez Canal. To the east they occupied the West Bank of the Jordan River. And to the south the Syrian guns no longer threatened peaceful farmers from the Golan Heights.

Much of the Israeli victory feeling was simply relief at the removal of the threat that had been so tangible only days earlier. Against an air of impending extinction Israelis could now match a decisive and astounding military achievement. The immense forces that had formed the noose around Israel's throat were now no more than dust and ashes to be covered by the desert sands, and all had been smashed by a citizen militia army—an army with inferior equipment and numbers but vastly superior motivation, the will to survive as a free nation. And as if that was not enough, the people of Israel could again look on the landscapes and shrines of their biblical history and heritage.

For Begin the sight of thousands of Israelis flocking to the Western Wall was a dream come true, the manifestation of that vision which his opponents had dismissed as unrealistic and fanciful. It was something of a personal victory—a proof that his fellow countrymen had not forgotten their link to the land of their biblical forefathers, a vindication of the program that his party had never abandoned.

The new situation offered Begin a fresh source of support. When the idea of an "entire Land of Israel" had referred to land that all lay beyond the frontiers of a garrison State, few Israelis had taken it seriously. But now that it was a reality, many people were discovering in themselves a new streak of nationalist fervor. Even among the radical left there were those who suddenly found they were not so different from Menachem Begin. The war also caused something of a religious revival. Rachel's Tomb, and the Cave of the Patriarchs, where Abraham, Isaac, and Jacob are buried, were now the object of regular weekend outings rather than vague memories to those who had been there before 1948, and less than that to newcomers after independence. Names out of a glorious past, such as Jericho and Solomon's Pools, were a reminder of the rich spiritual heritage.

The nationalistic-religious wave even managed to penetrate the impregnable Zionist left. It prepared Israeli minds for Begin's ascendancy to power ten years afterwards. The gospel he had preached for nineteen years did not seem so extreme any more. The seemingly unbridgeable gap between Begin and his opponents no longer existed. Apart from a handful of extreme leftists, all Israelis were now speaking the same language.

The *Herut* platform, too, which had seemed to extremist and totally unrealistic, was now suddenly a valid viewpoint in day-to-day politics. And Begin himself was in his element. In emotional speeches in the Knesset he spoke of Jerusalem as the "City of David," the conquest of which was a matter of historical justice, the correction of a wrong. To this he added a new phrase: the "estate of the forefathers." In his eyes the West Bank was not occupied territory but rather an inseparable part of that "estate," bequeathed to the Jewish people by the three gentlemen buried in the Cave of the Patriarchs. Though the West Bank was part of the area defined as the "Arab State" in the 1947 UN Partition Plan, the State had never been allowed to rise. The area was annexed, during the War of Independence, by the Hashemite Kingdom of

411

Jordan—an annexation never considered legitimate by Menachem Begin and his party.

The new circumstances also caused Israelis to view Begin in a different light. Looking back, people could see that in fact the Labor Party leadership of the coalition government had been actively pursuing policies *vis-à-vis* the Arab world very similar to those of Begin himself. Not only that, but people with keen political minds could see that the social policy of Labor had moved further and further from its socialist origins, and closer to the social concepts of Begin. On a personal level Menachem Begin reaped other harvests. One of them was his relationship with Moshe Dayan, a man he had always respected even though he was entirely different from him. Though associated for most of his lifetime with the Labor camp, Dayan has always been suspected of political opportunism rather than deep socialist conviction. Undoubtedly pragmatic, he is known to students of Israeli politics as a man capable of changing his opinions with each new dawn. Despite the obvious differences between them, he and Begin were quick to find common ground. While others were striving for ways to avoid war, these two were busy considering the moves to be made and the possible results, both military and political. Within the cabinet they were the nucleus of a "hawk" coalition that crossed party boundaries.

After the war Begin discerned that Dayan was not motivated by a sense of history, and that the restored territorial integrity of the homeland meant little to a man who was too cold-blooded for simple emotion. Yet he would hear the man say, publicly and in private, that Israel had not won in order to part from the areas that were the cradle of the Israeli nation.

412

They signed no formal pact, but they were allies—and it was perhaps this that paved the way for Dayan's leaving the Labor alignment ten years later in order to become Menachem Begin's Foreign Minister.

When Prime Minister Eshkol died, a few months after Israel's greatest military victory, it seemed for a moment that the national coalition was at an end. Golda Meir, chose by the Labor Party to succeed Eshkol, was also a member of the founding generation of the Israeli labor movement—and she brought with her a reminder of the traditional enmities and distaste for Begin and his politics. She felt the same hostility for her colleagues of Rafi, the men who had deserted the party along with Ben-Gurion. It was with an angry eye that she viewed the budding partnership between Dayan and Begin, and the legitimacy that it might accord the latter's party. Before the 1967 war she had led the opposition to a coalition government and to giving the Defense Ministry to Dayan. Moreover she was a far more forceful and resolute figure than her predecessor, so it was unlikely that her neighbors at the cabinet table were going to see the partnership flourish.

The people who expected to see cracks in the framework of the national coalition were soon to find that they had been mistaken, however. Golda Meir quickly proved to be an outspoken "hawk." Surprisingly she found a common language with Begin—and he reacted by calling her "a proud Jewess."

The general elections of 1969 took place in the shadow of the great victory. Nobody expected a political upset. Begin had achieved public legitimacy, but the government that led the nation to victory was after all a Labor government. Golda Meir reaped the harvest. Nevertheless national unity was as appealing to the electorate as it was to their representatives, despite voices that warned it could not last. The state of emergency that had created the national coalition had passed, but some instinct warned the leaders that vital decisions were still to come.

Force of circumstance, and perhaps the death of Eshkol, healed much of the rift between Rafi and the party to which it had originally belonged. Only Ben-Gurion and a handful of loyal followers remained outside. It looked as if the more leftist Mapam Party, which had presented a unified state with Labor at the election, and the Independent Liberals would be partners in the new coalition. Labor's almost traditional partner, the National Religious Party, was presenting conditions to which Golda Meir would not easily agree, and Begin's *Gahal* insisted that it would not join the government without the religious faction. While the negotiations for a new coalition dragged on endlessly, the position in Israel fast approached a new crisis. On the Suez Canal Egypt was waging a war of attrition, while terorists were keeping the army busy on the Jordanian frontier. On top of that, and perhaps as a result of the postwar boom, labor relations were worsening. Strikes and sanctions were becoming the order of the day.

Golda Meir's potential partners in *Gahal* insisted on the use of restraint against workers and demanded the inclusion into the coalition agreement of a clause calling for compulsory arbitration in vital industries and services. To Labor, the right to strike is as basic as any other fredom, and the party could not accept any restriction of it. As unhappy as certain of the

414

leaders were with the industrial unrest, they could not and would not use the tactic that *Gahal* proposed.

Even a few of Begin's colleagues were unhappy about *Gahal*'s conditions. Labor was leaning over backward to insert into the coalition agreement clauses that related to the occupied West Bank as the "estate of the forefathers." The division of ministries was also eminently acceptable. Begin's party was no longer a spare wheel in an emergency vehicle, but rather a potential full partner in a coalition constructed according to the size of parliamentary representation of the parties. Yet Begin personally was adamant: there would be no Labor-*Gahal* coalition unless Golda Meir included the compulsory arbitration of labor disputes in the new program of legislation.

"I think we're staying out. Nobody can change Begin's mind," Dr. Elimelech Rimalt confided to a fellow ministerial candidate, Yosef Sapir, who readily agreed. Both men had attempted to convince Begin that, with the IDF engaged in an escalating war of attrition on the Suez Canal, this was no time for *Gahal* to be away from the table where the decisions would be made. They pointed out that Egyptian bullets were not concerned with the party affiliations of the Israeli boys on the front line, and those boys needed to feel that the country was united behind them. Begin tended to agree with his two colleagues that the emergency was not over, and he knew full well that Golda Meir's new government would be the one to stabilize the achievements of victory. But he would not change his mind. Apart from the labor dispute issue, he could not see any reason to let his party be pulled in unconditionally.

After forty-two days of negotiation it appeared that

Gahal would resume its place on the opposition benches. And Begin seemed satisfied with that state of affairs. It was an indication of his status within *Gahal,* for many of his *Herut* colleagues would gladly have supported their Liberal Party partners in their reasons for joining the government, but did not do so because Begin was opposed to it.

On the forty-second day there came a turning point. Looking back one could say that U.S. Secretary of State William Rogers set up Israel's national unity coalition on December 10, 1969. That morning the chances for successful completion of the coalition negotiations were very slight. By evening the coalition was an established fact. The dramatic change was brought about by Rogers's public announcement that the United States was seeking to reach a Middle East settlement in conjunction with the Soviet Union—and over Israel's head. There was no longer any need to speculate over rumors and leaks from Washington. The Secretary of State was saying in effect that the United States no longer recognized the Israeli principle that it was up to the two sides involved to settle their differences in direct negotiation. And his alternative implied coerced settlement.

Rogers did not say what borders the United States intended for Israel, but it was clear that there would be no holding the territories. On the subject of Jerusalem his words were vague to say the least, and they conveyed no consolation to Israelis for whom the city was not negotiable. In brief, the Rogers declaration was a warning bell in Jerusalem. Golda Meir convened her "caretaker" cabinet that same evening.

Yosef Sapir, summoned from the Knesset cafeteria

to the cabinet meeting, commented: "Who knows? Perhaps this will convince Begin."

The extraordinary cabinet session was a long one, with plenty of disagreement between the ministers, but it did result in a consensus on the publication of a statement rejecting the Secretary of State's proposal. Menachem Begin, who according to eyewitnesses was smiling when the decision was taken, called Sapir as soon as the meeting was over.

"I have an idea. At times like these the human brain doesn't stop inventing ideas. I suggest that we propose that the clause on compulsory arbitration be dropped from the coalition agreement."

Next day, as a polite but adamant Israeli statement rejected Rogers's overture, the entry of *Gahal* into the new government became an established fact. At the same time Major General Ezer Weizman suddenly announced his resignation from the army to join the *Herut* faction of *Gahal*. To anyone who knew the general's decidedly hawkish opinions, the move could not have come as a complete surprise. In the army Weizman was not at liberty to express his views publicly, but he had made not secret of them.

Weizman's name was a household word in the Israeli army. Though he was not an aristocrat among the *Palmach* officers (like Yitzhak Rabin and his successor as Chief of Staff, Haim Bar Lev), he nevertheless fitted in with the aura that they created. He had risen through the ranks of the air force, eventually serving as Commanding General. Even though he was Head of Staff Branch in the General Staff during the 1967 war, he was considered to be the architect of the air force's impressive victory on June 5.

To some degree it was ironic that Weizman was

joining Begin's party. His uncle Haim Weizmann, the first president of Israel, had been Jabotinsky's bitterest enemy and a target of Begin's political arrows. However, the family relationship had never restricted Ezer Weizman.

The announcement that Weizman was taking the political plunge caused a sensation. Despite the prohibition on politics within the army, senior officers were known to have leanings that on occasion resulted in active party membership upon their retirement from the service. But so far there had been no question about which party they would join when the time came. Weizman was the first to turn his back on the Labor Party, and the first general to join Begin's party.

Menachem Begin threw an emotional celebration for Weizman at the party headquarters, Jabotinsky Tower. There, in front of television cameras, the two men hugged each other under a photo of Haim Weizmann's bitter adversary. Weizman joined the cabinet as the new Minister of Transport.

The new coalition had the widest backing of any Israeli government—102 out of the 120 Knesset members, who were united in their opposition to the Rogers announcement. Against the growing disagreements within the cabinet the American pressure provided a strong impetus for cohesion.

One decision taken by the government—on deep penetration bombing of Egypt—was to have its effect on the 1973 war. Begin, as Minister Without Portfolio, was a full partner in the decision, now considered by military analysts to have been a mistake. But in late 1969 the political-military echelon in Israel recognized that there was a need to escalate the war of attrition to a level where the Egyptians would be unable to follow. The war had done Israel more damage than her leaders were prepared to admit. One direct result had been the beefing up of the reserve army, which placed an almost intolerable burden on the economy of the country. Suddenly the army was compelled to abandon the *Blitzkrieg* warfare that it understood so well, and to fight a static war reminiscent of World War I in Flanders. In addition the daily casualty lists were taking their toll on national morale. Israel is a small country, almost one large family. That fact, together with the unhappy heritage of the Holocaust in Nazi Europe, has always combined to make Israelis exceptionally sensitive to casualty lists.

Unpredictably Menachem Begin did not immediately support the new military opposition. A hawk himself, he believed that the Arabs could be convinced by a show of force. But as a man with a sense of national responsibility, he tried to persuade his ministerial colleagues that the matter needed careful study before any conclusion was reached. The cabinet was fed mostly by reports from Chief of Staff Haim Bar Lev and the head of the Intelligence Branch, Major General Aharon Yariv. Begin suggested that other generals and Intelligence personnel should be invited to government sessions so that all sides could be heard. As far as the bombings was concerned, neither he nor his colleagues needed to look hard for experts. Ezer Weizman, the new Minister of Transport, was both an experienced combat pilot and the architect of Israel air force doctrine of warfare. He was in favor of deep penetration missions into Egypt and entirely convinced that the air force could perform the task.

Other ministers were coming round to the view that

bombing Egypt could topple President Nasser. There were indications that the Egyptian public, who were being given distorted information on the balance of power between the two countries, were becoming disenchanted with their president. If they were to see Israeli planes over the big cities of Egypt, they might well either depose Nasser or compel him to abandon his involvement in the Arab-Israeli conflict.

On January 7, 1970, Israeli aircraft flew the first bombing mission. The Egyptians could see that the intruders enjoyed complete freedom of the skies. Interceptors that tried to stop them were shot down. On occasion the people could even watch the Israelis flying low over Nasser's presidential palace. But the bombing only served to make Nasser dig in even more firmly. However, he was forced to call in the Russians, who promptly provided pilots for the Egyptian squadrons. Massive Soviet involvement was undobutedly a danger to Israel, even though a number of Soviet pilots were shot down by the raiders.

But in 1970, however, nobody foresaw the 1973 war. Despite the situation on the Canal, most Israelis believed that Israel had never been in a stronger position. The country was enjoying an unprecedented prosperity and its population believed almost blindly in the army's ability to repel any Arab aggression.

It was in this atmosphere that Golda Meir and Menachem Begin approached a relationship in which the old adversary status was completely forgotten. Behind his back, she referred to him as "a perfect gentleman." The prime minister was particularly impressed by Begin's talent for legal formulations. Her own speeches tended to make frequent reference to general concepts such as morality and justice, but precise wording had never been her strong point, and he came to her aid in this respect on more than one occasion. They also found a common language in internal policies. As a zealous socialist since her youth, Golda Meir could hardly be expected to accept Begin's overall view, but she was just as opposed to the growing labor unrest and strikes as he was. Considering this to be sabotage to Israel's war effort, she was ready and willing to do combat with the unions from which her party drew its main strength.

Summoned to the premiership when she could rightly have thought her political career over, Mrs. Meir was apparently determined to make her mark on history—and perhaps in this she was motivated by the ever-present patriarchal shadow of Ben-Gurion. Her route to history seemed to lie via the achievement of Israeli and Jewish unity in the ranks that followed her. It delighted Begin to hear this elderly heretic, brought up in the socialist tradition, referring favorably to the value of orthodox religious life.

It was not plain sailing. Differences of opinion between Begin and the rest of the government began to surface—at first over a question of semantics, to which sometimes Begin attached supreme importance. The nonparty organization calling itself the Entire Land of Israel Movement had come into being shortly after the Six-Day War. Its purpose being exactly as its name suggests, it was only natural that its members should look to Begin as their representative within the government. They expected him to insist that there must be no withdrawal from the "occupied" or "liberated" territories, no matter what inducement was offered by the Arabs. He did do just that; but not with the degree of vehemence that might have been expected. Led by Abba Eban, the "doves" in Mrs. Meir's coalition cabinet argued that the new movement could do great damage to Israel's international status since the world did not recognize Israel's right to annex the territories occupied in June 1967.

Cracks also began to show on a more practical level. Since Abba Eban's Foreign Ministry was the first to realize the failure of the deep penetration bombing policy, it was he who suggested to the prime minister that she open a "peace offensive." Golda Meir was skeptical. To her the world was either black or white: the Israelis wanted peace, while the Arabs sought the destruction of Israel. It was a popular view among Israelis, but one bitterly criticized by Nahum Goldmann, aging president of the World Jewish Congress. Goldmann, who enjoyed access to many important people in Europe and the United States, offered to go to see the president of Egypt on behalf of Golda Meir's government. The offer was refused.

The tension growing between Begin and the government in which he served paradoxically had nothing to do with Mrs. Meir, with whom he enjoyed almost complete understanding. It was the "dove" faction of the Labor Party that troubled him. Not only did they disparage the Entire Land of Israel Movement and support Goldmann's thesis; there were even mumblings among them that the time had come to dump Menachem Begin before his hawkish views involved the entire government. He responded with his usual aggressive rhetoric, taking care not to attack Golda Meir personally.

A new slogan was gaining acceptance: "Territories in return for peace." Golda Meir took up the challenge. In a long Knesset speech she insisted that the Arabs had no intention of compromising with Israel, no matter what the conditions. However, she repeated Israel's declared willingness to accept UN Security Council Resolution 242, which spoke of just and lasting peace in the Middle East. This caused a certain concern to Menachem Begin and his *Gahal* colleagues, for Resolution 242 also spoke of Israeli withdrawal from territories occupied in war.

Sidestepping a possible crisis, Begin argued that the subject of Resolution 242 had never been discussed by the government, and that most of its members would in any case support his view. At a meeting with Golda Meir he complained bitterly about her change of position, but she reassured him that there was no change —leaving him free to believe that her speech had simply been a gesture to the doves of her party.

The *Gahal* members of the Knesset then convened in caucus to discuss the position they would adopt in the forthcoming plenary session to debate the prime minister's speech. Apart from their annoyance at not being consulted on a matter so important to them, the party members were in a serious quandry. Coalition discipline required them to vote for acceptance of the prime minister's policy statement; yet such a step would imply a rejection of their own basic principles regarding the completeness of Israel within her new borders. On the other hand the Labor Party doves were putting pressure on Golda Meir not to retreat either from her statement or from its possible interpretation. She readily agreed that a concession to *Gahal* at this point would only be the beginning of a long chain of concessions in the future.

Begin knew that he could not support the government on this issue, yet he did not consider the time ripe for departure from the coalition. Though he was deeply insulted that Golda Meir had made the statement without consulting him, he believed that a continued *Gahal* presence in the cabinet could prevent capitulation to the Americans. *Gahal* abstained in the Knesset vote—and it was no longer possible to hide the cracks in national unity.

At this point, in June-July 1970, the situation on the Suez front was changing radically. Soviet involvement was becoming both massive and visible. Israeli Intelligence reported that the Russians were erecting a wall of ground-to-air missiles along the Canal. The Americans watched in growing anxiety. By a stroke of irony the man who had caused the establishment of the national unity coalition, Secretary of State Rogers, was now about to cause its dissolution.

Despite the efforts of the UN special envoy Dr. Gunnar Jarring to achieve a cease-fire, the war over Suez was escalating. To stop it, the United States through Mr. Rogers now offered a new formula that attempted to place a cease-fire within the larger context of the Arab-Israeli conflict. It suggested an end to belligerency in return for total withdrawal from the occupied territories, with an additional hint that the supply of U.S.-made weapons to Israel was dependent on acceptance of the new proposal.

At first it looked as if Israel would reject the Rogers Plan out of hand. Begin sat back and listened to his Labor Party colleagues attacking the idea. Initially the president of Egypt was not willing to accept Rogers's proposal either, but when he did so, the Israeli government was in a tight spot. Nobody was willing to return to the pre-1967 frontiers, which would place Arab artillery within range of Israel's heartland; yet

Israel could not afford a clash with the United States, on whom she was dependent for both military equipment and economic aid.

Begin's mood grew blacker. As he explained to a fellow cabinet minister: "You must understand, my party and I believed during all those years in opposition that we had a right to all of the Land of Israel, even when parts of it were not under our control. Do you really think that we can now agree to support the opposite of what we believe?" The minister, a confirmed "soft-liner," knew Begin well enough to appreciate that this man was not inclined to compromise—and certainly not with his principles.

A few days later the *Gahal* ministers met to coordinate their positions, Begin stressed that acceptance of the Rogers Plan, even with reservations, would imply withdrawal to borders that no sane Israeli could accept, and ended by saying that such a step would force *Gahal* to leave the government.

"Mr. Begin," said his Liberal Party colleague, Aryeh Dulzin, "I must say that your remarks are very logical, but your logic frightens me."

Dulzin and his fellow Liberal Yosef Sapir felt that *Gahal* involvement in the cabinet could still prevent political erosion and compel the government to maneuver away from total withdrawal. To Begin this was simply a tactic lacking in realism.

The next day Begin went to meet Dayan at the Defense Ministry, in an attempt to convince him of the justice of the *Gahal* case. Having explained their position, he added what must have sounded like an ultimatum: If the government accepted the American plan, *Gahal* would have no choice but to inform the prime minister that it was leaving the coalition. Dayan made no response to that, merely noting the Israel was too strong to be coerced into agreements that she did not like, but too weak to become embroiled in political confrontation with the United States.

Begin's next call, accompanied by Yosef Sapir, was at the office of the prime minister, where he told Mrs. Meir that continued participation of *Gahal* in the government was dependent on rejection of the Rogers Plan. But within hours there was a split in the *Gahal* ranks. The Liberal faction would not accept the ultimatum implied in Begin's remarks. Meanwhile Labor Party ministers were trying both directly and through mediators to convince Begin not to leave the government. Most of them were convinced anyway that the Arabs would eventually wreck the plan by refusing any political reward in return for withdrawal. Obviously any move back to the June 1967 frontiers would have to be matched by the defensible borders and lasting peace that the United Nations had already accepted as a principle.

Begin was not prepared to rely on Arab obstinacy. For him the point was clear. He would not be a party to any decision that returned the "estate of the forefathers" to non-Israeli hands. As he told a *Gahal* caucus in the Knesset: "I will cut off my right hand before I sign such a document."

The Liberals were not convinced that their best interests were served by departure from the Cabinet Room. Perhaps the biggest dilemma of all was that of confronting Ezer Weizman. As a "hard-liner" and supporter of Begin's views, he was totally opposed to any acceptance of the American terms; yet he was against leaving the government. Israel was faced with far-reaching decisions, and perhaps even with a military crisis caused both by the Suez war of attrition and the terrorist infiltration via Jordan. This was ample reason, so Weizman thought, to stay inside the government—since a party in opposition could do little more than criticize.

Begin would not be budged. He could not tolerate the idea that *Gahal* ministers would vote against the Rogers Plan, then continue in government as if nothing had happened. He even hinted that if the party decided against his view, he would no longer be able to represent is as a minister in the coalition. Meanwhile his attitude was causing consternation among some of his Labor Party allies, as Yisrael Galili would reveal to one of the Liberal ministers: "I don't understand what he wants. Does he want the representatives of Labor in the government to join *Herut?* After all, the two components of *Gahal* are having a hard enough time making one party."

The Liberal discontent was growing. Knesset member Gideon Pat, now a minister in Begin's government, criticized the *Herut* members of *Gahal:* "First they hesitate and debate. But when it comes to a vote, they watch Begin and do as he does."

"Do you remember," Elimelech Rimalt asked Ezer Weizman, "when you were in the army, you asked me why we don't unify the two halves of *Gahal?* I think that now you can understand for yourself."

In the first week of August 1970 the government of Israel unanimously decided to accept the American proposal for cease-fire on the Suez Canal, and accepted, by a majority vote, the Rogers peace initiative. In voting against the second point, the *Gahal* ministers had in fact sealed the fate of the National Unity coalition.

The central committees of *Herut* and the Liberal Party met in joint session to decide the future of *Gahal* in government. Begin himself later related that he came to the meeting with a distinct recollection of his mentor, Zeev Jabotinsky, leading his faction out of the Zionist Organization in 1933, because he did not agree with its policy. Behind the scenes the Liberals were trying to whip up support from among *Herut* colleagues. Some of Begin's closest associates, still trying to convince him to stay, suggested that he create a nonpartisan mass movement against withdrawal from the occupied territories, and use it as a counterbalance to Rogers. But Begin was resolute.

"I swear to you," he told the meeting, "that in all my life I have never been more at peace with myself and my conscience than I am now."

His motion was accepted by 117 votes to 112. Not much of a majority, but enough to return Begin to the wilderness of opposition after 1,000 days at the table of power.

CHAPTER 24

Union

The Menachem Begin who returned to the opposition benches in mid-August 1970 was not the same man. Involvement and partnership in the national burden seemed to have moderated his views, and had certainly moderated the tone of his speeches. His style was now polished and ironic rather than biting and inflammatory. Both inside and outside the Knesset he was speaking more of peace. It was not exactly the peace that the Arabs intended, or even that to which the government of Israel aspired, but it was a definite change from the zealot who had sought paths that could only aggravate the tensions between Jew and Arab. Perhaps it was because Israel now had under her control a larger area of the historic "Land of Israel." Be that as it may, he had certainly stopped referring to the IZL's old claim to the terrain east of the River Jordan.

One thousand days in coalition had done something to Begin, yet the break with the government disrupted personal relations within *Gahal*—and even within the *Herut* faction. Ezer Weizman fumed that the departure was unnecessary, and the Liberals continued to call it a major mistake. Nevertheless the sequence of events on the international scene was giving Begin a certain advantage over his opponents. The first in the series was President Nasser's decision to move ground-to-air missile batteries up almost to the Canal line within hours after the cease-fire over Suez. *Gahal* demanded an attack on the new missile sites while Begin, in accusing the government of inactivity, warned that the day would come when Israel would regret having done nothing.

His accusations and demands for an immediate military operation fell on deaf ears. The Israeli public were pleased that days passed without any bulletins listing the dead and wounded. Government information services were emphasizing the new tranquility. The country felt it could now settle back to enjoy prosperity in the confidence that the Arabs could never attack Israel—unless, of course, they were bent on suicide.

It was in this atmosphere that Israel heard on September 28, 1970, of the death of Gamal Abdul Nasser, the only man who had seemed capable of uniting the Arab world. His successor, Muhammad Anwar el-Sadat, seemed a pale stopgap figure beside his charismatic predecessor, and his threats were treated as a joke. Indeed Sadat himself would note years later that his opponents in Egypt had not expected him to occupy the presidency for longer than four to six weeks.

Within Israel the debate over the occupied territories had become almost a national pastime. Most Israelis now took the territories for granted. A minority still argued in favor of making an attempt to compromise with the Arab world based on the return of at least some of the new areas. And Begin saw himself as a knight in shining armor riding forth to protect the Chosen People's bequest from the Almighty.

"There is no separation between historic right, which is always actual, and the right to security, which is a daily affair," he wrote in his weekly article for an evening paper. "Were Judea and Samaria to be torn from us, the foundation of our security would be destroyed, and with it would collapse the chance for peace."

Begin tried to convince the Israelis that annexation of Judea and Samaria—he refused to refer to them as the West Bank—would advance the cause of peace and the Arabs were bound, sooner or later, to recognize the fact. This was the point at which he formulated the most important principle of his opposition party, and the foundation stone upon which his own coalition would eventually be built: No reparceling of the land of Israel.

There are those who claim that Hussein must get back Judea and Samaria. Because of the twists of time and fashion, there are those who argue that they should be transferred to a rule called "Palestinian." The moral and Zionist tragedy is that neither of these groups can conceive a third possibility: to maintain in the territories of the Land of Israel only a Jewish sovereignty.

In linking the historic and security issues Menachem Begin was also prepared to respond to the demographic argument—to those who claimed that Israel could not continue as a Jewish and democratic State while she controlled an extra half million Palestinians. The answer to that lay in a massive Jewish immigration. Begin had another argument: annexation of the territories would, in the final eventuality, also be in the American interest. "We must persuade our American friends," he wrote, "that if a Palestinian state comes into being in those territories, it will not be long before it becomes a Soviet base. I am convinced that the Americans understand that perfectly."

To those non-Israelis who drew a parallel between the groups that made up the Palestine Liberation Organization (PLO) and the Jewish underground during the British Mandate, Begin responded that the comparison was sacrilege. He fervently believed in the justice of the IZL's war and the injustice of Arab terror, primarily because the PLO did not hesitate to strike at population centers as part of its campaign "to destroy Israel," while the IZL only fought against the foreign régime. As he stubbornly contended, the talk of recognition of Palestinian rights of self-determination was the biggest hoax of the twentieth century, since the Palestinians are an integral part of the Arab nation.

"The Arabs have so many countries, and we have only one," he said in the Knesset. "Why do those who are called Palestinians persist in taking ours from us? Do they want to live here? They are welcome. Nobody is driving them out. But I can't understand why they insist that this is their land."

Begin used a historical argument. From the dawning

of history, the Land of Israel has been the homeland of the Jewish people. It was the estate of the Jewish forefathers, generations before the modern cities of Europe and America came into being, thousands of years before someone had argued for the existence of an Arab Palestinian nation. And Begin had not a shadow of doubt that, in the end, the world would recognize Israel's arguments were right, provided Israel presented them in the right way.

As the official attitude toward recognition of the Palestinian entity moderated, Begin's attitude hardened—and the Palestinians themselves were most helpful to him. The extremist propagandists of the PLO argued incessantly that their main purpose was the destruction of the State of Israel, and that their "secular and democratic" state would be built upon the ruins of the Jewish homeland. These are the PLO's principles, written in the Palestinian Treaty, which is considered their political program. "Listen to them," Begin said. "Listen to what they say. Why don't you believe them? They don't hide their intentions."

Meanwhile a drama was unfolding within Begin's party—and the main actor was Ezer Weizman. Weizman was an unusual specimen in the *Herut* collection: Israeli-born, and possessing the lack of formality traditionally associated with the "sabras," he was the antithesis of the overly courteous and formal Central Europeans of *Betar* origin. His penchant for speaking his mind in blunt terms had made him something of a national institution, and certainly one beyond the understanding of the party veterans and the members of Begin's "fighting family." Yet when *Gahal* left the coalition and Weizman vacated his seat as

Transport Minister, he was appointed chairman of the *Herut* Executive. Most of his effort was devoted to rejuvenating and broadening the party, but he soon found that the *Herut* pyramid of hierarchy—with Menachem Begin at its summit—was cast of reinforced concrete. As a general, Weizman had been brought up in a system where rotation through a number of positions, and then eventually out into the cold of the civilian world, was a strictly and even cruelly enforced rule. This was not the case in *Herut*.

"If you want to breathe fresh air you can't do it there," he told an interviewer. "Everything revolves around Menachem Begin. People vie with each other to guess what he's thinking and how he will react."

Weizman also contended that Begin had given up trying for power—that he was satisfied with an anachronistic party, unsuited to the changing spirit and needs of a modern country. These were hard ideas for Begin to digest. In his view Weizman was a political babe in arms and, as such, had to be restrained courteously but firmly. Unlike some others in the party, Weizman was not motivated by a driving ambition to replace Begin, but merely by the innocent conviction that *Herut* needed new ideas—that the days of the IZL were over.

Persuaded that Begin was a virtual dictator who could not tolerate criticism—a view hotly disputed by loyalists like Kadishai—Weizman resigned from his chairmanship of *Herut* at a time when new national elections were on the horizon. He turned to a new career in business, and would probably have considered politics a closed chapter of his life but for the intervention of an old colleague in arms, General Ariel Sharon.

Ariel Sharon was also somewhat of an anomaly in the Israeli army. His first appearance in the national eye was as a young major when, in the early 1950s, he was recalled to the army from university in order to lead a tiny unit of raiders operating across borders against the *fedayeen* terrorist gangs. At a time when morale in the ranks of the army was low, his exploits restored confidence and gave the troops a new sense of purpose. He quickly graduated from a fifty-man guerrilla-type detachment to command of the new paratroop army.

A favorite of the national leadership and the idol of his subordinates, Sharon was nevertheless the *enfant terrible* of the IDF, with a highly deserved reputation for impulsiveness and caustic public pronouncements. He had one driving ambition—to become Chief of Staff—and he was sure that his military ability and distinguished record would eventually bring him the coveted position. When he finally realized that the peak was unscalable, he decided to resign his commission before the normal rotation policy of the army made the step inevitable. Promptly, to the astonishment of many of his associates, he joined the Liberal faction of *Gahal.* One of his friends expressed the general reaction: "It's hard to grasp what a wild man like 'Arik' will do among those perfect gentlemen, who are interested mainly in economics."

Sharon made no attempt to explain, or even to justify, his move on ideological grounds. Simply, the Liberal Party seemed to him a field waiting for him to plow. As far as *Gahal* was concerned, Weizman had already provided a precedent for retired generals. And Begin was delighted; his partners in the alliance were bringing him a fine dowry for the impending elections

—a second general with a fine record. But Sharon was to have the same experience in the Liberal faction that had been Weizman's lot in *Herut*. His breath— or rather, gale—of fresh air soon proved too chilly for the perfect gentlemen, who were totally inexperienced in coping with earthy military style. Unlike Weizman, Sharon was imbued with the combative spirit, and he proceeded to sow the first seeds of the plant that was to bring Begin to power.

While still a raw civilian recruit to politics, in the summer of 1973, Ariel Sharon shattered the relatively placid political life of Israel. He convened a press conference and called for the union of all the right-wing parties into a force that might stand a chance in the contest against the Labor Party due to take place in October. At first glance such a union appeared to be a wild dream. The right wing of Israeli politics was not only split among itself, seemingly irreparably, but also did not in total possess even one-half of the electoral strength of the Labor Party and Mapam, which together comprised the Labor alignment. The union, therefore, did not seem worthwhile—far less possible. Yet Sharon, with his unusual instincts, had sensed the potential of the combination. He now issued an outrageous ultimatum: Either there would be union, or he personally would turn his back on politics and would urge publicly that others do the same.

The right wing of the political spectrum contained, apart from the Liberal and *Herut* alliance in *Gahal*, a tiny party known as the "Free Center" and led by the attorney Shmuel Tamir. This was a splinter faction of the Labor Party, which had followed Ben-Gurion into political exile, then strayed even farther right, and a number of individuals whose sole common denominator was their common interest in the Entire Land of Israel Movement.

Sharon's appeal was received enthusiastically among the younger generation of these parties and factions, who in any case had a vested interest in any change in leadership. The party establishments, on the other hand, were in a dilemma. The Liberals had already been burned by Sharon's crusading fire. Begin had no taste for yet another version of the Weizman experience. Tamir could not see himself in the same picture with Begin, whom he had left to form his own party and, if he had difficulty with this, it was nothing compared to what Begin thought. The very name of Shmuel Tamir was capable of giving Begin gooseflesh. As for the "National Party" of ex-Ben-Gurion supporters, all the others considered them to be merely a fraction of the Labor Party. But the pressures from the rank and file were too strong to be ignored; and there was much truth in Sharon's argument that this was the only possible hope of unseating Labor.

The right-wing parties were left with no choice but to enter cautious and suspicious negotiations with each other. They examined one another's intentions and plans very carefully but even as the negotiations moved into high gear, newspaper photographs still revealed frozen smiles on the faces of Begin and Tamir as they looked across the table at each other. There were moments when the whole exercise seemed futile, yet Sharon continued to use all his powers of persuasion. When *Herut* stood ready to torpedo the inclusion of Tamir in the coalition, Sharon again issued an ultimatum: all together or nothing at all.

By this time none of them wanted to appear before the electorate as responsible for wrecking their chances. And so, on the eve of elections, the party that Sharon named *Likud*—"Unity"—came into being.

Though Begin was not at first enthusiastic, he was quick to appreciate the potential advantages of the *Likud* coalition. Since all partners preserved a degree of independence, Begin enjoyed preferential status, in that *Herut* was the largest individual unit and *Gahal* could muster the loudest voices. The policies of all were close enough for cooperation, and that applied even to Tamir and Begin.

Thus a modified *Herut* election platform was put forward as the program of a united force that could at last claim to be an alternative to the party that had ruled Israel for twenty-five years. However President Sadat of Egypt decided to upset all the well-laid election plans. At noon on October 6, 1973, mere days before the election, the armies of Egypt crossed the Suez Canal into the Sinai Peninsula. At the same time Syrian armored units smashed through the thin defense line on the Golan Heights. The war caught Israel unawares and rocked the country's political and social system. People suddenly had doubts about the policies of the national leadership, which was forced to admit to having been taken by surprise by the Egypto-Syrian offensive. The myth of Israel's invincible army was almost shattered. Much of the blame was laid on the shoulders of Defense Minister Moshe Dayan, though Prime Minister Golda Meir publicly accepted her share. A public commission of enquiry resulted in the resignations of the Chief of Staff and other senior officers.

Few Israelis were untouched by the trauma of the Yom Kippur War, and Menachem Begin was no exception. When the war began, Begin was praying in the synagogue of Jabotinsky Building, close to his Tel Aviv home. His daughter Leah was the one who informed him of the general mobilization. He was thunderstruck. As a member of the Knesset Foreign Affairs and Security Committee, he was aware that the Egyptian army had been holding maneuvers close to the cease-fire lines, but he also knew of the Intelligence Branch appraisal that the probability of war was low. (Two days later Begin's first-born son, Benjamin, got off a plane at the Tel Aviv airport. Benjamin was completing his studies in Denver, Colorado, when news of the outbreak of war reached him. He left his wife and children, and took the first available plane to Israel to join his reserve unit. After the war he would stay on in Israel and volunteer for two years' service in the regular army.)

While the war lasted, Begin voiced no criticism of military or political mistakes. As he himself later observed, a responsible opposition does not engage in such games while the nation is fighting for its life. But his was not really a passive attitude. He made clear to the prime minister that he would remain silent only until the battles were over. Afterwards the wave of protest from soldiers and reservists on the line who had witnessed the terrible blunders reached a crescendo in demands to remove those responsible. Unlike many others, Begin did not join in the chorus against Moshe Dayan, although he considered him responsible insofar as he shared in collective responsibility. The war was over, and the interrupted elections were to take place almost immediately. Begin believed the public would have their own say, and it seemed likely that they would exact the required price from the government that had allowed all this to happen.

Sharon gave up politicking in October 1973, to return to the ranks of the army. As a reserve general he commanded one of three army corps that blocked the Egyptian offensive, and then led the assault force that crossed the Canal into Egypt. Ariel Sharon earned another full measure of glory. When he removed his uniform again to go back into politics, the interlude made a good election story, and the *Likud* took full advantage of it.

The Yom Kippur War itself was not enough to change the political map. The right wing took a considerable bite into the electorate, but Labor still won—apparently confirming that nothing could ever shift them from power. Certainly Begin seemed convinced of it.

"Had the reserve been mobilized in time . . . I don't doubt that the army would have dealt the enemy a crushing blow," Begin said in his election campaign, in his quietest tones ever. Most Israelis would have agreed with that, but they were not ready for a drastic change of régime. The wounds of war were still healing slowly, and national morale was at its lowest. The seven fat years were obviously at an end, and Israel was dependent on the United States for her survival under the staggering burden of the cost of the Yom Kippur War. It was perhaps symbolic that in these days of despondency, the man who had declared Israel's independence, David Ben-Gurion, died as a lonely, aged recluse in his desert kibbutz. A nation already saddened by horrible war watched in untold grief as the Old Man was laid to rest. Next to the grave stood a solemn Menachem Begin.

A few days after the state funeral on December 3, 1973, the daily press published a letter that threw a new light on the rivalry between the two men—a letter written by Ben-Gurion to Begin when he was Minister Without Portfolio in Golda Meir's government:

> Paula, my wife, was for some reason an admirer of yours. I opposed your road sometimes strongly —both before the State and after it arose—exactly as I would have opposed the road of Jabotinsky. I strongly objected to a number of your actions and opinions after statehood, and I do not regret my opposition. For in my opinion I was in the right; but personally I never harbored any grudge against you, and as I got to know you better over recent years, my esteem for you grew and my Paula rejoiced in it.

Another page of history was closed. It was perhaps also symbolic that the day Begin would choose four years later to extend Israel's invitation to President Anwar el-Sadat to visit Jerusalem was the anniversary of Ben-Gurion's death. Begin himself drew attention to the fact in his Knesset announcement of the invitation.

In the meantime the election results were a disappointment to Begin, even though he could draw encouragement from the fact that the vote in army polling stations was heavily in favor of the *Likud* coalition. Nobody attached particular importance to the fact at the time, though it should have given food for thought to the Labor Party. But they were still in power, and totally oblivious to the public time bomb. The nation had given a vote of confidence to Golda Meir and her colleagues; but the criticism of the handling of the war could not be silenced.

CHAPTER 25

"I, Menachem Begin, Do Solemnly Swear . . ."

The attainment of power by Menachem Begin was a long-drawn-out process. Its roots lay in the gradual disappearance of clear political distinctions between his party and its traditional rival, at the same time that he and his movement became the alternative to the government of the day.

This process took on particular momentum in the four years following the Yom Kippur War of October 1973. The widespread dissatisfaction with the Labor government, which was blamed for the October "earthquake," brought Begin finally to power.

These four years witnessed the growing disintegration of the Labor establishment. Golda Meir resigned and withdrew from political life, a bitter and disappointed woman, thereby creating a vacuum in the Labor leadership. Mrs. Meir belonged to the founding generation of the Israeli labor movement, and her heirs were only youths when she was already an established political figure. Great hopes were put in these younger leaders. Her successor as premier, Yitzhak Rabin, had been a military leader of great fame and a successful ambassador for Israel in Washington. Rabin's Defense Minister, Shimon Peres, had already considerable achievements to his credit, while Yigal Allon, who became Foreign Minister, enjoyed similar esteem, way beyond his glorious role as *Palmach* commander in 1948.

Rabin announced that his government would be one of continuity and change. Many Israelis did not take that promise seriously. For them it was enough that a younger man had finally taken over the helm of state from the aging "founding fathers." Rabin was an Israeli-born subject, who could be expected to be free of the inhibitions of a Diaspora background and upbringing, and also a military hero of proven capabilities. But the fact was that there was continuity without change. The style may have been different, and some of the old and tired faces were missing—yet the Labor Party was still unchanged.

The new leaders were typical in their constant quarrels with younger heirs of outstanding leaders. Rabin had reached the premiership after a struggle with Peres; and the latter never did get on with Allon. This was to have been the dominant trio that would provide Israel with national leadership.

Within a short time the personal rivalry of the trio began to overshadow everything else, and to supply headlines to the waiting newspapers. As a result none of the three enhanced his reputation. Throughout this period the relationship between the premier and his Defense Minister was especially tense, with Rabin accusing Peres of seeking to undermine him with the view of replacing him. Mrs. Meir retired to her Tel

Aviv home, became the Grand Old Lady of the Jewish people, and watched with growing anxiety what was happening in the corridors of power. She enhanced her moral authority by keeping out of political life.

It soon became apparent that the government of Israel was not working in harmony. The confrontation between the three top men reached its zenith at a most inopportune time, in the general elections.

Shimon Peres announced his candidature to the Labor Party nomination for the leadership, meaning the premiership. This was an unprecedented challenge to the incumbent party leader, and in the weeks preceding the nomination vote the campaigns of both candidates, Rabin and Peres, were particularly uninhibited in their mutual attacks and in their efforts to wrest support from the other side. With all eyes focused on this mighty struggle, the Israeli government appeared to be in a state of paralysis. As the fight grew even more bitter and the charges even more strident, the opposition members sat on the sidelines watching with glee. Later they were to quote both of the contestants against each other, concurring in each case.

In the end Rabin won the nomination by a narrow margin. But it was a bitter victory, for not only was he backed by a divided party filled with personal intrigues and hatreds, but his triumph was very short-lived. Only a few weeks elapsed before there burst on the world the news that the Rabins had a bank account in Washington, D.C. According to an Israeli law (since canceled) Israeli nationals were forbidden to hold accounts in foreign banks. An Israeli correspondent serving in Washington discovered by chance that Mrs. Rabin had transgressed this law.

445

Rabin, in a dramatic radio and TV appearance, withdrew his nomination for the party leadership. Peres was then voted as party leader by acclamation, while a still divided party began to fall apart.

The decline of the Labor Party was expedited by an increasing incidence of scandals among the establishment. With the Israel press adopting a crusading role, bribery and corruption appeared to be endemic throughout the most respectable financial institutions. The director of a large bank was charged with stealing $40 million, and the manager of a powerful government company was found guilty of a similar crime. The symbol of this crusade against corruption by the press became the chairman of the Israel trade union health organization, Asher Yadlin. Part of the inner circle of the Labor establishment, he was that party's nominee for the governor of the state bank just before the police arrested him. While representing trade unionists he was living a life more suited to a capitalist, all on public money. Yadlin was sent to jail. The next big news story was even more dramatic. His best friend, Housing Minister Avraham Ofer, committed suicide just as the press began to focus its attention on his past behavior. No charges were ever pressed against Ofer, mainly because of his sudden death, which in itself caused untold harm to the party's election prospects. Then came the accusation against former Foreign Minister Abba Eban, over bank accounts of his held abroad. Although police investigation never came up with anything incriminating against him, the row damaged the Labor Party's image even further.

On a higher level the party was also in trouble because it spoke with two tongues. While offering the voter a platform that sought territorial compromise in order to reach an accommodation with the Arabs, it also stressed that it would never give up all of the territories. The doves who might have been drawn to Labor were put off by the number of hawkish candidates; at the same time the hawks objected to the many doves to be found on the Labor parliamentary list. Another reason for Labor's losses was its opposition to big wage demands made during the previous year, resulting in labor disputes which the government tried to break. It was charged that the trades unions were instruments of the government.

Against this stormy background the prospect increased of the *Likud* providing an alternative government. It did not stand accused of the unpreparedness for the 1973 war, nor did it have an image of a party beset by intrigues. Rather it demonstrated a strong leadership, and it spoke in a clear and firmly hawkish voice, which appeared to be the right way to talk to an increasingly hostile world.

Besides, the more the voters studied the parties' programs, the more they managed to discern that few differences existed between them. Both sides strove for the same aim in similar ways. Historical differences were no longer relevant to the Israel of 1977.

Against this background a transformation began to take place in Menachem Begin. Those who remembered him from the time when he emerged from the underground and his first years in parliamentary life could hardly recognize the highly emotional leader. Begin had aged in the intervening years, and this is apparent in his external appearance. He has grown balder, and the mustache has disappeared.

It is fascinating to see how his appearance has become identical with his public image. He has cleaved to his hawkish positions, and thus strongly opposed the interim agreement between Israel and Egypt achieved by Dr. Henry Kissinger's mediation. He argued against what he regarded a one-sided Israeli withdrawal in Sinai. The Rabin government claimed that by signing the agreement, it would provide a dynamic momentum for further steps leading to a Middle East peace settlement. Begin said that such dynamics existed only in the government's mind, and that it had acted recklessly in foregoing two important strategic passes in Sinai. "We are giving up important strategic advantages for nothing," he argued in the Knesset debate on the subject. "We are presenting Egypt with our most essential security interest without getting anything in return. Such withdrawals, as sought by Kissinger, can bring the enemy to our very doorstep."

He had a most attentive audience, for any Israeli need only think of the Egyptian surprise attack in October 1973, and gaze at the map of the Sinai Peninsula, to see how right Begin's arguments were. Whoever dominates the two mountain passes handed over by Israel controls the entire Peninsula. If another attack came, it would require a much greater defensive effort on Israel's part.

On the other hand the fear arose that Israel's readiness for territorial compromise in Sinai might lead to similar concessions in the West Bank. While Sinai is far away from the centers of Israel's most populated area, the West Bank is only 15 kilometers off, and concessions there could lead to the positioning of Arab guns within firing range of Israel's main cities. In addition many people in Israel, particularly religious men, had begun to consider the area an integral part of Israel. They saw it as the ancestral homeland and therefore an area that was not negotiable. Huge demonstrations against the Sinai withdrawal accord were held, and while Begin did not participate in these protests, he gave them his blessing.

The government that signed the interim accord was caught in a whole series of internal and external dilemmas, and seemed ripe for a fall. It was just then that the *Likud* opposition, poised for a sure victory at the polls, sustained a serious blow. It came from the Yom Kippur war hero, General Sharon, who had been instrumental in forming the national-conservative bloc, and now seemed intent on its destruction. It is interesting to compare Sharon's behavior to that of General Weizman. As Weizman had found himself at odds with the veteran *Herut* leadership, so Sharon fell out with the senior Liberal Party politcians, *Herut*'s partner in the *Likud*. Apparently Sharon could not adjust himself to political life, considering the party rule anachronistic, and he stormed out of the *Likud* to form his own party.

Before doing so, he took an unprecedented and highly controversial step, agreeing to serve as Premier Rabin's advisor on security. The *Likud* took this as a great insult. Rabin and Sharon had been friendly since their army days, and Sharon thought that in this way he could return to the army command. However, while the general was biding his time in the prime minister's office, the government began to fall apart. Sharon found his position increasingly untenable, and decided to resign when the interim accord was signed with Egypt. Although he retired to his farm in the south, giving the appearance of one who had grown tired of public life, he told an interviewer, "I am not the type to sit by idly. I'm not built for it." And when the election campaign got under way, the restless general dived into the fray once more, this time at the head of a tiny party. Sharon claimed that while Labor was falling apart, the *Likud* was incapable of taking over for lack of political oxygen. He wanted his cut in the political cake, and he did not wish to share it with anyone else.

All this time Begin, who was simply sitting it out until the elections, continued with his time-honored custom of personal contact with his supporters. The weekly "open houses" held at his modest apartment in north Tel Aviv enhanced his reputation for modest living. Begin's near-puritan lifestyle was compared favorably by the public to the luxurious lifestyle adopted by some Labor ministers.

The many visitors at the Begin apartment were impressed by the warmth and harmony prevailing between Menachem and his wife Aliza. This charming woman never concealed her admiration for her husband. She tended to his spartan needs, keeping the children quiet when her husband had company or was at work in their lounge, which also served both as his bedroom and study. And she always saw to it that her husband had his glass of tea at hand.

Although they have been married many years, Mrs. Begin has taken care to keep out of the public eye. This is in stark contrast to the wives of former prime ministers, some of whom sought a share of power. In only a few cases did she ever grant interviews. She has always regarded her role as that of helpmate to her husband. At one time she began to study archeology, but soon gave it up. She is an erudite person and an accomplished linguist, speaking Hebrew, English, French, and German equally well. She still knows her Latin, and she and her husband both like the poetry of Virgil. She is an admirer of Agatha Christie's works, and a lover of classical music. To the outsider it is unclear how far her influence extends, but it is known that her husband consults her on his every move.

The Begins are a very close family. They firmly believe in the traditional values, and saw to it that their three children had the best education available. Begin is a strict but loving father. When his elder daughter, Hasia, wanted to study nursing, he insisted on her doing her army service first. By the time the younger daughter, Leah, came of military age, however, her father allowed her to study teaching instead.

Whenever he has the time to spare, Begin adores playing in the garden with his eight grandchildren. "It gives me a longer life," he says. His day, whether in Jerusalem or in Tel Aviv, begins at 5:00 A.M. with the daily newspapers. He goes through them all, even reading the letters to the editor. Over the years Begin accustomed himself to selective reading of material close to his heart, especially in domestic and foreign affairs. He is an avid reader of the world press, and in the past was a loyal subscriber to *Le Monde*, the *Manchester Guardian*, and *Pravda*. In recent years he has had to forego this pleasure, since inflation cut into his personal budget.

He lies in bed reading until about 6:45 A.M., then listens to the news on the radio. In the evening, at least before he became premier, he liked to read for pleasure. He particularly enjoys historical works and biographies; just before he assumed office, he was reading about the last years of President Roosevelt. He speaks of books as "expanding my horizons, and helping me to provide quotations for my speeches and articles."

Begin is also an avid reader of anything written about him. He is highly sensitive to criticism, whether oral or in print. Until he became prime minister, the *Likud* leader used to phone newsmen to comment on their reports. It is said that he gets angry when someone questions his decisions. Yehiel Kadishai disagrees. Begin does not say anything to those who annoy him, Kadishai maintains. So how is his anger expressed? "By his penetrating look," says Kadishai. "You can tell that he is angry. His gaze is most severe."

In recent years Begin contributed a weekly column to *Maariv,* the evening newspaper, but on becoming premier this practice ceased. He has told his confidants that he intends to retire at seventy in order to devote himself to writing about his generation, which witnessed the Holocaust and the establishment of the Jewish State. He wears dark suits and is always very careful with his appearance, in contrast to the casual dress of his Labor predecessors. He has a limited wardrobe, mainly due to the family's restricted income, as they live on his Knesset member's salary. All the same, one of Begin's pleasures is to give money away to the poor, or to any of the various beggars knocking at his door.

Aliza Begin is as modest in her lifestyle as her husband; she is a simple dresser, making most of her own clothes. She maintains a strictly kosher kitchen, and loves to cook. However her husband is no great eater, and his austere taste influences their meals. But on Saturday evenings, when friends come to one of the "open houses," which usually spread out onto the ground-floor balcony, they bring lots of cookies. Mrs. Begin is involved in fund raising for the Weizmann Institute of Science, and has been an active member of the Institute's Israeli Friends for many years.

Aliza Begin introduced few changes into the prime minister's official residence in Jerusalem. Most noticeable are the artistic photographs of swans, flowers, water lilies, and so forth—the work of their photographer daughter, Leah. Aliza is a popular figure with the public and deeply loved by those close to her, especially because her change in status has not altered her ways. She remains a simple person. Ever since she became the wife of Israel's prime minister, she has been fighting with her husband's security service bodyguards. They dislike her desire to continue traveling by bus between Jerusalem and Tel Aviv. But as she tells them: "That's how I have always traveled."

It was Ezer Weizman, with his unique intuitive power, who sensed the turning point. Just as he had stormed out of politics, so he dashed back into the center of things and assumed the direction of the *Likud*'s triumphant election campaign. When Weizman agreed to run the campaign, he had one condition: he must have complete power to run the show. This was a tremendous change for *Herut*, for in the past Begin had been in sole charge, drafting the major election material and personally setting all campaign details. Begin agreed to stand aside and let Weizman take over, and the *Likud* campaign was soon stamped with an entirely new image, reflecting the wishes of the native-born Israelis.

Then, at the height of the campaign, Begin collapsed. He was rushed to a Tel Aviv hospital emergency ward, not far from his home, with a severe heart attack.

"It was touch and go. He was a step away from death," a friend of the family was later to relate.

"It would seem that he did not like the next world too much, so he resolved to come back to us," his wife would say with a smile.

Israelis prefer a self-image of glowing youth, even though for so many years their rulers have been old men and women. But they concealed their illnesses and never published any announcement concerning their state of health. A besieged Israel would never allow herself to trust a leader in poor physical shape. For Menachem Begin this was a dreadful blow and one of the great testing times.

The Labor Party, now on the run, openly asked: Can a man with a bad heart really function as prime minister?

The question was quickly dealt with. Two days before the polls Begin stunned the nation by confronting Shimon Peres, the Labor Party leader, in a question-and-answer session on television. Begin seemed rather tired and pale on the screen, which modified his hawkish image, projecting a more relaxed appearance and one of great courtesy to his political rival. He emerged as the great fighter for parliamentary democracy. But above all the TV confrontation demonstrated to the voters that Peres was trying to be more Begin than Begin himself. When it came to the vote, they obviously preferred the original.

In that same TV appearance, Begin reaped the benefit of Weizman's political know-how. With the aid of one of the country's top public relations agencies, they sought to project an entirely new Menachem Begin—the ideal family man, the devoted grandfather, the man who preferred to give his time to reading or to visiting with family friends.

Although the image was near enough to the truth, its projection was indeed the success story of the 1977 election. By studying the results of previous elections, Weizman concluded that the young voters had no memory of the old Menachem Begin. This was especially noticeable in the 1973 general elections held immediately after the war, when the *Likud* won the majority of votes in army camps. So Weizman resolved to focus on the older generation, who still cleaved to the old image from the 1950s.

The *Likud* public relations campaign concentrated on the plethora of corruption scandals, which evoked just the right kind of reaction. Even Begin's sworn opponents could not deny his integrity and honesty. As the image of those in power grew more and more sullied, so those who had been out of office grew more appealing. But, this aspect was to complicate things for Weizman. Some time before the election campaign began, the troubles besetting *Herut*'s own "Tel Hai" party fund became public knowledge. Ever since the 1950s the party had been indebted to certain private individuals, who loaned *Herut* money that was used to aid the families of fallen IZL soldiers and to finance party operations and election campaigns. When the party organizers failed to pay off these debts they grew, particularly with the burden of high interest rates. This was just what the beleaguered Labor Party was seeking, and *Herut*'s debts became a hot issue. Whenever *Likud* speakers mentioned Labor leaders involved in corruption, hecklers would throw back the name of the "Tel Hai" fund. But however much the government propagandists pressed home this issue, it never touched Begin personally or affected his positive image. Everyone knew that the party chairman had always left financial matters to others.

"He doesn't even know how much money he's got in the bank," Yehiel Kadishai would relate. "Begin hasn't got a clue about financial matters." Begin himself was obliged to travel thousands of miles to raise money for his hard-pressed party in distant Jewish communities, and his confidants related that the "Tel Hai" fund affair "simply broke his heart."

It is difficult to know whether Begin would have left things up to Weizman and stayed in the background throughout the entire campaign, if it had not been for his illness. People who know him well say that if his health had permitted, he would certainly have stopped a number of the tactics adopted by Weizman and his professional advisors. One of the tactics used by his opponents in their TV spots were photographs from his early election campaigns, especially the notorious scene where he was accompanied by motorcycle outriders, and the well-known incident when *Herut* supporters threw stones at the Knesset building during the debate on German reparations. But they lacked impact on the voters, who seemed to consider them part of ancient history.

Israelis were more worried about the future. Before them they saw Menachem Begin as he had become in recent years—the politician who helped form the National Unity government on the eve of the Six-Day War in 1967, and who left the cabinet in 1970 when its Labor majority was about to adopt policies he opposed. For many Israelis, especially the younger ones, their political leaders had acquired the image of men only interested in retaining honors and power. Begin had acquired a contrasting image, one of political integrity and intellectual honesty, as a man who did not hesitate to resign from high office when his conscience dictated it. As leader of the opposition he emerged as a politician with a marked sense of national responsibility. Begin had enjoyed sufficient trust to be let into the greatest secrets by the Labor premiers. Thus Rabin told him of the rescue operation of the Israeli hostages in Entebbe just before the Israeli paratroopers left on their mission.

Begin's comment to Rabin on that occasion became famous throughout Israel. He said: "This operation is as courageous as anything we have achieved in this country. I pray for its success. But I want you to know that, if it should fail, then I will back you up. No one will ever be able to claim that we opposed this operation, and we will never use a possible setback as political ammunition." Rabin praised Begin after the operation's completion, saying, "He demonstrated a sense of real national responsibility."

On political issues, especially in respect to the territories, the Rabin government acquired an image of being incapable of making decisions. Indeed over the years it was accepted by the changing governments that their main decision was not to make a decision. Until October 1973, most Israelis applauded this position. It seemed as if in the confrontation with the

Arab world, time was on Israel's side, and that no one could budge them from the borders acquired in the June 1967 fighting. But the Yom Kippur War changed all that. Suddenly it became clear that the government must make a decision. Yet the delicate balance between hawks and doves made such a move unfeasible. As a result the public mood became more hawkish, the doves found it difficult to present their case, and the Arab world made things even more difficult. The PLO continued to talk of destroying Israel, and the heads of Arab states clung to the three no's of Khartoum (no recognition, no negotiations, no peace), refusing to make even one step in Israel's direction. Against this background more and more people preferred a clearly hawkish stance. Begin's known position earned him their support, for they trusted his uncompromising views.

The key plank in the *Likud* platform was the principle that the "Land of Israel," between the sea and the Jordan River, would never be partitioned again, and that a government led by the *Likud* would do its utmost to extend Israeli law throughout the West Bank. And this was undoubtedly the wish of many Israeli voters.

The large number of those Israelis ready to hand back all or most of the West Bank were only in favor of making such a far-reaching move in exchange for a real and lasting peace with the Arabs, one involving maximum security arrangements. But the Arab states and the PLO would not countenance such an arrangement, and without any positive response on their side, no Israeli thought there was a point to any such move. For most Israelis had learned to live with warfare; if the Arabs remained inflexible, there was nothing to lose.

Israeli observers believe that only a man like Begin, whom no one can accuse of being soft on Israel's basic interest or of being likely to abandon his principles, is capable of leading Israel to a territorial compromise even on the West Bank. They think that while not foregoing the historic right of his people to the area of the West Bank, he will of necessity explain to the Israelis that this ancient right does not hinge on the placement of a political boundary. Such a right can be attained in its religious, historical, and emotional aspects across an open border.

Begin's adoption of pragmatic rather than dogmatic decisions was apparent in the early months of his premiership. Thus he did not go so far as to apply Israeli law to the West Bank, although such a commitment was included in the *Likud* platform. It would seem that only a leader enjoying such authority as he does could do such a thing, irrespective of party pressures.

In the early part of 1977 Menachem Begin laid down the guidelines of the government he hoped to lead after the impending elections. He told his party convention that "If the *Likud* is asked to form a government, then its first concern will be to prevent war. A *Likud* government will adopt a number of peace initiatives. . . . We will ask a friendly country, which maintains diplomatic relations with Israel and her neighbors, to convey to them our proposal to open negotiations for the signing of peace treaties. Such negotiations must be direct, without prior conditions, and free of any imposed solution from outside."

Begin promised to give "special attention to Israel's relations with the United States of America," and said he hoped to see "the normalization of Israel's relations with the Soviet Union." He also expressed his hope that he would be able to repair Jerusalem's ties with Paris. It was at that party convention, too, that the future prime minister set out the underlying principles of his national policies, which included Judea and Samaria remaining an inalienable part of Israeli sovereignty, for

> whoever is ready to hand over Judea and Samaria to foreign rule will lay the foundations for a Palestinian state—the border between Israel and Egypt being delineated inside Sinai, and Israel's border with Syria being delineated on the Golan Heights; Arab inhabitants, whose national identity we recognize, will have a free option to receive either Israel citizenship or to hold their previous one. The refugee problem will be solved in a humanitarian manner, and proper understanding and regard, by the provision of suitable housing and employment. Arabs residing in the Land of Israel will enjoy cultural autonomy.

On the very evening that Begin presented his government to the Knesset and to the nation, the new premier called on King Hussein of Jordan, President Sadat of Egypt, and President Hafez al-Assad of Syria "to convene in order to discuss the achievement of peace." He then proceeded to enumerate the guidelines of his administration.

In domestic affairs the Begin government was much quicker in applying its social and economic election campaign commitments than anyone could conceive. The *Likud* had promised the electorate to sweep away the heritage of years of socialist rule and to liberalize the Israeli economy by removing foreign currency controls, by abolishing food subsidies, by encouraging private enterprise, and by stopping government intervention in the economy, which was to be given over to the players of the free market. Less than four months after the *Likud* took office, it proclaimed its new economic policy, soon dubbed "the economic earthquake."

Five months after its formation Begin's government, which had won by a bare majority, was strengthened by the addition of the moderate party of Professor Yigael Yadin, the Democratic Movement for Change. This middle-of-the-road party has its roots in the post-Yom Kippur War protest movements, and contains many disillusioned Laborites. Yadin became deputy premier, bringing with him Begin's old rival from *Herut,* Shmuel Tamir, who as a leader of Yadin's party now became Justice Minister. This meant that the government coalition led by Menachem Begin enjoyed the support of a comfortable majority of 78 out of the 120 Knesset members in Israel's Parliament, an all-important consideration for the success of Begin's peace plan.

Epilogue

President Anwar Sadat's dramatic journey to Jerusalem in November 1977, and Menachem Begin's return visit for their two-day Christmas meetings at Ismailia in the Sinai desert created high expectations that peace was almost at hand. But as the weeks went by, it became clear that it was impossible to solve generation-old problems in so short a time. The old enmities, complexities, and paradoxes still existed. There was still a lack of trust on both sides that no handshake could conceal. Personal warmth and good intentions could not be translated into political achievements overnight.

Israel and Egypt differed most sharply over two issues: Egypt demanded total withdrawal in Sinai to the internationally recognized border, while Israel wanted to maintain some measure of control over two large military airfields and the Rafah Salient, where there were the beginnings of a city (Yamit) and a few agricultural settlements. On the other hand, Israel demanded that after the withdrawal, most of the Sinai Peninsula be demilitarized, which Egypt made conditional on parallel demilitarization of the Negev. The major difference, however, was over Judea and Samaria. President Sadat was wary of the influence of the "rejectionist" Arab states that accused him of being interested only in a separate agreement that would exclude Egypt from the hard-line front against Israel. Therefore he wanted Israel at least to declare its readiness in principle to recognize the right of the Palestinians to self-determination, with all that implied. As Begin's government is pledged to the principle that the Land of Israel will never again be divided, this condition could not be accepted.

So although on the surface the peace momentum seemed to be continuing, to those aware of the degree of the differences it seemed likely that an impasse was inevitable unless something dramatic was done.

After the Ismailia meeting, to avoid admitting failure, Begin and Sadat had agreed—with American mediation—on the establishment of a military committee and a political committee to convene in Cairo and Jerusalem, respectively.

When the political committee met in Jerusalem on January 18, 1978, the Egyptian delegation, headed by Foreign Minister Ibrahim Kamel, rejected all attempts on the part of the Israeli delegation to conduct face-to-face discussions. All contact was through American mediators, and everything centered on the Egyptian demand to reach an agreed formula on the Palestinian problem before any other issues could be negotiated. Suddenly, two days after the conference had opened, Sadat recalled his delegation.

Although the military committee did not "blow up," it recorded no significant progress. The Egyptians were adamant in their refusal to grant any concessions at all in Sinai.

Those were difficult days for Menachem Begin. His illness, which had incapacitated him right after the elections, hit him again. There was widespread concern over his physical condition, and doubt was cast on his ability to function. His leadership was undermined. Peace Now, a new movement having no connections with the established political parties, maintained that the government's uncompromising rigidity was blocking the way to peace. Public-opinion polls showed a sharp drop in the Prime Minister's popularity.

It was not these polls that concerned Begin—he was well-schooled in unpopularity—but he sincerely feared for the future of the illusive peace initiative.

When the Americans proposed a meeting of the Israeli and Egyptian foreign ministers, Begin unhesitantly consented. The meeting at Leeds Castle near London on July 17 netted no tangible results. Nonetheless the Israeli Foreign Minister carried away the impression that the Egyptians wanted an agreement. Ezer Weizman returned with the same impression from meetings with Sadat. Secretary of State Cyrus Vance had a similar feeling, and it was on the basis of his report that President Jimmy Carter decided to convene a summit meeting at Camp David.

The President's decision to call such a meeting engendered much criticism. His prestige in the United States was at its lowest ebb. The failure of this meeting could well put an end to any chance of his being elected for a second term. Sadat's situation, too, was far from enviable. During the nine months since his visit to Jerusalem he had been under fierce and constant attack from the "rejectionist" states, and no Arab country, with the exception of Sudan, openly supported him. His acceptance of the invitation only increased his isolation and exacerbated the attacks on him. Many people felt that if the meeting failed, not only his political future but his very life would be in danger. The risk for Begin was less dramatic, but hardly less significant. The Peace Now movement had expanded its ranks, and the evening before his departure for the United States a hundred thousand Israelis congregated in Tel Aviv to demonstrate their conviction that "Peace is preferable to a greater Israel."

The Israeli delegation arrived at Camp David in two large helicopters on Tuesday afternoon, September 5. They were received at the landing strip by President and Mrs. Rosalynn Carter. Begin was invited to Aspen, the President's lodge, for a cup of coffee, and the rest went to their respective billets.

At seven o'clock in the evening Begin assembled the members of his delegation for their first consultation, and later that same evening Begin returned to Aspen for his first talk with President Carter. President Sadat, who had arrived before the Israeli delegation, was fatigued from the trip and had retired at once.

On Wednesday, September 7, while President Carter and President Sadat were closeted for their first meeting, Begin and the senior members of the Israeli delegation met with Secretary of State Vance. Later Begin went out for a walk along the trails and accidentally met Sadat returning to his lodge after his meeting with Carter. This was the first time the two leaders had met since Ismailia. They greeted one another courteously and paused to exchange a few words, but the atmosphere remained rather frigid.

That afternoon Begin and Sadat met at President Carter's for their first official discussion—and the first crisis.

Sadat presented an eleven-page document setting forth the Egyptian position on all the controversial questions. Egypt proposed not only a total Israeli withdrawal to the June 4, 1967 lines and the establishment of a Palestinian entity, but also reparations for all damages suffered by Egypt during the thirty years of war. The paper was peppered with harsh comments concerning Israel's intransigence.

When Sadat had finished reading the proposal, Carter asked: "And now what?"

"Let Begin study the document and give us his answer," Sadat said. Then he added in a more conciliatory tone that this time he wanted an effective framework for a peace agreement, not only a declaration of principles. But he stressed that he would not accept a settlement of the Sinai question before there was an agreement over Judea and Samaria.

A somber atmosphere pervaded Birch Lodge, where the Israeli delegation assembled for consultation. Some members felt that unless Sadat retracted his proposal, there was little point in continuing the conference. But it was decided that Israel would not cause a breakdown of negotiations, but would "play Sadat's game" and present a paper to counter his.

The Israeli paper was presented by Begin at the second three-way meeting Thursday morning. For about an hour he read his answer, point by point, to each issue raised by Sadat. The meeting lasted for some three hours. Reporting later to the members of his delegation, Begin described it as a "frank, cordial discussion punctuated with sparks," in which President Carter took an active part.

The argument over Sinai was intense. Sadat stated that under no circumstances could he leave sovereign Egyptian territory in Israel's hands. When Begin mentioned the possibility of a territorial compromise in Sinai, Sadat interrupted him. "Never!" He repeated the word three times for emphasis.

Sadat refused to discuss the demilitarization of Sinai. "Let the aides finish it . . ." he said. Of the settlements in Rafah Salient, Begin said, "There is not a person in Israel who will agree to dismantling them." His suggestion that this region be placed under supervision of the United Nations or of joint Israeli-Egyptian patrols produced no reaction from Sadat.

When Begin concluded, it was clear that agreement had not been reached on a single one of the disputed points. Nevertheless the atmosphere was not one of crisis. "It was a good sounding-out," Begin summarized.

Carter called the Israeli suggestions very generous, but asked, "Will there be no peace because of the settlements?" Begin's response was a comprehensive review of the security questions involved in the presence of the settlements. Still Carter declared that the settlement issue must not be permitted to deadlock the conference.

The parallel meeting headed by Vance hit the same snag. Moshe Dayan, Weizman, and the Israeli legal adviser, Professor Aharon Barak, immediately rejected the Egyptian demand, which had gained American support, to freeze new settlement plans, as well as the

Egyptian request to refrain from adding manpower reinforcements to the existing settlements.

When the members of the Israeli delegation assembled in Begin's cabin that evening, they agreed that the conference was deadlocked. It was clear now that there was no choice: the Americans had to bring forward their compromise suggestions.

The next day the Americans focused their efforts on the Egyptian delegation while the members of the Israeli delegation again met for consultation. Begin transmitted additional details of the three-way talks of the day before. He was encouraged by the fact that even President Carter clearly recognized that the Egyptian proposal was unacceptable. The delegation reached the conclusion that under all circumstances Sadat must be prevented from making it appear that the settlements in the Rafah Salient were the cause of the conference's failure.

That evening there was a Shabbat dinner in Begin's lodge. Carter, his wife, Vice President Walter Mondale, Vance, and National Security Adviser Zbigniew Brzezinski were invited. Sadat was not asked for fear he would refuse. Despite the heavy hearts everyone did his best to create a festive atmosphere.

Saturday was a day of rest. The Americans were closeted in Hickory Lodge, the residence of Vance and Mondale, working on the first draft of their proposal. The Egyptian delegation, too, was in conference. That evening the first of four chess games took place between Begin and Brzezinski (they ended in a tie—each won two games).

On Sunday the three leaders toured the battlefield at Gettysburg, and that afternoon the American "working paper" was ready for presentation. The proposals were prepared with utmost thoroughness. They separated the issue of Sinai from that of Judea and Samaria and dealt with them independently, trying to circumvent subjects and terminology that had been stumbling blocks in the past. But on the whole the American document was closer to the Arab position, particularly in its definition of the status of Jerusalem and on the question of new settlements.

When Carter met at night with the Israeli delegation, a discussion ensued that was later described as "difficult." Begin took exception primarily to the paragraph in the American paper referring to the "inadmissibility of acquisitions by conquest." He repeated the claim that Israel's conquests were gained in the course of a defensive war that had been forced upon her. He also objected to applying United Nations Resolution 242 to all the territories. He said, "That means an obligation in advance with respect to the Golan Heights. We cannot agree to that."

After returning to his cabin, Begin said to one of his aides, "I have experienced many difficult situations in my life. But never have I felt as strongly as now that I am doing the right thing, that I am protecting the interests of the State of Israel. Even if, as a result, no agreement is reached. I shall be able to say with a clear conscience that we defended a correct position."

Monday morning, before he went to see President Sadat, President Carter invited Dayan to clarify some matters, and a discussion ensued that lasted for over two hours.

Dayan was extremely pessimistic after that meeting. He reported that the President thought Israel must concede on the settlements because that was a matter on which Sadat could not give in. Dayan's feeling was that if Israel remained adamant, a showdown with the Americans was unavoidable.

Tuesday was the day of the "big crisis." During the Israeli consultation that morning Dayan said that although the President expected the Israeli delegation to present a new working paper which would enable the Americans to offer further compromise proposals, in the matter of the settlements and the Sinai airfields, the Americans supported the Egyptians. Most of the Israelis expressed the feeling that the conference was at an impasse. Nevertheless it was suggested that a new working paper be submitted, but only Begin retained a measure of optimism.

The turning point came that same day when, by chance, Dayan met the American ambassador to Israel, Samuel Lewis, and told him casually that he was scheduled to return to Israel the following day. These words startled the ambassador and, as it turned out, the entire American delegation, since the implication was that the Israelis had given up hope.

In the late afternoon when most of the members of the Israeli delegation were gathered in Laurel Lodge, Carter appeared, as if quite by accident. He said his people were already preparing the latest working paper and suggested establishing an ad hoc committee, consisting of Professor Aharon Barak as the Israeli representative and Dr. Osama el-Baz as the Egyptian and himself as chairman, to define and formulate all points of agreement that had been achieved until now. Begin then said, "Mr. President, I should like to talk with you this evening. On my part, it will be the most forthright discussion I have ever had, with the exception of those with my mentor, Zeev Jabotinsky."

Carter agreed, knowing Begin well enough to realize he did not mention Jabotinsky's name lightly. Their discussion lasted an hour and a half, and Begin returned satisfied, although no agreement was reached on any issue on which they held divergent views. He did not feel that the President accepted his stand, but he believed that he had succeeded in pointing up the problems and positions and that now something would happen.

On Wednesday came the initial breakthrough. Carter was closeted all day in his lodge with Barak and El-Baz. At ten o'clock he appeared and took Begin aside to express his esteem of Professor Barak. A few minutes later the typists finished copying the American working paper on Sinai, and the three delegations met for their first discussion of it.

On Thursday the conference was again bogged down by the question of Jerusalem and the settlements in Judea and Samaria. Begin invited Vance over and did not mince words with respect to the attitude on the settlements as reflected in the American proposal. Crisis was in the air. Friday marked the end of the ten days President Carter had set aside for the Camp David Conference, and there were no results. The President asked that the conference go on. It was decided to agree to his request, although Begin would not allow the Israeli delegation to work on Shabbat.

The delegation did indeed refrain from all work on Saturday, with the exception of Dayan who had a lengthy talk with Carter. The President told him that he wanted to reach an agreement on Sunday, no matter what.

That night Begin, who had intended to go to Washington to attend a gala concert of the Israel Philharmonic, was invited to meet with President Carter. Their talk lasted for four and a half hours. The concert was forgotten. A compromise formula for Sinai was worked out. Carter agreed to leave the issue of the settlements up to the Knesset, and Begin promised that members of the Knesset would be free to vote as they saw fit, without being bound by the coalition agreement. An accord was also reached concerning the airfields, after the United States agreed to assist in the construction of two substitute fields in the Negev. It was then not too difficult to reach agreement with respect to the time schedule of the withdrawal from Sinai.

Regarding those issues still in dispute, it was agreed that each delegation would submit letters of intent, formulating its position in detail, and these issues would be discussed later in the course of the actual peace negotiations. Carter set the close of the conference for Monday.

Sunday opened with a crisis: Egyptian Foreign Minister Ibrahim Kamel submitted his resignation to Sadat. Everyone awaited Sadat's reaction. Would he consider the resignation an indication of what was waiting for him at home, and pull back? No, Sadat was determined to accept the agreement.

Then at noon—another crisis, a very serious one.

The entire Israeli delegation was having lunch when Ambassador Lewis came in and handed Dayan a draft of the American letter of intent concerning the future of Jerusalem. Dayan perused the document and reacted immediately. "We cannot accept this." He passed it to Begin whose face clouded over.

"Under no circumstances," he stated categorically. Their objection was not only to the fact that Jerusalem was referred to as "occupied territory," but also to the American conclusions, based on this approach, concerning the future status of Jerusalem.

Hasty consultation was held on the spot and all agreed. "On this issue we will break up the conference," and Dayan added, "Let's go and pack."

Ambassador Lewis hurried to the President's lodge.

In a black mood the Israeli delegation gathered at Birch Lodge. Rain was falling in torrents. No one said a word.

And then, in the midst of the rain and the gloom, President Carter arrived to give Begin autographed pictures of himself as gifts for the Prime Minister's grandchildren. They referred briefly to the document. Begin declared, "May the hand that signs such a document wither." The President nodded, a grave expression on his face, but he left without saying anything.

A few minutes later, though, there was a telephone call from Aspen. The President asked for Professor Barak. And at five o'clock it was all finished. Between the Israeli legal adviser and the President of the United States formulas were found that both Begin and Sadat could sign.

Begin decided that it was time to put an end to the undeclared "mad" prevailing between him and President Sadat since their confrontation at the beginning of the conference. He phoned Dogwood Lodge and told the President of Egypt that he wanted to come over and thank him.

"*Ahalan w'suhalan*" [You will be welcome], answered Sadat.

Begin went out into the pouring rain. When he returned some twenty minutes later, his face glowed with satisfaction. As he came in, the phone rang. It was President Sadat asking to return the Prime Minister's visit.

Sadat arrived, altogether serene, pressed Begin's hand in a friendly manner, and then shook hands with everyone present. He embraced Weizman. Someone suggested a toast to the successful conclusion of the conference and Weizman offered a goblet of champagne to the President. He refused, saying, "I'm not an infidel like you, ya-Ezer. . . ."

At seven in the evening they dispersed to pack, and two and a half hours later the evacuation from Camp David began.

All the rest—the ceremony of signing the Framework Agreement at the White House, the victorious return to Israel, the dramatic session of the Knesset beginning on the morning of September 17 and ending in the early morning of the following day when the Framework Agreement was approved by a tremendous majority—are recorded on the pages of history and in our individual memories.

The morning after the long night at the Knesset, after one of his most brilliant appearances on the parliamentary stage, Menachem Begin was tired, satisfied, but pensive. His heart was heavy as he considered the great sacrifices he had been forced to make at Camp David, the struggles still awaiting Israel, and the concessions that would be expected all along the way. He knew, too, that even with the sacrifices and concessions, the way would be long and tortuous.

Nevertheless his expression was calm, the expression of a man at peace with himself. He knew he had taken a long step toward peace.

Framework for the Conclusion
of a Peace Treaty
Between Egypt and Israel

In order to achieve peace between them, Israel and Egypt agree to negotiate in good faith with a goal of concluding within three months of the signing of this framework a peace treaty between them.

It is agreed that:

(A) The site of the negotiations will be under a United Nations flag at a location or locations to be mutually agreed.

(B) All of the principles of U.N. Resolution 242 will apply in this resolution of the dispute between Israel and Egypt.

(C) Unless otherwise mutually agreed, terms of the peace treaty will be implemented between two and three years after the peace treaty is signed.

The following matters are agreed between the parties:

(A) The full exercise of Egyptian sovereignty up to the internationally recognized border between Egypt and mandated Palestine;

(B) The withdrawal of Israeli armed forces from the Sinai;

(C) The use of airfields left by the Israelis near El Arish, Rafah, Ras En Naqb, and Sharm El Sheikh for civilian purposes only, including possible commercial use by all nations;

(D) The right of free passage by ships of Israel through the Gulf of Suez and the Suez Canal on the basis of the Constantinople Convention of 1888 applying to all nations; the Strait of Tiran and the Gulf of Aqaba are international waterways to be open to all nations for unimpeded and nonsuspendable freedom of navigation and overflight;

(E) The construction of a highway between the Sinai and Jordan near Eilat with guaranteed free and peaceful passage by Egypt and Jordan; and

(F) The stationing of military forces listed below.

Stationing of Forces

(A) No more than one division (mechanized or infantry) of Egyptian armed forces will be stationed within an area lying approximately 50 kilometers (km) east of the Gulf of Suez and the Suez Canal.

(B) Only United Nations forces and civil police equipped with light weapons to perform normal police functions will be stationed within an area lying west of the international border and the Gulf of Aqaba, varying in width from 20 km to 40 km.

(C) In the area within 3 km east of the international border there will be Israeli limited military forces not to exceed four infantry battalions and United Nations observers.

(D) Border patrol units, not to exceed three battalions, will supplement the civil police in maintaining order in the area not included above.

The exact demarcation of the above areas will be as decided during the peace negotiations.

Early warning stations may exist to insure compliance with the terms of the agreement.

United Nations forces will be stationed:

(A) In part of the area in the Sinai lying within about 20 km of the Mediterranean Sea and adjacent to the international border, and

(B) In the Sharm El Sheikh area to ensure freedom of passage through the Strait of Tiran;

And these forces will not be removed unless such removal is approved by the Security Council of the United Nations with a unanimous vote of the five permanent members.

After a peace treaty is signed, and after the interim withdrawal is complete, normal relations will be established between Egypt and Israel, including: full recognition, including diplomatic, economic and cultural relations; termination of economic boycotts and barriers to the free movement of goods and people; and mutual protection of citizens by the due process of law.

Interim Withdrawal

Between three months and nine months after the signing of the peace treaty, all Israeli forces will withdraw east of a line extending from a point east of El Arish to Ras Muhammad, the exact location of this line to be determined by mutual agreement.

For the Government of the
Arab Republic of Egypt:

For the Government
of Israel:

Witnessed by:
Jimmy Carter, President of the United States of America.

Dell Bestsellers